Anthony B. Pinn has a Ph.D. in religion
from Harvard Divinity School and is
Assistant Professor of Religious Studies
at Macalester College, St. Paul, Minnesota.

Why, Lord?

WHY, LORD?

Suffering and Evil in Black Theology

Anthony B. Pinn

Continuum • New York

BT
732.7
.P46
1995

1995

The Continuum Publishing Company
370 Lexington Avenue
New York, NY 10017

Printed in the United States of America

Library of Congress Cataloging-in-Publication Data

Pinn, Anthony B.
    Why, Lord? : suffering and evil in Black theology / Anthony B. Pinn.
        p.   cm.
    Includes bibliographical references and index.
    ISBN 0-8264-0854-0 (hardcover : alk. paper)
    1. Suffering—Religious aspects—Christianity. 2. Good and evil.
3. Black theology. 4. Liberation theology. 5. Humanism—20th century. I. title.
BT732.7.P46   1995   95-19439
231'.8'08996073—dc20   CIP

Acknowledgments will be found on page 205, which constitutes an extension of the copyright page.

For Rev. Anne Hargrave Pinn

and the Ancestors

If God is not for us, if God is not against white racists, then God is a murderer, and we had better kill God. The task of black theology is to kill gods that do not belong to the black community, and by labelling black history as a source, we know that this is neither an easy nor a sentimental task but an awesome responsibilty.

—James H. Cone, *Black Theology of Liberation*

Contents

PREFACE

The theoretical framework and content of any book bespeak the concerns and values arising from the author's personal life journey, couched in academic language and categories. This is no less true for this volume. Such an acknowledgment alerts the reader to the complex nature of the author's viewpoints, the underlying assumptions and affirmations, and ultimately helps the reader assess the arguments presented in light of the interconnection between lived experience and thought. A reading of the text is, therefore, enhanced by a brief exploration of my personal motivations for and concerns in writing this volume.

My formative years were spent within the Black church tradition, specifically the African Methodist Episcopal denomination. Singing in the choir, participating in the Young People's Department activities, serving as an acolyte, and attending Sunday School formed the lion's share of my weekly interactions outside family and school. For me, at an early age, lay activity was no longer enough; I felt a "call" to Christian ministry, a need to serve the church through ministerial leadership. I started preaching at the age of fourteen, and the AME Church ordained me a deacon after my first year in college.

While in school, I worked as a youth minister in various AME churches and saw firsthand the efforts of Black Christians to make sense of their daily struggles in light of Christian theology and doctrinal structures. I will never forget hearing "church mothers" give testimony regarding the hardships of life and God's mysterious ability to "make a way out of no way." The words of Sunday morning prayers have stayed with me: "Lord, you never said it would be easy . . . and so, if I'm going to wear a crown, I must bear my cross." Experience in Black churches, where people struggle to make sense out of an apparently meaningless world and where I strove to help this process through sermons, prayers, and other ministerial functions, raised questions for me concerning the tension between lived reality and

Christian "truths." Does the Christian message say anything liberating to suffering humanity? Does theological conversation serve to make a positive difference in the way the oppressed respond to their existential plight? Do Christian explanations of human suffering make a "material" and concrete difference? I placed these questions within the framework of theodicy or, more generally, the problem of evil.

Undeniably aware of the existential hardship faced by African-Americans, I was and continue to be anxious to speak a liberating word to Black sufferers. An academic dimension was first added to my exploration as a Master of Divinity degree candidate at Harvard Divinity School. My master's thesis presents some initial thoughts on the paradoxical nature of God conceptions and human experience.* I argued in this thesis that the key to easing the tension between Christian belief and human suffering is a reworking of the God idea that shifts "responsibility" for moral evil to human misconduct. Within my Ph.D. course work, the importance of this question lingered, and I decided to pursue further research on this evasive theological concern, exploring in the process the theological "potholes" (to borrow William R. Jones' phrase) created by my earlier perspective. I wanted to understand the development of this problem within my context, my cultural venue—the African-American religious traditions—while using the tools of my theological training. A revised version of that dissertation is here presented.

Through this book, I illustrate and evaluate the "theodical game" (i.e., redemptive suffering) in which African-American religious thinkers have historically participated. A theological pothole which emerged in my master's thesis is inherent in Black theodical arguments which ultimately resolve the paradox between the continuation of Black oppression and the basic Black theological stance on God as a proactive force in the world through the concept of redemptive suffering: that suffering is intrinsically "bad," but has a secondary benefit ordained by God. This bothered me. I could not accept the idea that the suffering of those I saw on a daily basis had any value at all. The oppressive circumstances church mothers discussed and stewards prayed about could not hold, for me, any merit in the struggle for "liberation." I needed to explore an alternative response that uncompromisingly affirms—at all costs, even the rejection of such concepts as the Christian view of God—the demonic nature of

* "Cross and Crown: African-American Understandings of and Responses to Suffering," Harvard Divinity School, 1989.

Black suffering. I believe that human liberation is more important than the maintenance of any religious symbol, sign, canon, or icon. It must be accomplished—both psychologically and physically—despite the damage done to cherished religious principles and traditions. Holding to this belief, I will stand or fall.

I found a similar response to Black theodical questions in the little-explored area of Black humanism. Black humanism, as found in Black oral tradition and later, Black literature, denies the existence of God and holds humans fully accountable for the existence and removal of moral evil in the world.

I realize that an invitation to dialogue with "nontraditional" religious perspectives may be uncomfortable for many of my readers. However, those concerned with human recovery from oppression must demonstrate a willingness to investigate all avenues showing promise for securing this liberation—the removal of injustice and inequality, and the promotion of full and healthy life options. The reader will also discover that Black humanism is not separate from Black religious tradition; it is a forgotten component. The task is to explore and discuss, openly and freely, the nature and ramifications of this broadened discussion of Black suffering. We owe this much to those who shall follow the theological trails we blaze.

Finally, I stress that I appreciate the theological and theodical efforts of those who came before me, and I realize that their patterns of activity and survival made the luxury of writing within the relative comfort of the academy possible. Accordingly, I work out of a great deal of respect and love; and thereby, my efforts are marked by recognition of and reverence for my ancestors' trials. Moreover, such reverence necessitates a serious examination of all possible resolutions to the evil they and we struggle(d) with. It demands a determined movement away from patterns of religious thought that lessen the impact and significance of Black suffering by finding a benefit within it. To allow such an attitude to go unchallenged is disrespectful.

This project, although an extension of my wrestlings and questions, could not have been completed without the assistance and support of many individuals. I thank my editor Cynthia Eller for her careful reading of the text, support, encouragement, and patience as I negotiated the demands and pressures inherent in the first year of teaching, and Watersign Resources was a pleasure to work with during the final stages of production. William R. Jones helped me to think through many of these ideas and I greatly appreciate his timely response to my many questions and requests. Emilie M. Townes and

James H. Cone read the full manuscript and provided many helpful suggestions and comments. Stephen Angell graciously offered access to his files on Bishop Henry McNeal Turner and responded with kindness to my many questions and concerns. Dennis Dickerson, Lewis Baldwin, and Cheryl Townsend Gilkes helped in numerous ways.

Macalester College provided much needed financial assistance. Without this help, the securing of permission to reprint materials would have been impossible. I must also thank my colleagues in Macalester's Religious Studies Department for understanding my "closed office door" and helping me set aside the time needed to work on this text. Numerous colleagues and friends (especially Teresita Martinez-Vergne) outside the Religious Studies Department at Macalester College encouraged me and provided invaluable assistance; I thank them all. I must also mention two students in particular, Leif Johnson and Michael Vernon, who helped transcribe materials and cheerfully made numerous phone inquiries on my behalf.

The encouragement and guidance of Gordon D. Kaufman, David D. Hall, Kwame Anthony Appiah, and other members of Harvard's faculty were invaluable. Nisé Nekheba provided numerous hours of editorial assistance and encouraging words. Other persons, libraries, and organizations who assisted with the preparation of the dissertation and its later revised form are not mentioned here by name. However, they remain important, and I continue to appreciate their contribution to this project.

My family, immediate (Raymond, Joyce, and Linda) and extended (Frederick and Barbara Lucas), provided much needed encouragement and I will remain grateful to them. My mother, the Reverend Anne H. Pinn, to whom this volume is dedicated, is responsible for this project in countless ways: Thank you.

I owe a debt of gratitude to all those mentioned here. They helped me, in countless ways, to improve and refine the thoughts contained in the following pages. I, however, am alone responsible for any oversights or errors.

Anthony B. Pinn
Macalester College
St. Paul, Minnesota 1995

INTRODUCTION

Amid world conditions and mounting calamities, the religious-minded are forced to confront certain questions, nagging tensions, and paradoxes. Because of the intimate connection between faith structures and a priori theological assumptions, such questions often threaten to topple the relevance of religious systems and world views. One such threat arises regarding the issue of human suffering—understood as an aspect of the problem of evil or "theodicy."* Suffering and unmerited suffering are used interchangeably (with reference to African-Americans) to denote moral evil. Moral evil denotes oppression, injustice, inequality, and the resulting psychological and physical damage. The problem of evil and "theodicy" interchangeably connote attempts at resolving the contradiction between traditional Christian understandings of God as powerful, just, and good, and the presence of suffering (as defined above), without negating the essential character of the Divine. Liberation, because of my understanding of suffering and "theodicy," will mean a vision of life without the assumption of God or God-ordained and permitted moral evil (i.e., human responsibility for moral evil). Movement toward this goal of liberation entails, for example, the attainment of extended life options and a better-developed sense of healthy human worth. Liberation is distinguishable from the goal of survival in that survival is a prerequisite; it implies the necessities for life that do not include, but make possible the pursuit of, a full set of life options. In light of the above definition of terms, my methodological framework rests upon constructive theological appeals to context and strong ties between the doing of theology and pressing life issues.

The examination of African-American responses to the problem of evil begins with slavery, where the religious question of human

---

* The term theodicy is used with quotation marks. This is to show from the beginning of this book the uncertain nature of this term as a proper category of investigation.

suffering first emerges for Black Americans. Brought here as chattel in the early 1600s, African-Americans have faced the brutalities of dehumanization through the destruction of their culture, the ripping apart of family units, rapes, beatings, and other actions that linked the control of Black bodies with the increase of plantation profits. All this, the Africans who encountered Christianity learned, was rightly done in the name of God. Some slaves accepted their lot in life. Others questioned the religious doctrine given to them and searched for an explanation of their plight beyond the plantation minister's rhetoric. They faced the classic difficulty of reconciling God with the experience of evil: ". . . if God is perfectly loving, God must wish to abolish all evil; and if God is all-powerful, God must be able to abolish all evil. But evil exists; therefore God cannot be both omnipotent and perfectly loving."[1] The effort to understand God amid the contradictory messages of existential hardship and the Christian gospel continued during the movement from "hush harbors" to early Black churches, and into the late twentieth century. Continued oppression made this questioning inescapable.

As John Hick illustrates in *Philosophy of Religion*, the resolution to the problem of evil can take various forms: (1) a rethinking of the nature / purpose of evil; or, (2) the postulating of a "limited" God; or, (3) a questioning / denial of God's existence.[2] Although Hick does not address it, there is a fourth possible resolution that entails questioning God's goodness and / or righteousness. A traditional example of the first resolution is found in Augustine's "free-will defense."[3] In essence, Augustine argues that evil (both moral and natural) in the world results from perfect beings (i.e., angels and humans) freely deciding to turn away from God. Therefore, evil is a privation of the good, denoting the misuse of free will (i.e., "The Fall"). Furthermore, God remains unblemished by this privation of the good because God ultimately punishes this sin and by that restores a proper balance to the world.[4] In essence, evil in the world is either the result of sin or the result of punishment.

The Irenaean "theodicy" also rethinks the nature of evil while maintaining God's perfection. However, unlike Augustine, Irenaeus argues that humans exist at an "epistemic distance from God" which allows them to freely make choices.[5] God created humanity as imperfect beings. With this in mind, Irenaeus argues that the earth is a place of "soul making" where humans work to refine their character and by that develop into the "image" of God. Evil is a necessary part of this world because human development takes place, in part, through trials and tribulations. Furthermore, God's perfection goes unquestioned because God did not intend the world to be free of evil.[6]

Some thinkers find the resolutions to the problem of evil offered by Augustine and Irenaeus faulty.[7] For example, some question whether Irenaeus' rethinking of evil is adequate to explain events such as the Holocaust and the Middle Passage (i.e., the transporting of Africans to the New World as slaves). In addition, the spontaneous "Fall" argued by Augustine does not put to rest questions concerning the ultimate accountability of God for this action. An alternate resolution to the problem of evil mindful of such dilemmas is process "theodicy." In this system, God must act in the world through "persuasion" because "God is subject to the limitations imposed by the basic laws of the universe, for God has not created the universe *ex nihilo*, thereby establishing its structure, but rather the universe is an uncreated process that includes the deity."[8] In short, God is not all-powerful. Furthermore, the developing world contains both good and evil (understood aesthetically as discord and triviality);[9] however, the good resulting from the unfolding of the world will outweigh the evil.[10]

Thinkers who find the rethinking of God's power or the nature of evil inadequate have the option of resolving the problem of evil through a questioning/denial of God's existence. As Hick notes:

> The responsible skeptic, whether agnostic or atheist, is not concerned to deny that religious people have had certain experiences as a result of which they have become convinced of the reality of God. The skeptic believes, however, that these experiences can be adequately accounted for without postulating a God. . . .[11]

African-Americans have engaged in discourse concerning the problem of evil in a manner reminiscent of three propositions noted above, i.e., rethinking evil's nature, rethinking God's power, and attempts to rethink God's goodness/righteousness. One sees these resolutions in Black theological thought suggesting that: (1) unmerited suffering is intrinsically evil, yet can have redemptive consequences; (2) God and humans are coworkers in the struggle to remove moral evil; and (3) Black suffering may result from God being a racist. Using position number one, many spirituals understand suffering as a paradox and promote it as a temporary evil known to and manipulated by God for the Christian's ultimate benefit (i.e., some form of heaven). God works, in the Christ event, through unmerited suffering (or moral evil) to bring about good. Ministers and laypersons within

Black churches combined positions one and two by presenting suffering as inherently evil, yet usable by God to prepare Black people for their ultimate freedom. This freedom was secured through the joint efforts of God and humans.

Spirituals and church leaders, in many instances, have developed a theodical approach centered on the notion of redemptive or fruitful suffering. These terms are synonymous and define oppression experienced by African-Americans as inherently evil yet holding secondary benefit. That is, the existential hardships endured by African-Americans display the presence of destructive "will to power." However, God manipulates this moral evil and causes good consequences. Benefits may entail needed pedagogical lessons such as the correction of character flaws, the obtainment of invaluable skills and talents, or some good which God will make clear in the future (benefits shrouded in divine mystery). In this way, suffering strengthens African-Americans, so to speak, for divine plans such as the betterment of American society, the reorganization of African society, or a combination of the two. One thing seems apparent: suffering in the here-and-now allows for the ultimate fulfillment of a divine teleological design.

Although this important aspect of theological inquiry is present in nascent and current Black theology, no one, to my knowledge, has published an extended documentation and analysis of its historical progression. *Why Lord?* seeks to cover some of this ground. African-American thought concerning human suffering, from slavery to the present, is critically examined in a manner allowing for fulfillment of several objectives. First, a comprehensive survey of currently available Black responses to the problem of evil is presented in the first several sections—beginning with the spirituals and moving through other important responses which came later. The spirituals reflect the earliest recorded account of African-American consciousness of human suffering as a religious paradox. In this manner, many spirituals, such as "De Ol' Sheep Done Know de Road," open the discussion of suffering as redemptive and a prerequisite for salvation. The continued presence of racism and other moral evils into the nineteenth and twentieth centuries resulted in the continuing relevance of the problem of evil. And so, building upon the spirituals as a base, nineteenth- and twentieth-century church leaders and laypersons tackled this question, providing an updated redemptive suffering argument in which suffering prepares African-Americans for the work of racial uplift and the redemption of Africa and/or the United States. Bishop Henry McNeal Turner's argument for slavery as an evil allowed by

God to introduce Africans to the beneficial influence of the Christian gospel and civil government demonstrates this point. A recent incarnation of this theological position is Martin L. King, Jr.'s philosophy of unmerited suffering. Using resources such as Gandhian philosophy, personalism, social gospel theology, neo-orthodox thought, and Black church tradition, King argues that the nonviolent acceptance of undeserved (i.e., racially motivated) suffering will afflict the American conscience and foster the end of societal discrimination.

The second objective of this study involves a defining and problematizing of human suffering as an organizing principle for life options and activities. I critically reflect on the work of William R. Jones and Delores S. Williams because of their attempt to rethink the nature of Black suffering as a "source" for Black theology. Jones in particular argues the centrality of suffering (therefore "theodicy") to the Black theological enterprise, and he seeks to give this question a full treatment, while avoiding "theological potholes" and unsubstantiated religious assertions. He begins by raising questions concerning God's goodness ("Is God a white racist?") and concludes by arguing for a humanocentric theism, which removes God from responsibility for evil and for liberation from evil. He argues that humans must work with God to cause liberation; this is because God's power within human history amounts to positive persuasion as opposed to proactive manipulation and shaping of historical events. Williams makes a similar move. Reflecting upon the biblical account of Hagar, she argues that God's role in history entails providing humans with the tools for survival. Hence, humans accomplish liberation using the materials for survival God provides. In this way, the problem of evil vanishes by denying the relevance of critiquing God for continued oppression. However, I shall argue that Jones and Williams fail to remove the trappings of redemptive suffering.

As part of the second objective, I assess the underexplored category of redemptive suffering, understanding it as a major strand of Black theodical thought.[12] The final section of the book takes this task up. In this section I argue that the history of Black religious thought on suffering—Black "theodicy"—makes clear the dominance and unacceptability of redemptive suffering arguments. These arguments are unacceptable because they counteract efforts at liberation by finding something of value in Black suffering. In essence such arguments go against social transformation activity. Redemptive suffering and liberation are diametrically opposed ideas; they suggest ways of being in the world that, in effect, nullify each other. One cannot embrace suffering as redemptive (as defined earlier) and effectively speak of liberation. The detrimental nature of arguments for redemptive suffering requires constructive work toward a more appropriate response to Black suffering.

The final section of the book expands the scope of resolutions to the problem of evil examined by Black theology. The goal is to encourage Black theologians to reflect upon a fuller spectrum of Black responses to the problem of evil and to allow for the full range of Black opinion. Therefore, it is necessary to extend Black theological inquiry and outline a fifth phase of Black theology's development. (The first phase entails the initial period, before the twentieth century; the second is the intellectualizing of Black theology during the civil rights era; the third entails globalization through crosscultural dialogue; the fourth is the inclusion of excluded voices calling into question the sexism and heterosexism of Black theology.) I define this fifth phase as the problematizing of Black theodical arguments and the fostering of a more complex conversation regarding Black suffering, making use of a revitalized canon of Black religion, including nontheistic forms of expression. *Why Lord?* provides the initial construction of a resolution to the problem of evil positioned outside harmful redemptive suffering arguments. Here I will outline the third of the previously discussed resolutions to the problem of evil—questioning/denial of God's existence—namely, Black humanism.

A typology of humanism, including two essential categories, is presented. The first category is that of weak humanism. This position argues for questioning God's power in the world and declares that humans must not depend upon God for liberation; they must work *with* God to achieve this goal. Weak humanism is in keeping with Black church tradition and does not avoid the "theological pothole" of redemptive suffering; even a limited God can attach benefits to existential hardship. The other category—strong humanism—offers at least a provisional resolution to the problem of evil that does not collapse into redemptive suffering argumentation because it does not place (in importance) theological categories above the reality of suffering. Black existence has priority. Everything else stands or falls based upon its correspondence to what is "known" about human life. The words of James H. Cone receive new life from strong humanism: Truth is experienced.

Is Black humanism a religious system? Undoubtedly, some will argue that strong humanism rests outside "Black traditional" thought and is therefore of limited use by the Black religious community. This argument is incorrect. As the last chapter explains, strong humanism is in keeping with Black tradition (although it is not

Christian), when one recognizes the breadth of Black religious expression—which includes the full spectrum of theism and humanism. Implied here is a rejection of the secular/sacred dichotomy that typically exists regarding theistic and humanistic forms of Black thought. Using Charles Long's definition of religion in *Significations*, both theism and humanism are religious to the extent they provide "ultimate orientation" and the framework for values, morality, and ethical patterns of conduct and activity. That is, strong humanism is a religious system because it provides a framework that guides human conduct and connects this conduct to the larger reality of Black community. Strong humanism fulfills a fundamental requirement of any religious system in that it defines, explains, and provides functional guidelines for reality. In this way, strong humanism, like other religious systems, keeps humanity from collasping into a state of chaos. By providing a functional worldview, explaining "reality," and clarifying proper human conduct, strong humanism meets the basic definition of a religion. As Clifford Geertz asserts:

> . . . a religion is: (1) a system of symbols which acts to (2) establish powerful, pervasive and long-lasting moods and motivations in [humans] by (3) formulating conceptions of a general order of existence and (4) clothing these conceptions with such an aura of factuality that (5) the moods and motivations seem uniquely realistic.[13]

To the extent strong humanism projects an order larger than the individual (i.e., "cosmic order"), it does so through reference to the Black community and the need to connect with and operate for the good of this community. Note that I am not making a global statement about humanism's standing as a religion: I am strictly concerned with the religious connotations of humanism within African-American tradition.

The investigation of strong humanism cannot be addressed using "theodicy" as a methodological tool. "Theodicy" requires a compromise with suffering because it assumes the goodness of God and requires the finding of something useful in human suffering. Theodical games do not allow for a way out of the theological trap of redemptive suffering. And so, I outline nitty-gritty hermeneutics—present within Black cultural expressiveness such as the blues—which offers a more viable methodology. Nitty-gritty hermeneutics is an effective tool since it holds no allegiance to Christian doctrine or theological sensibilities. It is not contaminated with nostalgic feelings toward traditional ways of viewing religious questions. Church tradition is less important than is the reality of oppression. Its only commitment is to what Peter C. Hodgson calls "hard labor"—strong and aggressive inquiry. Nitty-gritty hermeneutics maintains as its priority a sober look at life as it is, and it seeks hard truth unsoftened by theological obligations.

The following pages encourage a dialogical effort firmly entrenched in Black tradition. However, multidimensional dialogue does involve a rethinking of the location of the Black (Christian) churches in relationship to the larger Black religious community. Such an exploration does not lessen the importance of the Black church; rather, it serves to balance the Black churches' authority in light of other practices, perspectives, and organizations within the community. Traditionally, those who investigated Black religion did not venture beyond the boundaries of Black churches, acknowledging that Black churches have been the backbone of African-American religious expression. The age and relative stability of Black churches eclipsed the presence of alternate expressions of religious belief. Hans A. Baer, Claude Jacobs, and Andrew Kaslow have expanded this discussion beyond mainstream denominations by uncovering the importance of "Spiritual churches" within the Black community. Efforts like this have also been present in studies on Sweet Daddy Grace, Father Divine, and others. Scholars such as C. Eric Lincoln and Aminah B. McCloud expanded the boundaries by seriously studying the varieties of Islamic practice in Black America. And Joseph M. Murphy has helped scholars to recognize the importance of Santería for African-Americans, and other traditions in which the African Gods have survived. Nonetheless, Black (Christian) church centered dialogue dominates academic Black religious thought. Consequently, much additional religious ground needs to be covered in order to recognize Black religious expression's full complexity. *Why Lord?* presents a prolegomenon on one aspect of this religious ground—Black humanism. This, admittedly, is a first step. Exploration and dialogue must eventually encompass traditions beyond those presented here if a full spectrum of Black religion—in its broadest sense—is to surface. Only in this way will we understand the full complexity of Black responses to suffering.

For Black suffering is so massive and Black "theodicy" so detrimental that all possible alternatives need exploring. Black theologians must address themselves to the larger Black religious terrain rather then limit their discussion to the context of Black (Christian) churches and theistic alternatives. Dialogue, not monologues, is essential. Such an expansion of thought is vital to Black theology's self-critical stance and communal relevance.

1

SPIRITUALS AS AN EARLY REFLECTION ON SUFFERING

African slaves were not introduced to Christianity immedi-
ately upon arriving in the New World. Factors such as a
strict concern with the economic utility of slave labor and fear that
"conversion" would disrupt the status of slaves resulted in an ambiva-
lence toward the spiritual condition of African chattels. However,
weak attempts at conversion are traceable to religious bodies such as
the Anglican Church and the Quakers. Prior to the nineteenth century, the Anglican Church's Society for the Propagation of the Gospel
in Foreign Parts engaged in unsuccessful attempts to "save" the
enslaved Africans. Few of these early missionaries kept detailed
records of their activity, but their proselytizing of the slaves undoubtedly was hampered by planters who felt threatened by the supposed
"freeing" nature of religious instruction.

The energy of the nineteenth-century camp meetings created
conditions which opened Southern plantations to the paternalistic
efforts of missionaries and preachers. Of course, plantation preachers, evangelists, and missionaries were certain to emphasize the fact
that religious instruction for the slaves would in no way hamper the
benefits of slave holding. According to religious workers, God was
concerned with the slaves' souls, not their physical circumstances.[1]
With this guarantee and supporting legal structures, plantation owners lost some of their reluctance to provide spiritual instruction for
slaves. Slave holders were not threatened by this revival brand of
religion; it simply promised salvation without endangering the slav-
ery-based system of economics. Spirituality, not social change, was on
the mind of these mission zealots. With these qualifications, even

slave masters could pray for the eventual salvation of their slaves—once their work on earth was done.

The revival-fueled attention to the souls of slaves did not affect all slaves equally: only a certain few received direct attention. In short, the gospel reached the slave quarters by means of the "trickle-down" process. Clarence Walker provides some insight into the workings of this process. He records:

> Every Sunday the coachmen, footmen and body servants sat in the slaves' galleries of the churches and attentively drank up the sermons, prayers, and hymns intended for their masters in the pews. Then the house servants, who worked all day in the "big house," heard, with the masters' children, the old Bible stories. . . . These privileged ones, when the day's work was over, hurried to the slave quarters to share with the field hands the priceless treasures garnered in the churches and parlors of their masters.[2]

Although covered by a fog of paternalism and racism, the religious meetings encountered by "select" slaves mark a period of white and Black religious interaction. In fact, prior to the Civil War, there was a tremendous amount of joint Black and white religious activity. These services were far from equal, however. Blacks were frequently forced to listen to services in galleries (referred to as "nigger heaven"), or by means of open windows. Or, they had to wait until whites had been spiritually fed, and then the preacher turned his attention to them.[3] This type of joint activity allowed whites to maintain surveillance of Black activity, and in this way it prevented rebellious, "unorthodox," or "barbaric" activity among the slaves.

Although slave owners and their approved preachers controlled, to some extent, the location and content of worship, they were unable to fully monitor the coded musical articulation of an African-American worldview. That is, the slaves brought to religious services music heavily influenced by their African cultural patterns—which lyrically wove together enslavement realities, pieces of scripture, and folk wisdom. Even attempts by white missionaries to end these "barbaric" songs, "nonsensical chants," and "wild songs," as whites often called them, resulted in the alteration of their hymns into a musical expression unique to slaves. Accordingly, formal worship services echoed with the dissonant tones which arose out of the life conditions faced by enslaved Africans.

Secret meetings, known as hush harbor meetings, allowed for a certain amount of religious and theological freedom and thereby fostered the creation of lyrics by which to make sense of and endure daily sufferings. Although the encounter with Christianity provided an important matrix, the development of spirituals and other forms of musical expressivity is much older. Concerning this, Lovell writes:

> As soon as [they] made the transition from Africa to America and from [their] native language to [their] adopted language, the black creature[s] naturally continued what [they] . . . had been [doing] all along–making songs about [their] life and [their] religion.[4]

Although these spirituals, for the most part, were created by individuals, they narrated the community's collective physical and psychological experience and development. Accordingly, those who provided the creative and illustrative content of songs based such endeavors upon the feelings and activities common among the larger Black community. For example, spirituals often developed extemporaneously in response to a fiery sermon. As C. Eric Lincoln records:

> In the early days of the Black church the spontaneous creation of spirituals during the preaching event was a common feature of Black worship. These spirituals undoubtedly grew out of the preacher's chanted declamations and the intervening congregational responses. Little by little it became a song. . . . The oral nature of the spiritual's transmission meant that the spirituals were constantly recomposed and rearranged, so that a single spiritual might eventually have numerous musical and textual variations.[5]

The act of praying also inspired the creation of spirituals. The following account exemplifies this spontaneous and "prayerful" creation of song:

> Minutes passed, long minutes of strange intensity. The muttering, the ejaculations, grew louder, more dramatic, till suddenly I [Natalie Curtis Burlin] felt the creative thrill dart through the people like an electric vibration, that same half-audible hum arose, emotion was gathering. . . . [T]hen, up from the depths of some sinner's remorse and imploring came a pitiful plea . . . sobbed in musical cadence. From somewhere in the bowed

gathering another voice improvised a response. . . . [T]hen other voices joined the answer, shaping it into a musical phrase; and so, before our ears, as one might say, from this molten metal of music a new song was smithed out, composed then and there by no one in particular and by everyone in general.[6]

The sense of "psychic oneness" expressed in this account is not uncommon. In fact, Dr. Benjamin Mays considers spirituals part of the "mass category of Negro literature" precisely because of this communality.[7] If this communal connection is missing, "a song is not likely to hold its audience and it probably will not pass into oral tradition, where acceptance means that consensus has taken place over and over again through time."[8] Those spirituals which did not meet with the approval of the community lost their place and have not been recorded. Additionally, the transference and assessment of spirituals was aided, when permitted, by inter-plantation visits. And so, by the mid-nineteenth century, a significant reserve of theological songs had developed within the slave community as a result of this creative and spontaneous "musicking."[9] These songs not only provided the musical base for worship, they also answered hard religious questions.

Amidst the brutal behavior of slave holders who claimed to be Christian and followers of the humble Christ, African slaves were faced with contradictions and a hypocrisy which profoundly troubled them. Accordingly, certain questions emerged: How could someone who claimed a relationship with Christ perform evil acts such as the enslavement of other humans? How could God allow this oppressive behavior to continue?

These and other fundamental issues reinforced themselves with each day and with each strike of the lash. As evidenced by the spirituals, many slaves responded to this irony with disdain for the world of slavery. In a conversation between J. Miller McKim and a slave, the process by which daily evils perpetuated against African slaves were turned into telling songs is described:

Dey make 'em, sah . . . I'll tell you; its dis way: My master call me up an' order me a short peak of corn and a hundred lashes. My friends see it and is sorry for me. When dey come to de praise meeting dat night dey sing about it. Some's very good singers and know how; and dey work it in, you know, till dey get it right; and dat's de way.[10]

Of necessity, the slaves shaped and described their responses to these issues using the tools available to them, namely pieces of the Hebrew Bible, the New Testament, African cultural patterns, their reality as slaves, folk wisdom, and "the world of nature." Concerning this, Harold Courlander points out that there was interpolation taking place; Hebrew Bible figures often found themselves in conversation with the forces of nature and New Testament heroes.[11] In addition, churches were instrumental in the development of song among the slaves because they provided a place in which slaves could experiment with composition.[12] One clearly sees in the spirituals a modified version of the Christian faith—modified, that is, by traditional African melody. Several scholars acknowledge that some of the material incorporated into these slave songs is also found in white revivalist songs. This is particularly true concerning the songs sung by "oppressed" whites. Other scholars have argued that the Black spirituals are merely a variation on white spirituals, picked up during the camp meetings and other evangelical gatherings.[13] Regarding these issues, Albert Raboteau writes:

> [O]ppression was not slavery. The slaves' historical identity as a unique people was peculiarly their own. In the spirituals, the slaves affirmed and reaffirmed that identity religiously as they suffered and celebrated their journey from slavery to freedom.[14]

R. Nathaniel Dett confirms Raboteau's assertion and adds this question:

> . . . how otherwise shall one explain the strong, unwavering note of hope of final recompense, and the assurance of the perfectness of another life to come, unless one is willing to admit that the slave brought with him from Africa a religious inheritance which, far from being shaken in any way, was strengthened by his American experience?[15]

The exact location of spirituals within the slave community is a more complex issue. That is, thinkers such as John Lovell, Jr. argue that the spirituals are not strictly religious. Rather, they are religious to the extent they address the origins of life; yet, the spirituals extend beyond expressions of religiosity because they grew out of general life experience.[16] In fact, Lovell suggests that the first spirituals had nothing to do with religion, and had no connection with camp meetings because they dealt with life conditions (as if religion is devoid of these concerns). He contends the melodies created by Africans during the Middle Passage—prior to contact with white churches—shaped the white spirituals, and served as the foundation of the Black spirituals. Moreover, Lovell asserts that the songs Blacks sang during the camp meetings were new only to white ears. They had been sung for some time by the slaves. During these meetings, however, the song was customized and adapted to the slaves' environment, which began to change—due to restrictions on preacher and missionary efforts.

With the restrictions placed upon Black preachers, including the fear of physical danger for the promotion of non-status-quo doctrines and the restrictions inherent in the slaves' very introduction to Christianity, the spirituals provided the safest means by which to discuss so-called "dangerous" religious themes and issues. Furthermore, Lovell maintains that the words of the spirituals frequently found their way into other forms of musical expression which were not in essence religious. As a result, the lyrics served many musical functions ranging from work songs and "hollers" to ring shout melodies. Consequently, the words to the spirituals were not always biblically based, but often arose out of personal (yet communal) experience. In short:

> The subject of a call or holler could well be addressed to the same God of the spirituals. . . . This uniqueness was caused by the fact that, unlike African traditionalism which restricted its music to appropriate functions and events, slaves were not allowed to freely participate in all aspects of life common to African notions. Consequently, worship, work and relaxation were often performed under identical surroundings.[17]

Apparently, some scholars are not convinced by Lovell's argument regarding the "mundane" grounding of the spirituals. For example, the discussion of Black spirituals by theologian James H. Cone suggests that the spirituals are religious songs which contain nuggets of theological truth that can be combined with other aspects of African-American culture, history, and experience to create a working Black theology. I suggest that the spirituals are not merely cogs; rather, they represent a complete, yet nascent, Black theology, from which the basic thematic framework of later Black theologies is gleaned. One can assess the validity of this claim by looking at the development of central theological categories within spirituals.

According to James H. Cone, Black theology is a contextual and particularized theology of liberation concerned with the "being of God ["ultimate concern"] in the world in light of the existential situation of an oppressed community, relating the forces of liberation to the essence of the gospel, which is Jesus Christ."[18] Questionable aspects of this theistic/Christocentric perspective are implicitly addressed in the final chapter. Although the strong Christian tone of this definition is open to debate, it, at this point, provides a somewhat useful gauge for accessing theological formulations that are self-consciously Christian (theistic). According to this definition, it is reasonable to consider the following categories endemic to many formulations recognizable as Black (Christian) theology[19]: (1) the full reality of the oppressed—history, culture, and experience; (2) conception of God and Jesus Christ; (3) conception of heaven; and, (4) appeal to scripture. My understanding of this music suggests that all of these elements, beginning with existential awareness, are found in the spirituals.

The genius of the Black spiritual is seen in its profound expression of the world's complexities amid dehumanizing forces. As Benjamin Mays writes:

> [T]hese songs are the expressions of the restriction and domination which their creators experienced in the world about them. They represent the soul-life of the people. They embody the joy and sorrow, the hope and despair, the pathos and aspiration of the newly transplanted people; and through them the race was able to endure suffering and survive. Clearly, the Negro Spirituals are not songs of hate; they are not songs of revenge. They are songs neither of war nor of conquest. They are songs of the soil and of the soul.[20]

The cultural heritage and story of survival of African slaves in America is emotionally depicted within the music:

> I'm a rollin'
> I'm a rollin' through an unfriendly worl'
> I'm a rollin'
> I'm a rollin' through an unfriendly worl'.[21]

As a part of this descriptive process, the past is remembered, the present discussed, and the future planned. As Ralph Ellison suggests:

> Perhaps in the swift change of American society in which the meanings of one's origin are so quickly lost, one of the chief

values of living with music lies in its power to give us an orientation in time. In so doing, it gives significance to all those indefinable aspects of experience which nevertheless help to make us what we are. In the swift whirl of time music is a constant, reminding us of what we were and of that toward which we aspired.[22]

In this respect, the spirituals present the misery of life as a slave and speak to the isolation and disjointedness resulting from physical bondage. In light of this, is there any wonder why the slaves sang:

> Sometimes I feel like a motherless child,
> Sometimes I feel like a motherless child,
> Sometimes I feel like a motherless child,
> A long ways from home,
> A long ways from home.[23]

The spirituals often speak to the bitterness of life and the sense of hopelessness this engenders:

> Sometimes I'm up
> Sometimes I'm down,
> Oh, yes, Lord;
> Sometimes I'm almos' to de groun'
> Oh, yes, Lord.
>
> Altho' you see me goin' 'long so,
> Oh, yes, Lord;
> I have my trials here below.[24]

These words express the uncertainty of existence for African slaves who could not be certain of life from one day to the next. It was quite possible that a misunderstood action or the whim of slaveowners would mean being sold away from family and friends. Furthermore, beatings and sexual assault were a constant threat. The spirituals are not totally defeatist. To the contrary, the spirituals qualified the hardships of slave life with exclamations concerning the rewards that awaited them in heaven or "Canaan."

Spirituals depicting hopelessness often conclude with a sense of hope and of God's ultimate righteousness. Along this line, Howard Thurman suggests that pessimism became material out of which to create a desire to persevere.[25] That is, harsh reality (i.e., oppression) was juxtaposed to a notion of divine justice and equality (e.g., freedom). This message rings clear in "Go Down Moses":

> Go down, Moses
> Way down in Egypt land,
> Tell ole Pharaoh, to let my people go.
> . . . .
> When Isreal was in Egypt land:
> Let my people go,
> Oppressed so hard they could not stand,
> Let my people go.[26]

This spiritual illustrates the effort to locate a source of hope and strength outside of the immediate existential reality of the faithful. Moreover, this music outlines the basis and substance of hope—as present yet not always acknowledged by the physically perceiving. As a result, the spirituals illustrate a strong faith in the belief that hardships and pain do not escape God's gaze.

The imagery and symbolism of scripture and Christianity took hold among the slaves. And it was from these two elements that the slaves frequently sang of "a just God, just principles, a son of God who lived and died to see to it that justice would come to all people, including the poor and the untouchable and those who made mistakes and those who had little to offer besides their mere small selves."[27] Within many spirituals God stands out as the all knowing, powerful, and omnipresent creator, to whom those in need make appeal:

> We have a just God to plead-a our cause,
>   To plead-a our cause, to plead-a our cause,
> We have a just God to plead-a our cause,
> We are the people of God.[28]

The slaves were convinced that God had something good in store for them beyond slavery, and that they only had to wait on God, trust in God, and persevere. Yet, it was recognized that victory often came with a heavy price. The community represented within the language of the spirituals realized that difficult days had to be endured. Nonetheless, God was understood to be strong, just, loving, righteous, compassionate, and powerful. All these attributes meant that God could be trusted.

> God is a God!
> God don't never change!
> God is a God
> An' He always will be God.[29]

The spirituals' portrait of God is supplemented by a deep connection with Christ. Jesus Christ is often portrayed as the crucified savior, who through his suffering provided a heavenly future for those who endured unjust treatment on earth. Christ was understood to be "a god of compassion and suffering, a promulgator of freedom and peace and opportunity, a son of an omnipotent Father"[30]:

> Walk [Ride] in, kind Savior [King Jesus]
> No man can hinder me!
> Walk in, sweet Jesus,
> See what wonder Jesus done,
> O no man can hinder me![31]

The spirituals demonstrate a firm confidence in the ability of Jesus to conquer any of the slave's difficulties and triumphantly bring her or him to a better life.

Through his rupture of human time and history, Jesus represents the "already" status of freedom which is historically "immanent" as a result of the teleological nature of history. Accordingly, there is a closeness between Jesus and the slave; ontologically perceived, both are children of God. Epistomologically, both have a working knowledge of "unmerited" suffering. This connection is so intimate, that the spirituals even depict a physical proximity to the crucifixion event. One spiritual demonstrates this when saying:

> Were you there when they crucified my Lord?
> Were you there when they crucified my Lord?
> Sometimes, it causes me to tremble, tremble . . .
> Were you there, when they crucified my Lord?[32]

Jesus is also viewed as the exemplar of conduct. And to the extent that Jesus' life and death seemed redemptive and fruitful, Christian slaves were able to see merit in their efforts. Furthermore, the spirituals encourage believers to follow Christ's example of self-giving as a means by which to gain the reward—the fruitful consequences of their suffering. In most cases, the reward is connected with heaven:

My Lord, I've had many crosses an' trials here
   below;
My Lord, I hope to meet you in de manshans above.[33]

Others sang:

If you meet with crosses, an' trials on the way
Just keep your trust in Jesus,
An' don't forget to pray.
Let us cheer the weary traveler (3x)
Along the heavenly way.[34]

Heaven is often viewed as a new world in which the abused African is relieved of all earthly burdens and given the humanity and treasures her/his labor had provided. In addition, heaven serves as a critique of the hypocrisy and injustice experienced at the hands of slaveholders. This injustice, acknowledged as inconsistent with God's will, is ultimately corrected. The new equality is evident in the following song:

I've got a robe, you've got a robe,
All of God's chillun got a robe,
When I get to heab'n goin' to put on my robe,
Going to shout all ovah God's heab'n.[35]

Or according to these lines:

Let God's children have some peace,
I know de udder worl' is not like dis,
Swing low sweet chariot into de Wes'
I know de udder worl' is not like dis.[36]

At times, the reward is located on earth—a new earth constituted by humanity, equality, and a fulfilling existence, or a return to African soil.

It was through the idea of heaven, in whatever form found fitting, that Christian slaves were able to address their pain and suffering in a world which, at every turn, attempted to dehumanize them. The profound meaning of heaven is further explored by Cone when he remarks:

For Black slaves, who were condemned to carve out their existence in captivity, heaven meant that the eternal God had

made a decision about their humanity that could not be
destroyed by white masters. . . . [T]hey believed that God nevertheless had chosen black slaves as his own and that this
election bestowed upon them a freedom to be. . . .[37]

Their present condition was not the last word, nor the final measure
of their worth. Their suffering at the hands of hypocrites would end
and God, the judge, would ultimately adjudicate justice:

> Sooner-a-will be done with the trouble of this world,
> Sooner-a-will be done with the trouble of this world,
> Going home to live with God.[38]

Others sang:

> Dere's no rain to wet you,
>   O, yes, I want to go home.
> Dere's no sun to burn you,
>   O, yes, I want to go home.
> O, push along, believers.[39]

In the mind of the slave, the interconnectedness between their
condition, God, Christ, and heaven implied a concrete and contextual
response to the problem of evil. God, through Christ, made victory
out of human suffering. One way or another, they knew their life
would mirror Christ's life and that they would be free in heaven—"no
cross, no crown" :

> Steal away, steal away home,
> I ain't got long to stay here.[40]

Suffering was seen as a condition God would not only rectify, but also
reward. That is, the evils experienced in life would be transformed
into a humanized and fruitful existence:

> O, Christians keep a-in-chin' along,
>   keep a-in-chin' along
> Massa Jesus is comin' bye an' bye.[41]

In like manner, the God who provides heaven as the reward for a "good
life," so to speak, also provides hell as proof of sin's destructiveness.

Biblical accounts of God's breaking into human history documented, for slaves, the perpetual presence of God with the oppressed. Through this contextualization of scripture onto Southern life, Christian slaves gleaned a consistency in God's dealings with humans. It was assumed that God's concern with and desire for righteous existence applies to the contemporary world of the slaves. Regarding this, slaves sang:

> Daniel faithful to his God,
> Would not bow down to men,
> An' by God's enemy he was hurled
>   into de lion's den,
> God locked de lion's jaw we read,
> An robbed him of his prey,
> An' de God dat lived in Daniel's time is
>   jus da same today.[42]

The process by which slaves made this juxtaposition of their condition and biblical accounts involves the use of a hermeneutic of suspicion and identification.

Slaves looked at their existential condition and were not satisfied with the so-called "Christian" explanations provided by slaveholders and their ministers. Many slaves could not believe that God condoned their condition and rejected their efforts at liberation. Obedience to unjust practices and laws could not be consistent with the divine design of a loving and just God. This suspicion resulted in slaves "looking into" scripture themselves in order to find the answers to the questions posed by the hardships of life, and treating with scorn practices which did not line up with biblical precedence.

When turning to scripture, the slaves naturally identified with the chosen people of God who encountered suffering at the hands of cruel task masters. This recognition of a similar existential condition extended to the assumption that God would work on behalf of African slaves as God had for the Children of Israel. God is consistent in God's dealings with humanity; and therefore, God is forever concerned with the liberation of the oppressed. This thinking is certainly in line with the theological outlook of contemporary Black theology.

Within *Spirituals and the Blues*, James H. Cone begins a constructive project, based upon experience and objective academic tools, which entails developing a Black theology of liberation based upon Black cultural resources and framed by Black history of oppression.

Within the spirituals, for example, Cone sees the "essence of Black religion" (i.e., the record of God breaking into human history) and he demonstrates this by outlining the concept of God, doctrine of Christ, and eschatology, exposed within the spirituals. In short, Cone argues that the spirituals understand God as involved in the world, liberating oppressed people. In addition, he notes within the spirituals an understanding of Christ as the risen savior who identifies with the oppressed because he has experienced their pain. And heaven is offered as the symbolic promise of a properly lived life. In short, spirituals take a theological position which suggest that any situation that does not amount to liberation is evil and therefore against the will of God.

Cone's analysis of basic theological elements within the spirituals differs little from the discussion of the same elements offered earlier in this chapter. My disagreement with him concerns his failure to see the way in which oppression forced an assessment of these theological categories in the form of "theodicy." Cone misses the crux of the spirituals' theological discourse—"theodicy." And as a result, he does not fully understand the self-contained and layered theological nature of the spirituals. That is, the spirituals not only speak of God, Christ, and heaven; they speak of God out of and in the context of Black suffering, using the language of "theodicy": What is God doing about our suffering? John Lovell, in *Black Song*, points to this by acknowledging the nagging question in the spiritual which forms the basis of "theodicy":

> Although the prevailing view is essentially optimistic, the spiritual is honeycombed with realistic doubts and fears. Sometimes, the poet is not sure he has what it takes, or that religion is strong enough to override evil . . . or that justice is not man's greatest illusion.[43]

Cone should see Lovell's point when Cone thinks about his own words: "the spiritual is the people's response to the social contradiction."[44] Yet this observation regrettably eludes him:

> The spirituals nowhere raise questions about God's existence or matters of theodicy, and it is safe to assume that the slave community did not perceive of theoretical solutions of the problem of evil as a felt need. Rather, their needs were defined by the existential realities which they encountered.[45]

Cone does not recognize the presence of the theodical question in the spirituals that harsh experience forces slaves to wrestle with. Yet, in all fairness, Cone does acknowledge the complex nature of thought within the spirituals. However, this recognition surfaces only with respect to the dual program of otherworldly and temporal liberation, a distinction he makes in response to Benjamin May's emphasis on the compensatory and otherworldly nature of the spirituals.[46]

Cone acknowledges the manner in which existential hardship raises questions concerning religion. Yet, he assumes only a certain class takes the time to philosophically and theologically formulate such questions:

> These are hard questions, and they are still relevant today. In the history of theology and philosophy, these questions are the core of the "problem of evil"; and college and seminary professors have spent many hours debating them. But black slaves did not have the opportunity to investigate the problem of suffering in the luxury of a seminar room with all the comforts of modern living. They encountered suffering in the cotton fields. . . . They had to deal with the absurdities of human existence under whip and pistol.[47]

The harsh conditions under which slaves reflected upon their religion and life does not negate the philosophical and theological nature of this thought. Their condition, in fact, makes such theodical questioning more vital and urgent than it is for the "leisurely" academics. Christian slaves faced a pressing crisis of faith which forces the existence of Black "theodicy"—"theodicy" grounded in the absurdity of Black oppression combined with Black faith.

In suggesting that spirituals do not speak to "theodicy," Cone limits the actual dimensions of theodical examination. He suggests an opposition between theoretical theism and a concern with existential reality. A defense of theism and existential reality are both necessary if the task is to reflect the content of "theodicy" defined as the justification of God in light of evil in the world. Although the former portion of theodical formulations (i.e., God) is often embedded in the latter (i.e., existential reality) both are implicitly present. In fact, moral evil is only a religious problem for the theist—the "faithful." Within the spirituals, one notices the assumed theism noted above.

Cone believes that the spirituals do not concern themselves with "theodicy" because they do not seek to blame God for evil.[48] His argument involves a misinterpretation of the nature and objective of "theodicy." It is fundamentally concerned with justifying God, not condemning God. "Theodicy" seeks to understand the mystery of God's activity and presence in a world seemingly gone wrong. The spirituals do not deny God as a result of Black suffering because they see God working through pain. Nonetheless, this continuing belief in God's justice is not a denial of philosophical inquiry ("theodicy").

Even Cone, who appears to vehemently reject the existence of "theodicy" as a concern for slaves, is unable to maintain his staunch opposition to the actual existence of Black "theodicy." Within *The Spirituals and the Blues*, Cone outlines the spirituals' response to "theodicy". However, Cone fails to recognize that logically, the spirituals must pose the question of evil if they suggest a response. He writes:

> That this theme of God's involvement in history and his libera-
> tion of the oppressed from bondage should be central in black
> slave religion and the spirituals is not surprising, for it corre-
> sponds with the black people's need to know that their slavery
> was not the divine creator's intention for them.[49]

The response to this need to know is presented in spirituals such as "Didn't My Lord Deliver Daniel?":

> Didn't my Lord Deliver Daniel?
> Deliver Daniel, Deliver Daniel.
> Didn't my Lord Deliver Daniel?
> And why not every man?[50]

This spiritual is often considered an affirmation of God's liberating presence in human history. This is how Cone reads it. However, I would suggest that the question posed in this spiritual is not rhetorical in nature; rather it is a genuine and pressing question, carrying with it the weight of oppression due to skin color.

Concerning the origin of evil, the spirituals' canon attributes it to the fall of humanity, in keeping with traditional theological anthropology. This proclivity of humanity toward error is manipulated by the devil. Suffering is not the result of providential design. Accordingly, humans must constantly work to avoid evil and the devil's lure. Suffering is evil and remains so; however, this evil does not conquer God's ultimate plan. The theodical key is found in the words I heard as a child: "Lord, troubles of ev'ry kind, Thank God,

I'll always find, Dat a little talk wid Jesus makes it right." God transforms "troubles of ev'ry kind" into the promise of heaven. In this way, God's ultimate plan is not conquered by evil. In fact, the Christ event is used to illustrate God's transforming power and heaven is revealed as the reward for endurance. Hence, on one level and as was mentioned above, heaven illustrates the Christian slave's response to "theodicy":

> Mos' done toilin' here, O, brethren,
> I'm mos' done toilin' here.
> I ain't been to heab'n, but I been tol'
> Mos' done toilin' here.
> De street up dere am paved wid gol',
> Mos' done toilin' here.[51]

The complete response to "theodicy," however, is found in the suffering itself as opposed to the final reward given to those who suffer (i.e., heaven). That is, the passion of Christ taught slaves that suffering has the power to transform situations when handled properly. Suffering can be redemptive, and suffering's redemptive nature is the slave's final response to "theodicy." This line of reasoning, resulting from an identification with Christ's passion, suggests that suffering is a necessary prerequisite for redemption and in this respect it is fruitful. Regarding this, Cone argues that slaves saw themselves in the passion of Christ, and within their music they expressed this relationship.[52] That is, because the faithful can experience the reality of divine presence, they can endure suffering and transform it into an event of redemption.[53] This is played out, for example, in the following spiritual which highlights God's redeeming power relative to communication with Christ:

> Sometimes de forked lightnin' an' mutterin'
>   thunder too,
> Of trials an' tem'tation make it hard for me
>   an' you
> But Jesus, is our frien',
> He'll keep us to de en'
> An' a little talk wid Jesus, make it right.[54]

The sufferings of life are seen as a part of the growth leading to spiritual maturity:

De young lam's mus' fin' de way.
Wid crosses an' trials on ev'ry side,
De young lam's mus' fin' de way.[55]

Clearly, the spirituals provided an invaluable form of theological analysis and communication. They presented creative formulations for many "hush-harbor" religious activities. Yet, the spirituals had neither the sensibilities nor the structure appreciated by many Black clergypersons. Therefore, spirituals found an uneasy audience in many nineteenth-century independent Black churches. Consequently, efforts were made to forget the folk culture developed in slavery as a means by which to forge a future based upon imitation of mainstream spirituality, complete with singing by note. Bishop Henry M. Turner of the African Methodist Episcopal Church demonstrates this attitude when remarking that Blacks "have a widespread custom of singing on revival occasions, especially, what is commonly called *Spiritual Songs*, most of which are devoid of both sense and reason; and some are absolutely false and vulgar."[56] Although the spirituals found an uneasy audience in Black churches during the nineteenth century, their message remained. As Eileen Southern points out, the spirituals survived among Black worshippers who experimented "with composing all kinds of religious music, from the lowly spiritual to formal anthems and similar set pieces."[57] The musical content of the spirituals is not all that survived; the basic theological outlook contained in the lyrics repeatedly presents itself.

2

NINETEENTH-CENTURY BLACK THOUGHT ON BLACK SUFFERING

E arly-to-mid-nineteenth century African-American religious thought was influenced in part by slave experience, abolitionist propaganda, and the fears of Southern planters. Most notably, planters feared the blurring of the line between economic productivity and the slave's humanity. And so, every avenue by which such ideas could enter the mind of Southern slaves had to be closed. This of necessity included the humanizing potential of the gospel. Therefore, in order to avoid contact between slaves and these dangerous ideas, religious instruction and activity for slaves were held to a minimum.[1]

Conditions for Black Christians in the North were not much better. However, in the North, free blacks took advantage of the surge in moral consciousness suggested in abolitionist rhetoric. In addition to the intellectual impetus provided, abolitionists also provided financial support for fledgling Black organizations. With this type of assistance and the determination of free Blacks to enjoy certain rights and privileges, independent Black churches (such as the African Methodist Episcopal Church) developed.

Black churches never restricted their activities to the realm of spiritual health. On the contrary, Black churches committed themselves to moral reform, sociopolitical change, and mission activity. For example, organizations such as the Society for the Suppression of Vice and Immorality (founded by Reverend Richard Allen and two others) sought to improve the moral condition of the Black community.

Among their goals was curbing of alcohol use and the fostering of virtues such as thrift and industry.[2]

In addition to the work of these organizations, the sermons of Black religious leaders stressed moral uplift. Reverend Allen's "Address to the People of Color" given in 1808 illustrates this point. After a tragedy involving several young black men, he says:

> Labour with thy hands and thou will provide things that are honest, and with a good conscience enjoy them. Fly for thy life from the chambers of the harlot. Know, O young man, that her steps take hold of hell. Secret crimes shall be dragged to light and seen by the eye of the world in their horrid forms. The solemn record is standing: "Whoremongers and adulterers, God will judge." Go not to the tavern; the song of the drunkard will soon be changed to weeping and wailing and gnashing of teeth. Drunkenness hurls reason from the throne, and when she has fallen, Vice stands ready to ascend it. Break off, O young man your impious companions. If you still grasp their hands they will drag you down to everlasting fire.[3]

Richard Allen and other Black leaders did not advise moral reform for its own sake. Rather, they saw an integral connection between proper moral conduct and the freedom of Black people. That is, these leaders believed that a proper moral standing among free Blacks would assist in the freeing of slaves and the increase in rights afforded to all African-Americans. That is, white Americans would not be able to enslave those who, by their actions, demonstrated themselves to be civilized and moral beings. Black religious leaders were determined to respond to all the objections whites gave to the granting of full rights to Black Americans. In this way, Black clergy-persons hoped to move the South toward freedom. However, the bulk of independent Black church activity took place in the North.

With the Civil War and Reconstruction, independent Black churches began to aggressively address the political, social, economic, and spiritual needs of Blacks in Southern states.[4] Bishop Daniel Payne (of the African Methodist Episcopal Church) and others undertook the establishment of churches in North Carolina, South Carolina, and other Southern states. In spite of the continued missionary activities of churches, such as the Methodist Episcopal Church (North) and the Methodist Episcopal Church (South), many Blacks exercised their new sense of freedom by leaving white denominations and joining

Black ones.[5] Chronicles such as AME Church histories written by Bishop Handy and Bishop Payne illustrate the expansion of the AME Church and the African Methodist Episcopal Zion (AME Zion) Church into Southern states such as Georgia and South Carolina.

The synthesis of the independent Black churches and the folk religion ways of the former slaves was not smooth. This was due, in part, to the reluctance of many Black religious leaders to approve of the ex-slaves' religious expression.[6] As chapter one argued, many Black religious leaders believed "corn field" religious practices merely reinforced negative opinions concerning Blacks. Therefore, many Black churches incorporated Eurocentric attitudes and practices, which included the replacing of spirituals with hymns. This attempt to remove spirituals from Black church worship appears to have been more a conflict with the form of the spirituals than their content. That is, religious leaders such as Daniel Payne objected to the physical display that accompanied the spirituals rather than the message contained in the lyrics. Accordingly, only the form of expression was altered. The opinions of Black Christians, such as David Walker, continued to echo and expound upon themes concerning suffering, which are rooted in the spirituals.

Walker (a Methodist) moved to Boston and became a shop owner and activist. Convinced that slavery must end, Walker spent a great deal of time spreading abolitionist doctrine among the free persons of Boston. However, Walker desired to take his antislavery message to a much larger audience, including enslaved Southern Blacks. He accomplished this through his famous *Appeal* (1829)[7] which he distributed by attaching it to the clothing he sold in his shop.

Within his book, Walker denounced the racist practices of the United States; and in so doing, he stirred strong reaction from both proslavery and antislavery forces. One sees the reason for such fiery response when examining the potent questions asked by Walker:

> . . . I say, if God gives you peace and tranquility, and suffers you thus to go on afflicting us, and our children, who have never given you the least provocation—would he be to us a God of justice?[8]

Walker asserted that God did not condone the brutal treatment of African-Americans. Divine sanction of Black oppression was impossible for Walker because he understood God as kind, just, loving, powerful, and righteous. As such, God works to bring about the freedom of slaves and the establishment of a society based upon proper moral and ethical codes of conduct. Walker argued that the evil inflicted upon African-Americans has no positive value because it is the result of human misconduct. Therefore, African-Americans, he continued, had a responsibility to fight against their oppression and obtain the enlightenment necessary for the uplift of the Black race worldwide. Those who failed to take advantage of every opportunity to free themselves from dehumanization and ignorance deserved the harsh treatment they received. Accordingly:

> The man who would not fight under our Lord and Master Jesus Christ, in the glorious and heavenly cause of freedom and of God—to be delivered from the most wretched, abject and servile slavery, that ever a people was afflicted with since the foundation of the world, to the present day—ought to be kept with all of his children or family, in slavery, or in chains, to be butchered by his cruel *enemies*.[9]

As a result of slavery's brutality and the continuing desire of whites to hold Blacks in bondage, Walker suggested that African-Americans be sure in their resistance:

> If you commence, make sure work—do not trifle, for they will not trifle with you—they want us for their slaves, and think nothing of murdering us in order to subject us to that wretched condition—therefore, if there is an *attempt* made by us, kill or be killed.[10]

The language of *The Appeal* suggests that Walker's "kill or be killed" attitude was given precedence by the biblical accounts of the Hebrew children. God willed their deliverance even by bloodshed[11] and God willed the freedom of God's oppressed dark children. However, at certain points in his texts, Walker suggested that slavery was allowed for pedagogical reasons—due to the disobedience of Black people. That is to say:

> Ignorance and treachery one against the other—a grovelling servile and abject submission to the lash of tyrants, we see plainly, my brethren, are not the natural element for the blacks, as the Americans try to make us believe; but these are misfortunes which God has suffered our fathers to be enveloped in for many ages, no doubt in consequence of their

disobedience to their Maker, and which do, indeed, reign at this time among us, almost to the destruction of all other principles: for I must truly say, that ignorance, the mother of treachery and deceit, gnaws into our very vitals.[12]

In this comment, one notices the degree to which David Walker found some value or fruitfulness in suffering. Yet, he did not directly attribute this to God. Ultimately, the reason for Black suffering remains a mystery:

> ... when I look over these United States of America ... and see the ignorant deceptions and consequent wretchedness of my brethren, I am brought ofttimes solemnly to a stand, and in the midst of my reflections I exclaim to my God, "Lord didst thou make us to be slaves to our brethren, the whites?" But when I reflect that God is just, and that millions of my wretched brethren would meet death with glory—yea, more, would plunge into the very mouths of cannons and be torn into particles ... in preference to a mean submission to the lash of tyrants, I am with streaming eyes, compelled to shrink back into nothingness before my Maker, and exclaim again, thy will be done, O Lord God Almighty.[13]

To some degree, David Walker resolved his doubts by locating God's will in resistance to slavery, as opposed to seeing it in the existence of slavery. And accordingly, white Americans challenged God's vengeance by attempting to hold Blacks in perpetual bondage. Walker believed such acts of defiance only resulted in destruction:

> Can anything be a greater mockery of religion than the way in which it is conducted by the Americans? It appears as though they are bent only on daring God Almighty to do his best— they chain and handcuff us and our children and drive us around the country like brutes, and go into the house of the God of justice to return him thanks for having aided them in their infernal cruelties inflected upon us. Will the Lord suffer his people to go on much longer, taking his holy name in vain? Will he not stop them, *preachers* and all? O Americans! Americans!! I call God—I call angels—I call men, to witness, that your *Destruction is at hand*, and will be speedily consummated unless you *Repent*.[14]

Because Walker understood God as good and justice, blame for slavery could not rest ultimately with God. To hold God responsible would require a rejection of God's goodness or a denial of God's existence. (These entail propositions three and four outlined in the introduction.) In addition, Walker is unwilling to suggest the existence of a limited God, one incapable of positively shaping human history. This type of God is not in keeping, according to Walker, with the scriptures. Therefore, he is forced to find an alternative approach to solving the problem of Black suffering—a rethinking of the derivation and nature of suffering.

It is reasonable to assert that Walker's *Appeal* presents an understanding of Black suffering which fluctuates between (or perhaps combines) three possibilities: (1) suffering is the result of white America's misconduct; (2) suffering is pedagogical in nature; and, (3) suffering is divine mystery. The second option suggests a beneficial function to suffering. This redemptive suffering theme is more consistently developed by subsequent figures such as Maria Stewart.

The thought of Black women concerning the issue of Black suffering—informed by their experiences—served as a corrective, expanding and critiquing the materials provided by Black men. During the years of slavery, Black women's bodies were forced to fulfil the economic, sexual, and nurturing desires of white slaveholders.[15] In the fields, Black women worked as hard as men. In the "Big House," they raised white children; and, in their cabins, they raised Black children. When their actions displeased their owners, Black women's punishment was as severe and demonic as that given to Black men.

The middle class aspirations within nineteenth-century United States society resulted in women being forced to model their behavior in accordance with Victorian principles of "true womanhood" (i.e., "the cult of true womanhood"). According to Paula Giddings in *When and Where I Enter*, women were required to maneuver within prescribed parameters of submissiveness, purity, and piety, in order to be considered true and moral women. Many African-Americans upheld this Victorian ethic as a means by which to remove the stigma of slavery and advance the race. In some instances, Black men strongly encouraged Black women to limit their activities to the traditional—a false notion to be sure—roles of homemakers and helpers. However, for some Black women, these parameters were difficult to maintain because of the relationship between class, race, and morality. In other words, Black women were perceived as a different and inferior type of humanity; they were relegated to the status of "mammy" (an asexual servant) or jezebel (one ruled by uncontrolled sexuality).

In order to counter the oppressive connotations implicit in the Victorian ethic, Black female activists argued that Black women were true women; it was their historical situation that determined their condition. As Sojourner Truth indicates (during a women's rights gathering in Akron, Ohio, 1851), their harsh past does not make them less than women:

> That man over there says women need to be helped into carriages, and lifted over ditches, and to have the best place everywhere. Nobody ever helps me into carriages, or over mud-puddles, or gives me any best place! And ain't I a woman? Look at me! Look at my arm! I have ploughed and planted, and gathered into barns, and no man could head me! And ain't I a woman? I could work as much and eat as much as a man—when I could get it—and bear the lash as well! And ain't I a woman? I have borne thirteen children, and seen the most all sold off to slavery, and when I cried out with my mother's grief, none but Jesus heard me! And ain't I a woman?[16]

If Black women were given the educational opportunities afforded to others, their inherent value and beauty would be evident. Consequently, many Black women asserted that their suffering did not suggest an inherent inferiority. Slavery and its ramifications had not nullified the moral fortitude of Black womanhood. Rather, as metal is refined by fire, the ethical and moral fiber of Black women was strengthened by their suffering. This argument suggests the response to Black suffering offered by many Black women. Black men asserted that the enslavement of Africans was known by God and would result in the redemption of "America" and Africa. Suffering, then, was pedagogical, providing tools and strength for a great work. In addition to acknowledging this resolution, Black women also suggested a unique role for themselves in the redemption project—as a result of their experiences. Maria Stewart is the first African-American woman to publicly make this argument.

Taking upon herself the prophetic mantle of race uplift and criticism, Maria Stewart gave a series of public lectures in Boston (1831–33). In so doing, Stewart was the first woman of color to lecture publicly on political issues. Like David Walker, Stewart was not a preacher. However, as a committed Christian, her writings contain a theological framework, heavily rooted in scripture. For Stewart, scripture has two effects. On one level, it points to the workings of God in history—illustrating the power, righteousness, and justice God brings to the world. On another level, scripture notes the consistency and transhistorical nature of God's contact with humanity. The exodus was a major marker of God's devotion to human freedom, and Stewart latched on to this as representative of God's concern with all oppressed peoples. The United States would never have a secure existence until it began to deal properly with African-Americans. Until then, it faced the same fate as the land of Egypt which held God's other chosen people in bondage.[17]

As with the spirituals and Walker, Stewart suggests that the actions of God presented in the Bible provide for an understanding of moral and ethical conduct excluding the possibility of slavery (and sexism). Scripture, then, becomes a measuring rod for human relations. Appeal to scripture provides the rubric for a rethinking of Black identity and purpose beyond the distorted view from slavery. The information provided by the word of God and Stewart's personal conviction as a Christian necessitate both an end to slavery and the stifling of women's aspirations.

As Clarice Martin insightfully points out, the autobiographical writing of Stewart sheds light upon her religious (and theological) outlook. That is, the presentation in literature of Stewart's experiences not only serves to humanize the history of African-Americans, it also sheds light on the nature and function of religious thought and practice within Stewart's activism.[18] They are intimately linked because God requires this dual commitment.

The God who sparked Stewart's conversion and commitment to social reform seeks the freedom of African slaves. The scriptures make this view of God a necessity. Furthermore, such a God could not be the agent responsible for oppression. That is:

> Stewart's reflections on the tension of how to reconcile her experience of racial oppression with belief in the all-powerful Judeo-Christian God focus less on attempts to "absolve the deity of responsibility for injustice," or to "protect the deity's honor," pronouncing a "not guilty" verdict over God for that which destroys the affairs of human beings, and the world; rather, Stewart assumes both ontologically and epsitemologically that God is near to and acts on behalf of the powerless and the disenfranchised in the interests of divine justice.[19]

She, like Walker, was unable to hold this position without also suggesting that suffering had a function which (to some degree) rendered it fruitful. At times, Stewart claimed that suffering was pedagogical in nature:

> Why is it, my friends, that our minds have been blinded by ignorance, to the present moment: Tis on account of sin. Why is it that our church is involved in so much difficulty? It is on account of sin. Why is it that God has cut down, upon our right hand and upon our left, the most learned and intelligent of our men? O, shall I say, it is on account of sin![20]

Stewart further argued that the condition of African-Americans helped them recognize their shortcomings and move toward God's will:

> That day we, as a people, hearken unto the voice of the lord, our God, and walk in his ways and ordinances, and become distinguished for our ease, elegance and grace, combined with other virtues, that day the Lord will raise us up, and enough to aid and befriend us, and we shall begin to flourish.[21]

Stewart claimed that African-Americans had been foolish, and God needed to provide them with a painful education. This refined African-Americans, freed them from their ignorance and sin which hampered the attainment of rights and privileges. Once cognizant of these short-comings, and determined to correct them, African- Americans can function as God's coworkers, helping bring about justice.

Stewart found a special place in this process for Black women due to the many difficulties they faced. In a word, their hardships provided them with a "specialness," a unique ability or inner strength needed to uplift African-Americans. The unique character and fortitude of Black women creates a cycle of dependency on them by others. They are expected to shoulder the burdens of the day because they have pro-claimed their unique qualifications for doing so. Stewart's response to human suffering maintains a version of the redemptive suffering argument—tailored, of course, to Black women. In this way, Stewart resolves the problem of evil using the first of the four approaches outlined in the introduction—a reevaluation of suffering. This place for Black women, carved out by their suffering, is not limited to the domestic sphere. On the contrary, it expands into all realms:

> If such women as are described here [e.g., Jewish prophetesses and Greek women who delivered the Oracles] once existed, be

no longer astonished then, my brethren and friends, that God at this eventful period should raise up your own females to strive, by their example both in public and private, to assist those who are endeavoring to stop the strong current of prejudice that flows so profusely against us at present. No longer ridicule their efforts, it will be counted for sin. For God makes use of feeble means sometimes, to bring about his most exalted purposes.[22]

Ending her public lecturing career in Boston on a defeatist note, Stewart concluded that the oppression of African-Americans was ordained by God (i.e., providential) and that it would end only with God's decree:

It is the sovereign will of God that our condition should be thus and so. "For he hath formed one vessel for honor, and another for dishonor" [Rom. 9:21]. And shall the clay say to him that hath formed it, why hast thou formed me thus? It is high time to drop political discussions and when our day of deliverance comes, God will provide a way for us to escape, and fight his own battles.[23]

Nonetheless, this pessimisim—based upon personal trials and rejection as a speaker, rather than rethought theological perspectives—does not hamper her teleological views. Stewart continues to view suffering as temporary; yet, it is a temporary evil that her personal efforts suggests is best resolved by God.

In subsequent years, Frances Watkins Harper and other Black women activists suggested a unique position for women within the basic redemptive aura of Black experience—a continuation of Stewart's early theme. This position was not based upon their sex; rather, it was the result of their strong—tried by fire—character. This position was clearly presented by Fannie Barrier Williams, who stated that "Black women have a special sense of sympathy for all who suffer . . . offering the other cheek of reason, since they have suffered so long and so deeply."[24]

Frances Harper is in agreement when writing the following lines:

I am not sure that women are naturally so much better than men that they will clear the stream by the virtue of their womanhood; it is not through sex but through character that the best influence of women upon the life of the nation must be exerted.[25]

Women (particularly Black women) had the requisite character, skills, and divine favor to secure basic rights for all. They had a sensitivity which was manifest in an awareness of oppression's multilayered structure. In keeping with her contemporaries, Harper did not believe that slavery was a virtue in and of itself. Rather, out of the fiery furnace of slavery and suffering, African-Americans had refined and toughened themselves. This redemptive aspect, it should be noted, is most recognizable in a postslavery moment. Once this evil is stopped, such fruitful consequences become abundantly evident. One sees this, for example, in Harper's story entitled "The Two Offers." In this tale, Janette Austin, the protaganist, grows and is strengthened as a result of life's troubles and suffering. Concerning Janette's suffering, Harper writes:

> . . . and so, pressing back the bitter sobs from her almost breaking heart, like the dying dolphin, whose beauty is born of its death anguish, her genius gathered strength from suffering and wonderous power and brilliancy from the agony she hid within the desolate chambers of her soul.[26]

Harper did not suggest that one should seek opportunities to suffer nor that oppressive situations go unchallenged. Janette's movement beyond lost love illustrates this point:

> . . . Life, with its stern realities, met her; its solemn responsibilities confronted her, and turning, with an earnest and shattered spirit, to life's duties and trials, she found a calmness and strength that she had only imagined in her dreams of poetry and song.[27]

In a word, Harper suggests that situations resulting in suffering are not ideal; however, until they are removed they do "make us tough."

A similar perspective is found in the writings of Anna J. Cooper, Ph.D. Within *A Voice from the South*,[28] she developed her understanding of race relations and the steps and resources necessary to correct this oppressive encounter. Cooper recognized that slow developments were normative as long as the unique talents of Black women were ignored. These talents could not be matched or substituted by others.[29] That is to say:

> . . . as our Caucasian barristers are not to blame if they cannot *quite* put themselves in the dark man's place, neither should

the dark man be wholly expected fully and adequately to
reproduce the exact voice of the Black woman.[30]

Tainted with Victorian ethical standards of "women's place," Cooper
charted out the unique role of women in race uplift. Unable to see as
clearly as does Harper the reason for this "specialness" outside of
gender roles, Cooper believed the unique role of Black women
resulted from their "feminine flavor"—informed by the multidimen-
sionality of their sufferings.

> Everything to this race is new and strange and inspiring.
> There is a quickening of its pulses and a glowing of its self-con-
> sciousness. Something like this, it strikes me, is the enthusi-
> asm which stirs the genius of young Africans in America; and
> the memory of past oppression and the fact of present
> attempted repression observed to gather momentum for its
> irrepressible prowess. . . . What a responsibility then to have
> the sole management of the primal lights and shadows! Such
> is the colored woman's office. She must stamp weal or woe on
> the coming history of this people.[31]

Accordingly, the depth of Black women's influence was yet to be
understood. Thus:

> . . . to be a woman of the Negro race in America, and to be able
> to grasp the deep significance of the possibilities of the crisis,
> is to have a heritage, it seems to me, unique in the ages. In the
> first place, the race is young and full of the elasticity and
> hopefulness of youth. All its achievements are before it . . . and
> the memory of past oppression and the fact of present
> attempted repression only serve to gather momentum for its
> irrepressible powers.[32]

Many of Walker's and Stewart's contemporaries held a perspective on Black suffering which suggested that slavery in and of itself
was evil, but it was a providential evil out of which God would bring
ultimate good. This opinion was in keeping with notions of
American manifest destiny developed with the coming of the first
European settlers to North America. One version of this theory
translated into a desire to establish the colonies as a moral example
to the rest of the world. The more damaging translation of this

thought concerned the doctrine of white supremacy and the providential role of white Americans in spreading Western civilization and Christianity.

The latter translation of manifest destiny theory allowed many proslavery spokespersons to justify their treatment of Africans (and Native Americans) by asserting that slavery provided these "heathens" with civilization. However, abolitionists also saw the usefulness of these theories. As Wilson Moses remarks in *Black Messiahs and Uncle Toms*, "The holy war against slavery and their [slaves'] ultimate deliverance from it was associated in the minds of black people and in the minds of other Americans with the sacred mission of the United States to extend freedom to all persons within its boundaries."[33]

Black Christians manipulated this theme and combined it with biblical imagery, to express a solution to the apparent paradox of their enslavement. Like many white Americans who argued that they were ordained by God to civilize the world, African-Americans suggested that God had set them apart to be tested. Reverend William Miller of the AME Zion Church certainly believed this. Although he did not perceive suffering as being inherently good, Miller proclaims its refining quality. In spite of slaveowners and their behavior, Miller "was still tempted to cry with David, 'It is good for me that I have been afflicted, that I may learn thy statutes.'"[34] Some African-Americans saw this affliction (or learning process) as preparation for the task of redeeming Africa.

Absalom Jones, the first Black ordained Episcopal priest and founder of St. Thomas' Church in Philadelphia, alluded to this point (1808):

> Perhaps [God's] design was, that a knowledge of the gospel might be acquired by some of the [slaves'] descendants, in order that they might be qualified to be the messengers of it, to the land of their fathers.[35]

Jones acknowledged the possibility that slavery was providential and a tool by which Africans gained the desire to return to Africa and the skills necessary to redeem it. This notion was refined by prominent Black nationalists[36] such as Reverend Alexander Crummell.

Reverend Crummell was an Episcopal priest. In 1852, having fully experienced the cruelties of white racism and discrimination, Crummell was attracted to the African mission field where he remained until 1873. Crummell, like many nineteenth-century Black nationalists, believed that Africans had been brought to America to procure Christianity and civilization.[37] In keeping with other Black leaders, Crummell manipulated manifest destiny theory and biblical imagery to provide this line of reasoning. Crummell saw a relationship between the Hebrews and African-Americans. Concerning this he stated, "In a sense, not equal, indeed, to the case of the Jews, but parallel, in a lower degree, such a people are a 'chosen people' of the Lord. There is, so to speak, a covenant relation which God has established between Himself and them."[38] Like David Walker before him, Crummel maintained a concept of God as just, righteous, and powerful. The plight of Africans and African-Americans required the presence of such a God. And the teleological nature of events points toward the divine plan of a "civilized" Africa.

This, however, would not be a pain-free process. Similar to the Jews before them, Crummell defined the suffering of African-Americans as providential—a process of refining by means of ordeals. In addition, the suffering of African-Americans pointed to their special role. That is, God provided their suffering as a means by which to prepare Blacks for a great destiny:

> The fact that black people in the United States had not been destroyed by slavery demonstrated that the sufferings of the "captive exiles from Africa" were meant not as a judgement but as a discipline. Their tribulations were not intended to punish or destroy but to prepare the black race for a glorious destiny. It was obvious that the black race in America had "risen superior to the dreaded infliction of a prolonged servitude."[39]

Crummell believed that this "glorious destiny" involved God's historical use of indigenous people to spread the gospel to foreign lands. Accordingly, Crummell asserted that indigenous people possess a disposition similar to the "natives" of the land and were thereby better equipped to gain a foothold for Christianity. Thus, African-Americans had been brought to the United States as "serfs for centuries, on the plantations and in household," and by this contact "they have, themselves, been somewhat permeated and vitalized by the civilization and the Christian principles of their superiors."[40] Thus, African-American Christians that were trained properly served God's design to "send Christianity to Africa" and "invite attention to it [Christianity]."[41] Although Crummel eventually lost hope in the idea of redeeming Africa, he maintained his conviction that African-American suffering was redemptive. This knowledge, however, should be directed at circumstances in North America.

Many Black religious leaders were influenced by Alexander Crummell's position on the destiny of African-Americans and Black nationalism. Among those inspired by the words of Crummell was the young African Methodist Episcopal Church minister, Henry McNeal Turner.[42]

Turner was born to free parents on February 1, 1834, in New-berry, South Carolina. Although free by birth, Henry Turner was familiar with the degradation slaves encountered; he learned early that the South was willing to use any means to maintain the existing economic and social structure. Nonetheless, Turner had aspirations which, he recounts, were reinforced by childhood visions and dreams. These early "signs" and exposure to Southern missionaries and revivalists, sparked his interest in Christianity and his eventual entrance into Christian preaching.

In 1848, he joined the Methodists in the neighboring town of Abbeville. Shortly after his conversion experience, Turner sought active ministry and was licensed to preach in 1853. During the 1850s, Turner undertook numerous evangelistic trips to South Carolina, Georgia, Alabama, Louisiana, and Missouri as a member of the Methodist Church, South. Turner's ministry within the Methodist Church, South lasted five years, until a trip to Saint Louis in 1858 brought him into contact with the African Methodist Episcopal Church. (Prior to this, Turner had ministered to Southern churches which were bi-racial or Black churches under white control.) He was extremely impressed with the Black-run church and, in his writings, stated that he was more than willing to accept the church's offer to sponsor his ministerial preparation in Baltimore.[43]

At this early point in his career, Turner played the role of the fiery revivalist. His theological position revolved around the Bible, the saving power of grace, and a stringent moral code.[44] He concerned himself with issues of individual righteousness and salvation, heaven as a reward for proper conduct, and hell as punishment for evil living.[45] Turner combined this sense of individual spiritual progress with a sense of divine intervention and guidance. Accordingly, evil—in the form of slavery—is established by God for a specific function. He believed that many factors needed to be left to God to resolve because they were beyond the grasp of humanity. Ultimately, moral evil was a matter of mystery. This perception influenced Turner's early opinion concerning the Civil War—only God could solve it.

However, the Civil War's carnage and brutality forced a modification of Turner's beliefs. As a U.S. Army chaplain (a reward for service as a military recruiter) Turner witnessed belligerent acts by those who passionately attempted to maintain a system which belittled a multitude of African-Americans. Consequently, his early optimism was tempered. His contentment with remuneration, for current wrongs endured, in heaven is replaced by a commitment to divine restoration in the temporal sphere. The teleological nature of history must have immediate, penultimate signs and symbols marking its path. Turner's perspective necessitated historical outcomes.[46] In essence, he began to aggressively connect religiosity with sociopolitical concerns.

Turner's moves toward a liberal theological perspective included a rethinking of scripture. He begins to understand scripture as inspired by God, but containing many human flaws. Through the process of interpretation, the human element in scripture surfaces. Connected to this, theological anthropology according to Turner paints humanity as responsible for world conditions. Humans are active agents who work with or against the divine plan (i.e., progress).

The most noted aspect of Turner's theological system is his conception of a Black God. The Divine Being remains powerful, just, and righteous. God's mind is "stayed on freedom," so to speak. However, Turner strengthens this connection to freedom fighting by identifying God with the oppressed: God is Black. God identifies with dark humanity and supports their efforts to gain freedom in the same way God supported the Children of Israel's efforts. In part, this proclamation is a response to white theologians who portray God as ontologically and epistomologically white—condoning of racism.

God, connected to Black people, must have something to say about oppression. Being so intimately linked to those suffering, God must have a justifiable reason for allowing their pain. Slavery's end eliminated some of this questioning; however, signs of continuing poor treatment forced them to resurface. Turner maintained the concept of a strong and good God, and attempted to resolve the paradox caused by evil through a re-evaluation of suffering's purpose. In an 1870 speech concerning the Fifteenth Amendment, Turner remarked that suffering is a tool of progress and in this way is redemptive:

> Nevertheless, it seems to be the order of Providence to purge all reformatory schemes by carrying them through the fires of persecutions. Even Heaven itself cannot be entered without great tribulations. Oppression appears to be the counter poise

that secures equality of action, the balance-pole of steadiness and uniformity. The strength of the negative increases the force of the positive.[47]

During Reconstruction, Turner's position on the redemptive nature of "great tribulation" continued to evolve and began to reveal a deeper pessimism. Racism which prevented Black Americans from realizing concrete political participation[48] combined with socioeconomic hostility led Turner to integrate an emigrationist twist to his redemptive suffering argument.

As part of his emigrationist "theodicy", Turner suggested that Africans had been brought to the United States as slaves in order to gain Western civilization and Christianity. Educated Blacks were then to take this information back to Africa to save the "heathen." This argument distinguishes Turner from Walker and Stewart who argued that Black suffering did two things: (1) teach white Americans a lesson by which they will awake to their moral and ethical responsibilities with respect to Black Americans; and, (2) rectify the past and present misdoings of Black Americans. Turner argues that the context of Black suffering provides African-Americans contact with civilizing principles (e.g., democratic government) and Christianity which are necessary for their development as a great people. In addition, this "schooling" enhances the mental outlook of African-Americans and focuses them on their part in the divine plan for the world. Without the sufferings of slavery, important lessons would have gone unlearned. Turner wrote (1875):

> There is no more doubt in my mind that we have ultimately to return to Africa than there is of the existence of a God; and the sooner we begin to recognize that fact and prepare for it, the better it will be for us as a people. We there [sic] have a country unsurpassed in productive and mineral resources, and we have some two hundred millions of our kindred there in moral and spiritual blindness. The four millions of us in this country are at school, learning the doctrines of Christianity and the elements of civil government. And as soon as we are educated sufficiently to assume control of our vast ancestral domain, we will hear the voice of a mysterious Providence, saying, "Return to the land of your fathers."[49]

Furthermore:

God, seeing the African stand in need of civilization, sanctioned for a while the slave trade—not that it was in harmony
with his fundamental laws for one man to rule another, nor did
God ever contemplate that the negro was to be reduced to the
status of a vassal, but as a subject for moral and intellectual
culture. So God winked, or lidded his eyeballs, at the institution of slavery. . . .[50]

Turner asserted that white Americans were to be punished
because they attempted to make slavery a permanent device, and
failed to give Blacks full rights and resources. If slavery had been
used as God intended (i.e., a period of training), it would have ended
without war and damage. That is, "the white man had exploited the
Negro; this had been a historical necessity of natural growth [the
refinement of Africans], but the white man defaulted his obligation to
God and the Black man by forbidding his servants [Blacks] to
improve themselves."[51]

Turner lost faith in the special role of the United States in God's
providential plan. White America had failed. As a result, God's ultimate plan did not depend on the cooperation of whites. God would
bring about the restoration of the Black race without the assistance
of white Americans.[52] The evil deeds of white men would not prevent
the greatness of Africa.

Turner believed that Africa held great promise that African-
Americans would be fools to ignore.[53] Accordingly, Turner asserted
that if African-Americans were to make gains, it would only be accomplished in Africa. Turner found a willing audience among poor and
Southern Blacks. As far as many Blacks were concerned, Africa had
to promise a better life. "For the would-be emigrants . . . the decline in
their farm income, the background of increasing racial tension and
violence, and the general conclusion that the United States was a
white man's country combined to make them ready to emigrate."[54]

With all the merits of Turner's Black nationalism, his reliance
upon redemptive suffering arguments made it unsustainable. In finding some comfort in Black suffering, Turner undercut his aggressive
Black uplift agenda. In addition, he created a sense of double consciousness (i.e., beautiful Black bodies vs. Anglophilic cultural leanings). That is to say, the tension fostered by Turner's support for
blackness while denigrating Black cultural markers as less than civilized, served to paralyze liberative activity. How does one confirm one's
blackness while denying the cultural manifestations of said blackness?

3

BLACK SUFFERING IN
THE TWENTIETH CENTURY

Theodore Roosevelt seemed to be genuinely concerned with the condition of Black Americans. For example, Roosevelt demonstrated interest in the needs of Black Americans when he dined with Booker T. Washington in order to discuss race issues. This move shocked and angered many whites, while serving as a ray of hope for Blacks. However, as John Hope Franklin points out, this optimism was short lived. Roosevelt's "friendship" was not consistent; rather, it was expressed only when politically expedient, and this inconsistency brought with it additional hardships.[1] This desire to remain a viable political figure by acquiescing to racism continued during the administrations of Presidents Taft and Wilson. Not only did these leaders submit to pressure from Southern supporters, they actively contributed to segregation machinery and legislation. In effect, they decreased Black Americans' life options and attempts at progress with the stroke of a pen.

The already delicate situation of African-Americans made them a ready scapegoat; a means by which to unite various factions of the estranged white community.[2] The South was socially and politically fractured by the Civil War; and logically it looked for a convenient causation. Even destitute white Americans could compare themselves to the scapegoat community (even middle-class Blacks) and perceive advantages resulting from whiteness. If not politically and economically, these poor white Americans were psychologically comforted by their status in the New South.

In addition, the economic sphere was a constant source of difficulty. Due to factors such as the destruction of cotton crops by the boll wëevil, many African-Americans were forced off farms and into cities. The bulk of this migration took place between 1914 and 1930, spurred in part by the promise of opportunity.[3] In Northern cities Blacks were able to obtain industrial jobs made available, in part, by restrictions on immigration. However, it was not long before the number of people migrating far exceeded the number of available jobs. This, combined with the hostility of organized labor and the racist attitudes of employers, resulted in Blacks having to take jobs which were inferior to the opportunities they expected. The problems associated with adjustment to city life and inadequate employment were heightened by the exploitation of landlords and the depression of the 1930s. To make matters worse, housing difficulties were further increased by the practice of segregation sanctioned in many areas by law. In light of the period of calm that preceded it, African-Americans had no way of anticipating this harsh socioeconomic and political treatment. Yet, after a short period of toleration, Blacks began to face quick and rapid negation. With no interference by the North in Southern affairs, the twentieth century marked persistent hostility toward Black Americans.

Hatred and fear of Black Americans expressed itself in efforts to vilify them. Examples of this are readily found in pseudoscientific documents and literature. One famous author of this literature is Thomas Dixon, whose *Clansman* (1905) was the basis for the racist film *The Birth of a Nation*. Within this text, as well as in his other writings, Dixon ignored the reality of Black humanity and consciousness. Instead, he created an animal-like and savage creature, one deserving contempt and destruction. This is seen, for example, in Dixon's description of a Black man accused of rape:

> He had the short, heavy-set neck of the lower order of animals. His skin was coal black, his lips so thick that they curled both ways up and down with crooked blood-marks across them. His nose was flat and its enormous nostrils seemed in perpetual dilation. The sinister bead eyes, with brown splotches in their whites, were set wide apart and gleamed ape-like under his scant brows. His enormous cheekbones and jaws seemed to protrude beyond the ears and almost hid them.[4]

Undoubtedly, this perception of Black men made lynching and other forms of destruction that much easier to exercise. As was presented in chapter two, such depictions of Black men as sexually aggressive beast were often supplemented with images of Black women as sexually loose temptresses ("jezebels") who "force" men (particularly white men) into unseemly and lustful acts. If not cast this way, Black women were presented as asexual "mammies" content to care for white families.

Pseudoscientific proscriptions reinforced negative literary depictions of African-Americans. As Cornel West illustrates in *Prophesy Deliverance*, faulty science and philosophy provided a normative gaze used to define white superiority and Black inferiority on biological and physiological grounds. Through procedures made available by pseudoscience,[5] North American scientists argued that "negroes" inherently lacked the biological structure necessary for productive cohabitation with Anglo-Saxons. That is, Black bodies betrayed distinctions from the Greek ideal of beauty and intelligence which marked Blacks as physiologically and mentally inferior creatures. With the blessing of scientific and popular "proofs," the racist onslaught had concrete intellectual and refined social force.

Many Black Americans believed helping to secure democracy, through service in World War I, in other parts of the world, would result in better treatment at home. Yet, Black soldiers were subjected to verbal insults, poor housing, unhealthy working conditions, and denial of promotion. In addition, German officials took full advantage of every opportunity to point out the dilemma of Black soldiers. Propaganda encouraged them to lay down their weapons because

> . . . .they should not be deluded into thinking that they were fighting for humanity and democracy. . . . "Do you enjoy the same rights as white people. . .or are you rather not treated over there as second-class citizens?"[6]

Nonetheless, Black soldiers continued to fight in hopes of proving their loyalty and their merits. Regardless of their efforts, once back on American soil, it became clear that nothing had changed. As the editor of the *Crisis* magazine stated, "This country of ours, despite all its better souls have done and dreamed, is yet a shameful land. It lynches. . . . It disenfranchises its own citizens. . . . We return from fighting. We return fighting."[7]

Blacks continued to have their societal activities proscribed by Jim Crow laws and U.S. Supreme Court "separate but equal" mandates. These laws made Black Americans second-class citizens and placed restrictions on Blacks with reference to public accommodations, transportation, restaurants, and stores.[8] It is certain that psychological belittling and physical subjugation were unavoidable for most African-Americans. As David Nielson remarks:

> The color line was wavy here and there, and where ill defined, its customs were not consistent. But that a color line existed and that it affected their daily lives, all Black Americans could attest to. Daily the color line served to focus the Afro-Americans' attention on—to make him more conscious of—cultural differences the dominant society's attitudes created.[9]

The racial environment and its various twentieth-century incarnations were not without religious consequences. The radical edge of the Black church marked by Henry M. Turner (d. 1915) came to an end early in the twentieth century[10] and in essence, Black churches became "de-radicalized." Damaged by war and the Depression, Black churches tended to turn inwardly and address spiritual issues. Economically stable churches concentrated on becoming mainstream while distancing themselves from the problems ravaging the neighborhoods of less-well-off Black Americans. The sociopolitical maintenance of Black people, in large measure, was left to secular organizations such as the National Association for the Advancement of Colored People (NAACP). A notable exception to status quo Black churches is found in the institutional churches motivated by the social gospel, and headed by figures such as Reverend Reverdy Cassius Ransom.

Ransom, born January 4, 1861, in Flushing Village, Ohio,[11] was raised with the assistance of an extended family. From a young age, Ransom was told by his mother that he was to make something of himself and not be restricted by the difficulties encountered by other Blacks. He was taught that white American values and education were necessary for success. After completing his schooling at Wilberforce University, Ransom began his service as an itinerant minister in the African Methodist Episcopal Church. His work as a "travelling" AME minister took him to several cities including Cleveland (1893–96); Chicago (1896–1904); New Bedford, MA (1904); Boston, (1904–7); and, New York (1907–12). Within the early years of his work as a pastor, Ransom began to recognize the need for full community services:

> My first vision of the need of social services came to me as my wife and I almost daily, went through the alleys and climbed the dark stairways of the wretched tenements, or walked out

on the planks to the shanty boats where our people lived on the river.[12]

He continues:

> The number of these people increased so rapidly that the colored clergymen of the city were bewildered. They were unprepared by training, experience and vision, to cope with the moral, social, and economic conditions so suddenly thrust upon them. I soon realized that the old stereotype form of church services practiced in all Negro churches fell far short of meeting the religious, moral, and social conditions that confronted them.[13]

Daily contact with those who were suffering raised questions for Ransom concerning the relationship between human suffering and the Christian God.[14] Making use of the social gospel and its implicit liberal theology, Ransom constructed a working response.

Although the framework of social Christianity existed prior to this period, a formalized social gospel emerged in the years after the Emancipation Proclamation as a result of home mission efforts and other such activities. Tired of war and the strain upon life it creates, Southern and Northern religious leaders began to emphasize the Christian message's transformative influence on social existence. This work was conducted under the leadership of figures such as Josiah Strong, Washington Gladden, and Walter Rauschenbusch.[15] Unfortunately, social gospelers, preferring to concentrate on issues of poverty,[16] spent little time applying their version of the gospel to the removal of American racism. Even those who responded to the plight of African-Americans restricted their efforts to making Blacks over in the image of European-Americans. In fact, it was believed by many "gospelers" that Blacks could only find their place in American society when they possessed the values, culture, and ideas of European-Americans. According to "gospelers" such as Washington Gladden, African-Americans who avoided the lure of emigration to Africa must undergo a profound cultural, psychological, and ultimately ontological change in order to prosper. With respect to this opinion, a sympathetic reading of Washington Gladden asserts that:

> His acceptance of segregation was not based on racism but on his assumption that Negroes could not exercise social equality fully until they achieved the standards of the white majority.

> Nevertheless, he might have neglected the plight of American
> Negroes altogether. . . . He was a busy pastor with more imme-
> diate social problems to preoccupy him. His interest testifies to
> the breadth of his humanitarianism.[17]

The above apology for Gladden offered by Jacob Dorn falls short in
that it seeks to downplay, if not justify, Gladden's paternalistic commentary regarding Black Americans. The existence of strong racist
activities or overt neglect by others does not lessen or justify the dis-
tastefulness of Gladden's presumptuous "burden" any more than comments to the effect of "Some of my best friends are Black" soothe
racial tensions and bridge culture gaps.

The acceptance of Social Darwinism and cultural norms in relation to African-Americans is more clearly expressed in the writings of
gospeler Josiah Strong. Strong, an associate of the American Missions
Association, believed that the United States was the best of all coun-
tries populated by European blood. That is to say, the U.S., armed
with the gospel and democratic ideals, had been set apart by God for a
special mission—the redemption of the world. In a word, ". . . to be a
Christian," Strong argues, "and an Anglo-Saxon, and an American in
this generation is to stand on the mountain-top of privilege."[18] It is in
relation to this "chosen people" notion that one catches a glimpse of
Strong's position on African-Americans. They, along with other less-
civilized groups, prepared the way for the Anglo-Saxon.[19] True, Strong
saw a coming brotherhood of all humans. Yet, for much of his life, this
was based upon a Darwinian chain of events leading to the Anglo-
Saxonizing of the world. Regarding this Strong writes:

> Thus the Finns were supplanted by the Aryan races in Europe
> and Asia, the Tartars by the Russians, and thus the aborigines
> of North America, Australia and New Zealand are now disap-
> pearing before the all-conquering Anglo-Saxons. It seems as if
> these inferior tribes were only precursors of a superior race. . . .[20]

It must be noted that Strong did recognize flaws within this superior
group. Nonetheless, these flaws are not fatal because of Christianity's
soothing influence. And so, negative elements within American civilization do not negate the dominance of the Anglo-Saxons. Hence, the fall
of "inferior races before the advancing Anglo-Saxons" is inevitable.[21]

While Ransom found the concern for the relationship between
the gospel of Christ and the daily dilemmas of humans vital, he was

troubled by the racist tone of Strong and other social gospelers. Nonetheless, Ransom turned this racist perspective on its head. He argued that the proper practice of Christian principles, seen through a liberal theological and democratic lens, did not allow for the avoidance of hard race issues. Thereby, the social gospel and its implementation provided Ransom with the theoretical framework for an evaluation of the Black existential situation.[22]

Social Christianity's commitment to meeting the full range of human needs is enacted in the creation of his Chicago Institutional Church and Social Settlement (1900). Using the model provided by Chicago aquaintances such as Jane Addams (founder of Hull House), Ransom sought to provide material assistance and spiritual guidance: working for God is synonymous with working on behalf of humanity. Such a church "made plain the gospel" by placing the essentials of the Christian message within a contemporary and relevant language and context (e.g., the urban, industrial environment). In a *Christian Recorder* article defending this style of church, Ransom provides a clear picture of its nature and function. Ransom is firm in his conviction that working for God is synonomous with working on behalf of humanity:

> The institutional A.M.E. Church of Chicago was not born
> before its time. It comes to meet and serve the social condition
> and industrial need of the people, and to give answer and solu-
> tion to the many grave problems which confront our
> Christianity in the great centers of population of our people. It
> is not a dream spun out of the gossamer web of fancy, it is not
> an evasion, an abridgement, or a short cut method for the real-
> ization of Christ and the Christ life in the life of the people. It
> is a teaching, ministering, nursing-mother, and seeks through
> its activities and ministrations to level the inequalities and
> bridge the chasms between rich and poor, the educated and
> the ignorant, the virtuous and the vicious. . . .[23]

The narrowing of the economic, social, intellectual, and spiritual gap between humans serves two purposes. It, on one hand, enacts the gospel's call to unity—the manifestation of Jesus' conduct code; and secondly, it mirrors the best of the democratic principles espoused by the United States. Herein one finds Ransom's sense of collective salvation as a radical reworking of the quality and dynamics of societal life.

Like many social gospelers, Ransom recognized the manner in which industrialization, while having positive consequences, erodes

the individual's ability to enjoy life. That is to say, the poor conditions faced by the working class are a direct result of capitalism.
His desire to improve the conditions faced by workers lead to the
espousing of socialism as the necessary corrective for capitalism-
induced misery. Casting it in terms of communal cooperation and a
Christian code of ethics, Ransom and others argued that socialism
allowed for the unity and selfless sharing earmarking the gospel of
Christ. Socialism's emphasis upon equalizing production and the
benefits of production was in keeping with God's commitment to the
downtrodden.

Much of his thought on socialism is presented in "The Negro and
Socialism."[24] In this text, Ransom argues that the nineteenth century
is marked by the industrial age, complete with technological
advances which put the earth's wealth at the disposal of humanity.
The resulting economic windfall, in theory, should provide all citizens
the wherewithal to secure a fulfilling and meaningful life. However,
the current economic system denies workers access to the means and
benefits of production, resulting in inequality and poverty. He argues
that socialism resolves alienation from production through the
removal of greed and selfishness. One should not, according to
Ransom, equate this removal of selfishness with a rejection of individual interests nor a rejection of government. In fact, socialism
places its ultimate interest in humans over and above wealth.
Nonetheless, it does not provide complete equity in material holdings;
rather, socialism encourages mutual compassion and it

> affirms that altruism is a principle sufficient to govern the
> relations of men in the sense it is opposed to individualism and
> does not regard society as composed of an army of warring
> atoms, but believes that social system to be the best in which
> the interests of the individual are made subordinate to the
> interests of society, while allowing freedom for the highest
> development of his own personality.[25]

It is only within socialism that individuals obtain and are thereby
assured the materials by which to fully develop themselves. Whereas,
capitalism continues to create "have-nots" who dwell in misery,
within urban ghettos, and have not the time nor energy to develop
their full range of capabilities.

Ransom is convinced that socialism is the solution to the problems faced by African-American laborers and that the "battles of

socialism" must make use of all available hands—regardless of color.[26] A civilization based upon unity of all peoples, and the full expression of their talents, only comes through the implementation of this system. And African-Americans must play their role in the creation of this social transformation. However, Ransom soon discovered that racism pervaded the socialist agenda. African-Americans found themselves excluded from brotherhoods and labor unions. Their sufferings at the hands of an unjust system and its self-proclaimed reformers seemed perpetual. The continuing oppression of Black Americans regardless of reform efforts made it imperative that Ransom address the issue of Black suffering within the context of his social gospel and socialist platform.

Why were Black Americans facing such disproportionate suffering? Using the theory of chosen status provided by social gospelers like Josiah Strong, Ransom created a doctrine concerning the special role of African-Americans in North American life. He asserted that African-Americans provided a sense of spirituality that was missing, a sense of spirituality that was vital for the further development of the United States and beyond. That is to say:

> [The Negro's] deep emotional nature will be the foe of tyranny and oppression and as a religious vehicle will convey the triumph of the King of Kings into the seats of pride and power, and over the dark and barren regions of the globe.[27]

White Christians had forgotten the mandate of the gospel thereby relinquishing to African-Americans, who maintained a true sense of Christ's teachings, the fate of the United States. Ransom also argues, in *The Negro: The Hope or the Despair of Christianity* (1935), that African-Americans' contribution to culture also rests in the vitality they instilled in a rather dry religion.[28] To this extent, Blacks were responsible for a nascent theology of spirit which maintained some sense of continuation with African customs of dance and song. African-Americans' contribution to culture combined with Ransom's sense of an immanent and active God sheds light on his response to the problem of evil.

Regarding this, Ransom was convinced African-Americans learned valuable lessons from their suffering, lessons necessary for their improvement and the fulfillment of their role in the development of North American society.[29] Related to this, Ransom provided Black Americans with a creed: "We believe God to be not a cruel monster, but a loving Father, training and testing under severe discipline, the weakest and most unenlightened of his children." To this he added:

> America is God's proving ground for the possibilities of the Negro's capacity to win with faith and love what others have failed to hold with wealth, privilege and power.[30]

In this way, the power and righteousness of God are proven through the fruitful suffering of God's dark children. The divine plan set out in historical garb was certain, but not without costs. That is, "the pain and travail through which the Negro has passed must produce results worthy of the things [they have] suffered."[31] In a word, God had used severe means to accomplish divine goals. The nature of Ransom's perspective on the problem of evil was also shaped by his reliance on manifest destiny theory, liberal theology's sense of human progress, and pseudo-Darwinian perspectives regarding people of color. One observes his manipulation of these theories in the following lines from "Heredity and Environment" (1898):

> God took the barbarians and fashioned them upon the anvil of Rome into what we now know as European civilization. God brought naked barbarians from Africa, put them upon the anvil of American Christianity and Democracy; under the white heat of denial and persecution, he is fashioning them with sledge-hammer blows into a new pattern from American civilization.[32]

Ultimately, it is through Black Americans that the teleological design is completed and global brotherhood (i.e., the Kingdom of God) established. In addition to general statements concerning African-Americans, Ransom makes a statement concerning the special role of women in redemption. He writes:

> A few generations hence, when the womanhood of America, which constitutes its glory and its crown, shall be faithfully recorded by history, none shall outshine the achievements of the black women of America, who have cleansed their garments out of the fire of degradation and humiliation to shine forth in triumphant beauty as the choicest fruits that the American home and family life has produced.[33]

One notices that Ransom's analysis did not progress beyond nineteenth-century reaction to the "cult of true womanhood." Perhaps this results from the continued threat to Black families and the desire to maintain certain perceptions concerning Black family structure and middle-class status.

Maintaining the problem of evil argument forged in the nineteenth century, Ransom did not locate benefits within slavery itself; rather it was the aftermath, so to speak, of oppression that was fruitful. That is to say, Ransom nuances his solution with a variation on the common theme of redemptive suffering. He asserts that Black suffering is God's refining of African-American collective character in order to equip them for a special role in world progress. In a manner reminiscent of Henry M. Turner, Ransom acknowledges that oppression provides valuable lessons and tools which cannot be obtained otherwise. Although God does not directly inflict this suffering, all of the figures examined to this point affirm that God allows oppression to serve God's purpose; God controls human history, and brings structure to seemingly chaotic occurrences.

Not all African-Americans agreed with Ransom's assessment of the Black American's situation. Even some who supported a social activist church, and who agreed on the practical merits of the social gospel, were apparently at odds with his analysis. One can include in this category Ida B. Wells-Barnett.[34]

Wells was born in Holly Springs, Mississippi, in 1862. Growing up in the South, she knew first hand Southern hatred, a knowledge further refined during years of teaching school in the South. Wells combined this knowledge of social injustice with church involvement. Her devotion to social justice stems from her strong sense of Christian moral standards and ethical codes. As Emilie Townes points out, available diary entries portray Wells as a worker motivated by a strong sense of religious duty and guided by a justice-minded God. Wells continuously prayed for God's help in becoming a good Christian evidenced through good works:

> Mr. Ames preached about our religion costing us something and I thought of the beautiful Easter time coming, that my thoughts had strayed away from the true significance of the time to less important matters of dress; that I have made no preparation for an Easter offering, but must do so and instead of spending my holiday in fun and pleasure for myself will fast

for my many sins of dereliction and remain home to work, watch, and pray, and praise for the wonderful goodness of my Father to an unworthy servant.[35]

Wells requires this same relentless devotion to God and humanity from all who consider themselves servants of Christ. On this score, Wells is critical of preachers who fail to realize the social implications of the gospel by not encouraging African-Americans to stand up for their rights.[36] This criticism includes those who rely upon otherworldly recompense and thereby acquiesce to injustice. One comes across this, for example, in Wells' comments to a group of Black men who have been convicted of murder and sentenced to death. She says:

> I have been listening to you for nearly two hours. You have talked and sung and prayed about dying, and forgiving your enemies, and of feeling sure that you are going to be received in the New Jerusalem because your God knows that you are innocent of the offence for which you expect to be electrocuted. But why don't you pray to live and ask to be freed? The God you serve is the God of Paul and Silas who opened their prison gates, and if you have all the faith you say you have, you ought to believe that he will open your prison doors too.[37]

Wells' sense of obligation to address pressing social concerns in light of Christian duty is most clearly focused within her anti-lynching campaign.

While Wells-Barnett was teaching in Memphis (and working as an editor for the *Memphis Free Speech*), three Black shop owners were lynched. This hate crime sparked Wells' campaign against lynching. She was angered by the demonic business of lynching African-Americans, and she was determined to bring this atrocity to the public. Wells did not confine her mission to the United States, she also tried to gather international support for her anti-lynching campaign by speaking to British audiences. However, the eventual dwindling of financial support resulted in an end to her campaign (1895). Nonetheless, her dedication and outrage continued; and so she re-entered the anti-lynching campaign in 1900, armed with a strong sense of commitment and statistical evidence for her views.

The urgency of the situation, her commitment to justice, and the keenness of her analysis were without question. Within *Southern Horrors*, she wrote:

There is little difference between the Ante-bellum South and the New South. Her white citizens are wedded to any method however revolting, any measure, however extreme for the sub-jugation of the young manhood of the race. They have cheated him out of his ballot, deprived him of civil rights or redress therefore [sic] . . . robbed him of the fruits of his labor, and are still murdering, burning and lynching him.[38]

White Southerners suggested that Black men were lynched when they committed crimes, in particular the rape of white women. However, Ida Wells-Barnett pointed out that the actual motivation for lynchings, in most cases, is the desire by white Americans to maintain social control. She suggested that the real criminals were white men who, for centuries, had raped and abused Black women without legal consequences.[39] In addition, white women were not without blame. According to Wells-Barnett, there were white women who entertained sexual relations with Black men until societal pres-sures forced them to mask such activities with cries of rape. In this respect, Wells-Barnett saw Black suffering as the result of humanly misguided "will to power." Unlike Ransom, Wells did not find the suf-fering undergone by Black Americans redemptive; it did not speak to a divinely providential and redemptive scheme.

Although Wells-Barnett did not find suffering fruitful per se, she did allude to the specialness of African-Americans, emerging as a con-sequence of their ability to survive. For example, the survival of African-American women pointed to a vitality fully capable of sup-porting the upward mobility of Black Americans and meriting the curiosity of the world. In general, Wells-Barnett posited that African-Americans exhibited a profound strength that caused "The world [to look] on with wonder that we have conceded so much and remain law-abiding under such great outrage and provocation."[40]

Whereas redemptive suffering is theoretically rejected,[41] Emilie Townes suggests a perspective on pain in Wells-Barnett's work that parallels the notion of suffering's fruitfulness. Regarding this, Townes finds Audre Lorde's distinction between pain (a "process pointing toward transformation") and suffering (a continuous "cycle" of reliv-ing pain) particularly insightful.

Townes is rightly concerned with the manner in which the lan-guage of suffering has been used as a support and remedy for issues that actually merit more profound struggle. Using Wells and Lorde, Townes seeks to provide an alternative that moves Black Americans closer to full existence. This movement involves a linguistic shift from the language of suffering to that of pain, in hopes that this shift will spark new forms of leadership and action. The question concerns whether or not Townes' project on the language of suffering amounts to a semantical shift that does not provide a substantive rejection of redemptive suffering.

For Lorde, suffering results in a passive and short term response to one's environment which does not actively seek liberation by ending the cycle of oppression. To the contrary, concern with suffering betrays an interest in treating symptoms rather than transforming existence. Ultimately, the root of this suffering is "unscrutinized" and therefore pedagogically empty pain.[42]

Using this framework, Townes sees in Wells-Barnett's social activism a movement toward transformation which rejects suffering as evil and embraces pain. That is, according to Townes,

> she [Wells-Barnett] saw the challenge for the African-American community to work in partnership with the intention of moving from suffering to pain. Within the framework of Lorde's model, Wells-Barnett understood suffering as a way of being that prevented effective action and denied the individual or the group the ability and right to say "No" to their oppression.[43]

Townes locates the theological basis for this embracing of pain in the Christ event. Herein, God demonstrates the importance of pain and struggle as the avenue to liberation. In fact, "the resurrection is God's breaking into history to transform suffering into wholeness."[44] For those who understand God's presence and activity in the world and its radical consequences, there is the assurance that suffering has been fully dealt with by and in God. Pain serves to confirm rather than negate the love and presence of God. As a result, we are free to struggle out of our pain.[45] Townes is certain that

> Wells-Barnett's stance illustrates that one must learn to move from the reactive position of suffering to that of the transforming power of pain. Wells-Barnett lived her life through the critical stance of pain.[46]

My reading of Townes' argument does not reveal an epistemologically substantive distinction between pain and suffering. Townes does not convince that pain is ontologically anything other than what

Turner and others labelled suffering. Pain, like suffering referred to as redemptive, fuels efforts to break the cycle of oppression using past experience and lessons. That is to say, pain denotes the consequence of socially transformative activity:

> Pain promotes self-knowledge which is a tool for liberation and wholeness. . . . Pain names suffering as sin and plots a strategy to defeat sin.[47]

In the long run, pain provides the pedagogy and strength necessary to achieve liberation. Substituting the term pain for suffering, it appears that Wells-Barnett would agree with the spirituals and figures such as Turner and Ransom in regarding discomfort as strength-producing and redemptive. Both redemptive suffering and pain suggest the examination of oppression with the hope of finding something useful, something helpful in the achieving of liberation.

Townes' analysis simply suggests a linguistic shift. The substance of the argument regarding Black oppression remains the same. To illustrate this point, compare the following statements. The first is from Ransom, the second concerns Ida Wells-Barnett; one notices a strong connection, broken only by word selection. Ransom states:

> The pain and travail through which the Negro has passed must produce results worthy of the things [they have] suffered.[48]

Ransom suggests that African-American tragic experience is capable of producing worthwhile ends. Townes makes a similar statement concerning Wells-Barnett:

> . . . Wells-Barnett's stance illustrates that one must learn to move from the reactive position of suffering to that of the transforming power of pain.[49]

Ida Wells-Barnett does not, in actuality, make a clean break with the redemptive suffering (read redemptive pain) idea. However, she does not make this argument as strongly as some. Dr. Martin Luther King, Jr. provides an example of a contemporary and strongly stated redemptive suffering argument.

Martin Luther King, Jr. was born January 15, 1929, in Atlanta, Georgia.[50] King lived a middle-class life, guided by his mother and father ("Daddy King," the pastor of Ebenezer Baptist Church) who stood up against a racist South for the rights of his family. As a result of his father's stance, Martin King never experienced first hand the socioeconomic and educational hardships encountered by poor Blacks and whites in Atlanta.

King, at the age of fifteen, enrolled in Morehouse College. Here he was first introduced to the intellectual resources, most notably Henry David Thoreau, that shaped his perspective on North American society and society's relationship to the existential situation of Black Americans. King was impressed with the argument presented by Thoreau in "On the Duty of Civil Disobedience." He later combined Thoreau's notion of noncooperation with oppressive systems, and the Black church protest tradition.

Another major development during his time at Morehouse involves King's decision to enter the ministry. As with his conversion, this calling was "not a miraculous or supernatural something, on the contrary it was an inner urge calling me to serve humanity," an urge not without familial influence.[51] It should be noted that this interest in the ministry was not without intellectual modifications of traditional and fundamentalist religiosity he encountered in his father's church. This transformation was based on the new models of intelligent ministry found in Benjamin E. Mays and George Kelsey which offered King examples of social Christianity in action.[52] They exemplified an intellectually informed perspective of the gospel which allowed King to combine the best of his Baptist tradition (e.g., commitment to activism) with the richness of contemporary theological and philosophical inquiry. Both men encouraged King to use his skills and training for the betterment of the Black community. And so, King was ordained at Ebenezer Baptist Church in February of 1948.

After completing his degree at Morehouse, King enrolled in Crozer Theological Seminary in Pennsylvania. Here King encountered the social gospel, personalism, and liberal theology which would help him as he continued to rethink traditional Black church thought. Mays and Kelsey had introduced King to the social gospel during his Morehouse years. However, Crozer's George Washington Davis expanded King's awareness within the course "Christian Theology for Today." Through his reading of social gospel theology, particularly Walter Rauschenbusch's work, King clarified his understanding of the social responsibilities placed upon the followers of Christ. The prophetic appeal to social harmony and justice exposed by the Hebrew Bible prophets and Jesus is an inherent element of obedience to God. And so, King understood that religious people must live the ethical stance outlined in scripture because their religiosity must have temporal effect.

King also began pursuing an interest in the nonviolent philosophy of Mahatma Gandhi. As John Ansbro points out, the praxis initiated by Gandhi helped King respond to the critique of Christianity offered by Nietzsche. Nietzsche argued that Christian ethics glorified weakness rather than encouraging and nurturing vital characteristics such as pride, knowledge, and anger. The Christian devotion to love flys in the face of basic human instincts to remove weakness and promote strength through aggression.[53] This critique troubled King in that it forced an understanding of love as ineffectual and contrary to human progress. However, a sermon by Mordecai Johnson on Gandhi and subsequent readings reemphasized love's value as an active agent of transformation. That is, King recognized through Gandhi's activities the strength and power lodged within *agape* love. He would later use Gandhi's philosophy of nonviolent resistance within his civil rights efforts because it provided the philosophical base for his commitment to transformation through the appeal to the human conscience and active resistence of evil.[54]

The personalism he was introduced to at Crozer reinforced religious devotion's dual nature—spiritual and temporal—due to the transcendent and immanent nature of God. The personalist notion of God, for example, suggests a God who is intimately connected to human history. (This emphasis upon the practical presence of God in the world harmonized with Black church notions of a personal/immanent God who values all humanity.) King added to the presence of God in the world liberal theology's optimistic stance concerning human progress. Another example of King's growing liberal theological leanings is seen in his "divinity through moral struggle" analysis of Jesus Christ. In keeping with liberal theology's hope in eventual progress, King wrote a seminary paper entitled "The Humanity and Divinity of Jesus" in which he said:

> The appearance of such a person [Jesus], more divine and more human than any other, and standing in closest unity at once with God and man, is the most significant and hopeful event in human history. This divine quality or this unity with God was not something thrust upon Jesus from above, but it was a definite achievement through the process of moral struggle and self-abnegation.[55]

The personalist theology of Edgar S. Brightman at Boston University intrigued King; and as a result, he decided to pursue a Ph.D. in theology under Brightman's tutelege. Under the guidance of Brightman and L. Harold DeWolf, King wrestled with and continued to synthesize, by means of Hegel's dialectic, the theological and philosophical systems encountered at Morehouse and Crozer.[56] In terms of Brightman's personalism, King responded to the idea of humanity's ability to experience God. From this, King gathered that God's plan for the world is monitored through historical occurences. In this way, there are certain principles which guide the universe and which humans must live up to. Combined with this is Brightman's notion of altruism which requires a respect for and proper conduct toward all humanity.[57] One is required, then, to exercise high moral and ethical standards when dealing with others. For King, this did not involve a passive acceptance of injustice; rather, a concern for and appreciation of humanity requires effort to remove injustice so that all humans live with dignity and value. The moral code established in scripture and exemplified in Christ demands this proactive stance from free and responsible human beings. This idea fit well with his social gospel concern with Christ's impact upon the human condition and his strong sense of communal teleology.[58] An appreciation for liberal theology is apparent here; however, as was the fate of most concepts King encounters, this appreciation is tempered and the concept is modified.

Race problems within the United States brought into question liberal theology's optimistic view of human nature. Violence against African-Americans seeking basic human rights points to the strong human potential for evil. In light of this, King used Reinhold Niebuhr's neo-orthodox perspective on human sinfulness to temper liberal optimism. Niebuhr argues that individuals are capable of good; but as groups, they are prone to tremendous evil. Only radical love exemplified in the ethical stance of Christ provides a possible solution to flawed human interactions. Yet, King is careful to temper the neo-orthodoxy of figures such as Karl Barth because he is unable to accept the irreversible distance between God and humanity. King is too committed to personalism's appeal to human and divine interaction to accept such a chasm. In essence, King wants to balance or hold in tension humanity's potentiality and sinfulness.

The year prior to completing his dissertation on Tillich's and Wieman's conceptions of God, King accepted the pastorate of Dexter Avenue Baptist Church in Montgomery, Alabama (1954). It was also during his pastorate of this church (December, 1955) that the actions of Rosa Parks sparked the development of a bus boycott and the Montgomery Improvement Association.[59] During the turmoil of this bus boycott and subsequent activities, King further refined and put into action his views on the existence of a personal God, Niebuhrian anthropology, and Gandhian nonviolence (in light of the Black church tradition).[60]

King encouraged members of the protest movement to recognize God's presence in their struggle for justice.[61] Furthermore, he assured them that an appeal to their oppressors through *agape* love would affect the oppressor's moral conscience and result in the ending of racism. He was convinced that love, hope, and redemption were the essential values that Black Americans must demonstrate in order to achieve justice (and establish the "beloved community"). Yet, he recognized that this did not entail passivity, but rather resistance to evil through defiant nonviolent activity.

Intimately connected to *agape* love and nonviolence is the power of unmerited suffering. This is King's response to the problem of evil. In addresses and sermons, King remarked that Black suffering was redemptive when encountered and dealt with nonviolently.[62] One gleans this notion in rudimentary form within his seminary papers, such as "Religion's Answer to the Problem of Evil" (1951). Considering the pedagogically fruitful outcome of many evils, King said:

> Who can deny that many apparent evils turn out in the end to be goods in disguise? Character often develops out of hardship. Unfortunate [sic] hereditary and environment conditions often make for great and noble souls. Suffering teaches sympathy.[63]

King would come to recognize that unmerited suffering was redemptive because it led to the reconciliation of Black and white Americans. Furthermore, it was redemptive because God was on the side of those who suffered. That is, when God sided with the oppressed, suffering could not result in frustration or despair. King clarifies the type of suffering considered unmerited and redemptive. It is any of the racially motivated (later economically orchestrated) pain felt by people of color (later enlarged to the poor). One senses this understanding of suffering, for example, in a 1959 speech to the Montgomery Improvement Association:

> As victories for civil rights mount in the federal courts, the angry passion and deep prejudices . . . will be further aroused.

These persons will do all within their power to provoke us and make us angry. But we must not retaliate with external physical violence or internal violence of spirit. . . . As we continue the struggle for our freedom we will be persecuted, abused and called bad names. But we must go on with the faith that unearned suffering is redemptive, and love is the most durable power in all the world.[64]

King's theory on redemptive suffering was not solely the result of collective history; rather, his personal experience provided impetus for this stance. Reflecting upon numerous death threats, King discusses with the *Christian Century* (1960) his perspective on suffering:

As my sufferings mounted I soon realized that there were two ways that I could respond to my situation: either to react with bitterness or seek to transform the suffering into a creative force. . . . Recognizing the necessity for suffering I have tried to make of it a virtue. If only to save myself from bitterness, I have attempted to see my personal ordeals as an opportunity to transform myself and heal the people involved in the tragic situation which now obtains.[65]

It should be noted that an analysis of King's philosophy of redemptive suffering suggests that he was interested in the consequences of suffering rather than the substance of suffering. In keeping with early thought on this issue, King distinguished the cause and substance of suffering from the results of suffering, labeling the latter fruitful and the former the Tillichian demonic. That is:

Suffering in itself is not redemptive nor is it ordained by God; rather, it is contrary to Christian principles of unity and proper behavior.[66]

This hermeneutical analysis of Black suffering makes Christlike engagement of endemic hardship synonymous with bravery, values, and redemption. In short, suffering is an evil that God is able to manipulate and use for positive ends.

In later years (1962–68), King recognized that the inhumanity of white Americans towards Black Americans was more systemic than he initially realized. As a result, King shifted his emphasis away from love (and moral persuasion) as the counterbalance of dwarfed moral conscience to justice (and "nonviolent coercion") as the demand of love. Hence, love had to be combined with acquired power and full participation in a reformed society. That is, ". . . power without love is reckless and abusive and . . . love without power is sentimental and anemic."[67] This rethinking of power and love did not alter King's notion of unmerited suffering. King continued to believe that the acts of racism endured by African-Americans provided the avenue by which God's reconciling and redeeming love came into action (1961):

> The nonviolent say that suffering becomes a powerful social force when you willingly accept that violence on yourself, so that self-suffering stands at the center of the nonviolent movement and the individuals involved are able to suffer in a creative manner, feeling that unearned suffering is redemptive. . . .[68]

Acceptance of suffering allowed the oppressor to recognize the web of mutuality: damage done to the oppressed was done to self. On the other hand, this unmerited suffering enabled the oppressed to recognize their worth and humanity without causing the oppressor physical harm. In short, King pragmatically decribes Black suffering as both a tool by which to prick the conscience of the larger white society and a device to refine Black character. As with the other figures examined, King does not directly attribute Black suffering to God; rather, suffering is the result of human misconduct, but God uses it for fruitful ends.

The internal and external healing promoted by redemptive love, exercised through nonviolence, does not merely affect those who directly participate. The scope of its transforming power is larger than that. Even those who never march or protest take part in suffering that is potentially redemptive. The young girls killed by a bomb while in Sunday School (at Sixteenth Street Baptist Church in Birmingham) illustrate this. During their eulogy (1963), King says the following:

> So they did not die in vain. God still has a way of bringing good out of evil. History has proven over and over again that unmerited suffering is redemptive. The innocent blood of the little girls may well serve as the redemptive force that will bring new light to this dark city.[69]

The redemptive force of suffering is related to the notion of African-American's specialness. Lewis Baldwin refers to this as King's "messianic vision."[70] Using Kantian and biblical allusions, King explores this theme in the following remarks (1967):

> Let us be those creative dissenters who will call our beloved nation to a higher destiny, to a new plateau of compassion, to a more noble expression of humaneness. We are superbly equipped to do this. We have been seared in the flames of suffering. . . . So in dealing with our particular dilemma, we will challenge the nation to deal with its larger dilemma.[71]

By no means was King alone in his analysis of the Black situation. He received a great deal of intellectual support for his activities from other intellectuals.[72] Much of this support is explicit in statements made and affiliations forged with King's movement. However, there is also a level of agreement between King and those who, on the surface, might seem to be in disagreement. A case in point concerns Joseph Washington's critique of King.

Washington was widely criticized in the African-American community after the publication of his text entitled *Black Religion: The Negro and Christianity in the United States* (1964).[73] In this text, Washington is critical of King's lack of theological formulation. Essentially, he argues that King is not a theologian, but rather an advocate of philosophical nonviolence. Regardless of how beneficial and church-related King's social protest movement is, this protest (i.e., "militant noncooperation") is Gandhian; and therefore, it lacks Christian theological grounding.[74] That is to say:

> It is both Christian and human to choose to do what is clearly right, but nonviolence does not allow for this choice in either its methods or its results. Nonviolence as a philosophy wishes to be God in defining the boundaries, a desire which is not Christian though it is perhaps human.[75]

The Christian way involves the right to choice, to make decisions without being forced in a particular direction. (Free will is fundamental and essential.) In other words, the goal of justice is Christian, the method used to achieve it is not;[76] in fact, coercive protest methods suggest a "pseudoreligion".[77] Authentic Black religion, begun during slavery, seeks brotherhood (i.e., freedom and equality) under God. This brotherhood is achieved through faith, protest, and action—but without coercion.

The coercive practices of "pseudoreligion" serve to alienate Black Americans from other communities and result in Black stagnation and defensiveness. This is problematic because Black religion and white religion must learn from each other. White religion must learn justice and Black religion must gain "roots" and inclusion in the larger context of Christian faith.[78] However, Washington's critique appears to revolve around methodology rather than deeper issues of function and content. One sees this in his book *The Politics of God* (1967).

Within this text, Washington concludes that white religion has lost its appeal due to the replacement of Christian principles with capitalistic and oppressive interests—the status quo and material gain. Therefore, the world's hope is to be found in African-Americans whose religious structures preserve Christian principles of brotherhood vital for human existence. In this capacity, African-Americans are God's chosen people, called to follow in the tradition established by the children of Israel:

> God has called the Negro as the "suffering servant"; whereby humankind the world over will consciously, not accidentally, voluntarily, not by force as in times past, affirm first in principle and then in practice a life of full human oneness. . . .[79]

By means of this suffering, Black Americans will redeem themselves and white America. Washington concludes that African-Americans are the chosen people of God based upon the suffering they have endured, suffering which parallels the experiences of ancient Israel. It is important to note that denial of this chosen status does not negate its existence. To the contrary, it serves as further evidence of the Black community's distance from the atrocities of white folk religion and its logic.

As Washington's text *The Politics of God* indicates, he is, in many ways, in agreement with King's redemptive suffering argument. Both argue for Black suffering's usefulness as part of a divine plan. However, a point of disagreement concerns the targeted evils King attempts to elevate. Washington writes: "Surely it is presumptuous to believe that God has called the Negro to redeem mankind from war, nationalism, pride, and other human weaknesses."[80] According to Washington, Dr. King's philosophy forced Black Americans to place their sights upon coerced material gain rather than the more substantive components of the divine plan—brotherhood and unity. (He seems to forget King's discussion of the "beloved community" as the ultimate goal of the civil rights movement.) In so doing, Black religion moves dangerously close to the misguided capitalist interests of white religion. Granting methodological differences regarding action, Washington's argument essentially agrees with King in that both speak of suffering as a redemptive process which contributes to the improvement of American life. Although there is some agreement between King and many Black thinkers of his era, there were certain activists who voiced complete disagreement with King's theological analysis of Black suffering. Reverend Albert Cleage falls into this category.

Reverend Cleage, the founder and pastor of the Shrine of the Black Madonna, believed that Jesus, like Black Americans, was Black and angry—revolutionary. This is the message of the gospel. However, white Americans have perverted the true message and nature of the Christian gospel and use it to exclude and oppress African-Americans. According to Reverend Cleage, Black Americans must see through this perversion and seek liberation. Yet, unlike King who highlights God's involvement in liberation, Cleage believes that Blacks must seek change for themselves through revolution. God simply provided strength for this fight.[81] This is how Cleage implicitly resolves the paradox of the Christian God and Black suffering. He removes God from blame by arguing that God's role is not to provide revolutionary change. Humans must do this. However, this solution— as the reader will see again with Delores Williams—leaves questions. If Black suffering is utterly useless, would not a good God who is somewhat powerful work towards liberation as opposed to simply providing strength? Why does not God use God's own strength to help bring about much needed change? Cleage's "cover-up" falters because it leaves substantial questions concerning God's role in human suffering without satisfying answers.

In light of Cleage's emphasis on aggressive action, it is reasonable to assert that he found King's approach benign. That is, "In spite of all the loving [Blacks have] been doing, [they are] still second-class citizens."[82] The Black nation (the equivalent of the Kingdom of God) could not emerge out of self-destructive love and talk of redemptive suffering.

Advocation of redemptive suffering is not in keeping with the revolutionary nature of God's plans for African-Americans. God requires courage, not suffering. Therefore, "We don't pray for the strength to endure any more. We pray for the strength to fight heroically."[83]

Concerning the inner workings of suffering, Cleage argued that King's actions contradicted King's rhetoric.[84] Although King spoke of redemptive suffering, his activities taught people courage and self-respect. That is, the activities sponsored by King point to the value of dignity and do not suggest an important role for suffering:

> Now I suppose we can say that he [Dr. King] was engaged in redemptive suffering. You're suffering when you walk all the way across Montgomery, after working all day. You're suffering, and your suffering redeems white folks. But it wasn't really redemptive suffering. It was black courage. Black folks were learning that they had power, and they were willing to do the things that were necessary to use it. And they won.[85]

Cleage is clear: suffering occurred as a result of Black activity. However, this suffering only serves to reinforce the barbarity of American racists. The only redemptive elements of Black American action are the courage, strength, and nationalistic unity demonstrated. In other words:

> . . . what [King] said had no relationship to what was happening in the hearts and minds and souls of black people. . . . This was a movement inside black people. It had no relationship to what Dr. King was saying, either in his speeches or in his books. It was something that black people were learning. They were learning that they could stand up against the white man, that black people could come together as a group and could find unity in their struggle against oppression, and in their desire for justice.[86]

In the spirit of Cleage, theologians such as James H. Cone, within the emerging radical branch of Black theology, had difficulty accepting Dr. King's banal "beloved community" and integration philosophy.

Born in Bearden, Arkansas, in 1938, James H. Cone and his two brothers were well aware of racism and its social incarnation—Jim Crow. However, their father taught them to think highly of themselves and fight against racism. In keeping with this tradition of resisting inferior status, James H. Cone attended college against the odds. While a college student, he developed a strong interest in reading Black history and literature (e.g., W. E. B. DuBois, Booker T.

Washington, and Frederick Douglass). This study gave shape to the sense of pride and accomplishment that informs his writings.

Cone never lost his interest in the Black church tradition. And, in 1958, Cone continued his training for ministry at Garrett Biblical Institute. In this setting, Cone continued his readings in theology, with emphasis on neo-orthodox thought and, with the encouragement of William Hordern, a professor in systematic theology, Cone decided to pursue the Ph.D. at Northwestern University. After completing his degree, Cone taught at Philander-Smith College and Adrian College. While teaching at Adrian College, a predominantly white school, Cone had the time to think through the issues that had interested him since childhood. There, in his free hours, he expanded his knowledge of Black culture and the need for theological change—in part, as a response to the violent outbreaks in cities such as Detroit and Los Angeles.

He had his first opportunity to present these thoughts in a lecture entitled "Christianity and Black Power," given at Elmhurst College in February of 1968. In this paper, Cone brought Jesus Christ into harmony with the struggle for justice and social change. This was done by suggesting that Jesus' ministry indicates a strong commitment to the sociopolitical and spiritual liberation of the oppressed. In this vein, Cone rejected efforts to spiritualize the transformation spoken of by Christ. Instead, Cone argues for a socially conscious and materially liberating interpretation of Christ's teachings:

> If Christ was not to be found in black peoples' struggle for freedom, if he were not found in the ghettos with rat-bitten black children, if he were in rich white churches and their seminaries, then I wanted no part of him. The issue for me was not whether Black Power could be adjusted to meet the terms of a white Christ, but whether the biblical Christ is to be limited to the prejudiced interpretations of white scholars.[87]

This connection between the gospel and liberation allowed Cone to lessen the tension between the Christian orientation of the civil rights movement and the secular Black power movement. In both movements, one sees the divine mandate for freedom—liberation. Therefore, both demonstrate God's siding with the oppressed over and against unjust circumstances.

As a result of this Elmhurst lecture, Cone made important contacts and received several invitations to lecture. These added opportunities for critical reflection and comment, coupled with the assassination of King (April, 1968) gave a new urgency to Black power which Cone would express in his first book *Black Theology and Black Power* (1969).[88] Within this text, he outlines a response to white racism and the need for Black liberation, a theological perspective based upon and suited for Black life.[89] To some extent, it was an extension and strengthening of his existential self in theological terms.

> When a person writes about something that matters to him or her existentially, and in which his or her identity is at stake, then the energy for it comes easily and naturally. The writing is no longer being done for someone else but for oneself as a requirement for survival. . . . It is like the call to preach or to testify. The spirit of another invades one's being and compels one to tell the truth. That was something of what I felt in writing.[90]

Cone reconciled the emerging cries of Black power with the gospel of Christ: "Christianity . . . is Black Power!"[91] He argued that God sided with the oppressed and worked for their liberation. Furthermore, only those identifying with the oppressed were capable of understanding the mandate of this God. Of necessity, this connection with Black Americans involves a surrender of privilege and a commitment to liberative work. To make such a commitment to the oppressed is to reenact Christ's involvement with the poor of his society; it is to be Christlike, Christian. Cone uses Moltmann to explain his point. He says:

> If the gospel of Christ, as Moltmann suggests, frees a man to be for those who labor and are heavily laden, the humiliated and abused, then it would seem that for twentieth-century America the message of Black Power is the message of Christ himself.[92]

Some might label this commitment to Blackness racist in that it casts "Black" as normative. Cone disagrees. He argues that charges of Black racism are feeble attempts to cloud the issue of oppression, to mask the true culprits:

> It is important to make a further distinction here among black hatred, black racism, and Black Power. Black hatred is the black man's strong aversion to white society. No black man living in white America can escape it. . . . This feeling should not be identified as black racism. Black racism is a myth created by whites to ease their guilt feelings. As long as whites can be

assured that blacks are racists, they can find reasons to justify
their own oppression of black people. . . . Black Power then is not
black racism or black hatred. Simply stated, Black Power is an
affirmation of the humanity of blacks in spite of white racism.[93]

As the above quotation demonstrates, Cone's brand of Christianity
allowed for a commitment to the demands for nationalistic Black
power voiced by the Student Non-violent Coordinating Committee
(SNCC).[94] In this manner, Cone forged a spiritual and ideological
link, a bond between religion and Black radicalism. In fact, in *A
Black Theology of Liberation*, Cone strengthens this claim by asserting that Blackness exemplifies the contemporary metaphor for
oppression. Therefore a God who sides with the oppressed, who identifies with the oppressed, must share their Blackness. Hence, God is
Black. For Cone, this Blackness is ontologically and epistomologically
understood; and therefore, any who identify and work with the
oppressed become Black.[95]

The anger in the Black community had to be addressed, and the
church and its theologians had to avoid the impotency characteristic
of much of their history. Clergy and secular activists believed that the
church had to make a stand beyond the nonviolent love of King. Cone
gave full theological voice to this project by rethinking the civil rights
movement's religious thought and imagery. For example, love was
reformulated as a firm commitment to fight for freedom.[96] This radical nonsentimental love does not preclude violence. However, Cone
alters what is commonly understood as violence by refusing to understand violence from the Western perspective, which is concerned only
with denouncing the steps taken by the oppressed to gain liberty.
This Western, or oppressor, orientation fails to take account of the
harm perpetuated against the oppressed, the violence needed to
maintain "order." The issue then is not the existence of violence;
rather, it is who uses it and for what purpose. On this point he writes:

> It is this fact that most whites seem to overlook—the fact that
> violence already exists. The Christian does not decide
> between violence and non-violence, evil and good. He decides
> between the lesser and the greater evil. He must ponder
> whether revolutionary violence is less or more deplorable
> than the violence perpetuated by the system. There are no
> absolute rules which can decide the answer with certainty.
> But he must make a choice.[97]

In addition to the issues of love and violence, the need for Black power required a reworking of eschatology. Along this line, Cone's sense of the eschatological does not concern itself with another world. Rather, the eschaton means the complete liberation of Black people and the accompanying restructuring of society. Although the time frame for this is uncertain, the liberation event is guaranteed because God desires it to be and has ultimately achieved it on the cross. That is, "the crucial battle has been won already on the cross, but the campaign is not over. There is a constant battle between Christ and Satan, and it is going on now."[98] Cone's language seems harsh. Yet, this harshness is understandable considering the sense of urgency with which he addresses the issue of Black liberation. In a word, it is a matter of life or death for Black America; and so, careful maneuvering around white sensibilities is pointless. In fact it is deadly. Revolution is naturally uncomfortable for whites but necessary for Blacks.

In spite of Cone's call for new revolutionary praxis, much of his thought suggests allegiance to the very ideas he claims to reject. More to the point, Cone's rhetoric of revolution betrays a sense of special mission based upon suffering reminiscent of previously discussed positions. With respect to this, Cone argues that:

> All the black church has to do is to accept its role as the sufferer and begin to follow the natural course of being black. In so doing, it may not only redeem itself through God's Spirit, but the white church as well. The black church, then, is probably the only hope for renewal or, more appropriately, revolution in organized Christianity.[99]

This, however, does not constitute a divine sanction on the causation or substance of suffering. To the contrary, Cone argues that the atrocities faced by African-Americans (i.e., the causation of suffering) are not related to anything ultimately good. That is:

> In traditional eschatology, suffering is often interpreted as the means for heavenly entrance. . . . (Matt. 5:10–12). Evil and injustice are transformed into temporary good in view of the apocalypse. Black theology rejects this interpretation. . . . This is the key to Black theology. It refuses to embrace any concept of God which makes black suffering the will of God. Black people should not accept slavery, lynching, or any form of injustice as tending to good.[100]

Within the above quotation Cone suggests the dimensions of negative suffering: the oppressive (i.e., racist) structures of society produce a suffering which must be denounced and fought (negative suffering). On the other hand, movement against these forces results in struggle or positive suffering which should be embraced. In a word:

> The free Christian man cannot be concerned about a reward in heaven. Rather, he is a man who, through the freedom granted in Christ, is ready to plunge himself into the evils of the world, revolting against all inhuman powers which enslave men [negative suffering]. He does not seek salvation, for he knows that to seek it is to lose it. "He that would save his life would lose it. He who loses his life for my sake will gain it."[101]

With the basic theological tenets presented in *Black Theology and Black Power* still in place, Cone continues his theological project in *A Black Theology of Liberation* (1970).[102] Cone again argues that suffering is not ordained by God; nor is it providential and fruitful. Rather, providential understandings of suffering are demonic.[103]

> And God has chosen them not for redemptive suffering but for freedom. Blacks are not elected to be Yahweh's suffering people. Rather we are elected because we are oppressed against our will and God's, and God has decided to make our liberation God's own undertaking. . . . it is against our interest . . . to point out the "good" elements in an oppressive structure. . . . There are no assets to slavery.[104]

Cone rejects divine approval of suffering which makes necessary an attitude of grateful acceptance or passivity. Nonetheless, his critique fails to destroy the argument for redemptive suffering in that it leaves intact a sense of contentment with (positive) suffering. That is, Cone rejects the causes of negative suffering such as racism and restrictive social institutions while envisioning the suffering resulting from struggle as a positive phenomenon:

> To be elected by God does not mean freely accepting the evils of oppressors [negative suffering due to racism]. The suffering which is inseparable from the gospel is that style of existence

that arises from a decision to be in spite of nonbeing. It is that type of suffering that is inseparable from freedom, the freedom that affirms black liberation despite the white powers of evil. It is suffering in the struggle for liberation.[105]

This positive suffering is associated with Christ and his followers:

> The life of Jesus also discloses that freedom is bound up with suffering. It is not possible to be for him and not realize that one has chosen an existence in suffering. "Blessed are you when men revile you and persecute you . . . falsely on my account."[106]

By making this statement regarding the Christ event, Cone (like King) frames in Christ the perfection of life through tests and trials. Thereby, progress or freedom are intimately connected to suffering because Christ's suffering is mirrored in the suffering of African-Americans.[107] This connection to the Divine (e.g., as coworkers) forces the acceptance of suffering as redemptive:

> Because the faithful can experience the reality of divine presence, they can endure suffering and transform it into an event of redemption.[108]

Cone indicates in comments like the above quotation that African-American Christians, by their positive suffering participate in God's liberating plan. In short, out of suffering (properly addressed) comes a closeness to God and liberative consequences.

In *God of the Oppressed* (1975)[109] Cone offers his most complete and explicit discussion of the problem of evil or human suffering. Yet, it is essentially the same as his treatment of suffering in the two earlier texts. However, in this text, Cone must respond to the 1973 challenge of Black theology (and "theodicy") presented in William R. Jones's *Is God a White Racist?: A Preamble to Black Theology*. Cone remarks that philosophical notions on the problem of evil and humanism (e.g., Camus and William Jones) fail because they do not recognize the strength of the biblical faith. Philosophers and humanists are primarily concerned with abstract justification rather than concrete activity on behalf of the oppressed. For Cone, time need not be spent exploring the origin of evil.[110] The existence of evil is already a given but destroying it is the real issue. It is a matter of conceptualization versus eradication.

Cone uses the Christ event to respond to those, like William Jones, who question his perspective on the problem of evil. It is the ultimate answer because it recognizes suffering as being against God's will. As with earlier texts, an analysis of Cone's views on the problem of evil suggests a much closer connection to redemptive suffering than Cone acknowledges.

According to Cone, suffering is dualistic in nature. Negative suffering, which arises as the substance of socioeconomic and political oppression, is evil and must be fought. In opposition to this, there is positive suffering, which is the result of the Black community's struggle for freedom. Cone urges his readers to move from an acceptance of negative suffering to positive suffering (i.e., struggle).[111] African-Americans must not be passive, but rather, doggedly active in this movement toward liberation:

> Black people, therefore, as God's suffering servant, are called to suffer with and for God in the liberation of humanity: this suffering to which we have been called is not a passive endurance of white people's insults but rather, a way of fighting for our freedom.[112]

However, even Cone's aggressive tone betrays a willingness to accept suffering. Cone writes:

> The final victory will take place with the second coming of Christ. In the meantime, Christians are called to suffer with God in the fight against evil in the present age. This view gives us a new perspective on suffering. The oppressed are called to fight against suffering by becoming God's suffering servants in the world.[113]

As with *Black Theology of Liberation*, this text fails to demonstrate how African-Americans outside of the academy make the distinction between forms of suffering. It is still likely that negative and positive suffering will collapse, during existential dilemmas, into one category. And this category will most likely be redemptive suffering because it is, for the religious-minded, easily tied into Black church tradition and requires less confrontation with authorities. It is the path of least resistance.

I am not suggesting an idealistic stance on Black oppression premised upon the idea that a world without suffering can exist. Nor am I merely concerned with sematics. There are pragmatic grounds for my stance. My critique of Cone and the others addressed in this chapter relates not to questions concerning the existence of suffering but rather their understanding of suffering's nature and consequence. Along this line, Cone's category of positive suffering is reducible to redemptive suffering. Cone attempts, unsuccessfully, to draw a distinction between suffering *with* God (positive suffering) and suffering *because of* God (redemptive suffering). However, positive suffering maintains the possibility of divinely sanctioned oppression. It is because of this possibility that any religious explanation for suffering that hints at redemptive suffering should be avoided. Even Cone's slight appeal to redemptive suffering leaves the oppressed vulnerable and open to the embracing of their suffering as fuel for liberation. This position does not move toward the lessening of oppressive circumstances; rather, it lessens a sense of accountability and responsibility on the part of oppressors. The possibility of redemption through suffering, although not removing a sense of guilt, significantly reduces any urgent need to change behavior oppressors might feel. And, for the oppressed, it blurs a proper understanding of suffering as demonic, thereby significantly softening the perception of suffering as irreducibly and existentially damaging. In short, movement toward liberation should involve a desire for change brought about by a proper understanding of suffering as unquestionably and unredeemably evil.

4

ALTERNATIVE PERSPECTIVES AND CRITIQUES

Not convinced by the theological apologetic of popular Black theologians such as James Cone, Albert Cleage, Major Jones, Joseph Washington, and J. Deotis Roberts, William R. Jones wrote his first major work, *Is God a White Racist?*, as a prolegomenon to Black religious reflection. That is, Jones seeks to stimulate thought on the present condition of and inconsistencies in Black theology. The logically and historically unsound theological map offered by major Black religious thinkers makes this corrective necessary. That is to say, Black theologians have constructed a theological system which is full of deficiencies in logic and format.[1] The presence of unbending theological presuppositions has rendered silent questions concerning God's involvement in suffering. Accordingly, many theologians

> started [their] work in theodicy with a specific and assumed concept of God. Thus the view that God is one, creator, benevolent, etc. is the presupposed framework into which the evil is forced.
>
> This traditional approach has a dual effect: It obviously eliminates by definition other explanations of suffering and evil, for example dualism. . . .The accumulated effect of this traditional approach is to create a theological climate hostile to the consideration of categories such as divine racism.[2]

Jones' critique centers on an analysis of Black theology's response to the issue of evil[3] because the theodic issue is the foundation (recognized or not) of Black theological thought. In fact, the centrality of oppression within Black theology combined with talk of a sovereign

God makes Black theology an extended Black "theodicy."[4] Concerning this, Black theologians assume God is concerned with the welfare of the oppressed and is working toward their liberation. Consequently, "their [Black theologians'] own presuppositions and conclusions make the question 'Is God a White racist?' and its refutation the necessary point of departure for the construction of their respective systems."[5] With this statement, one begins to see the degree to which Jones' critique rests upon the fourth possible resolution to the problem of evil, i.e., rethinking God's goodness/righteousness.

Black experience has many layers and is open to a host of possible interpretations. This being the case, feasible resolutions to the vexing paradox of the problem of evil, with respect to Black Americans, are not restricted to mysterious yet honorable divine intentions. It is also plausible that God's concern lies outside of the Black community. And so, for Black liberation theology to legitimately speak of liberation it must acknowledge and disprove divine misconduct regarding African-Americans.[6] Thoughtful theological treatments therefore must demonstrate an awareness of the "multi-evidential quality of material" and the resulting interpretations.[7] In short, Jones contends that Black thinkers must not be so wed to their theological assumptions and structures that they are unwilling to raise hard questions about oppression and God's relationship to it. They must first disprove divine malevolence prior to proclaiming divine compassion for the oppressed.[8]

In spite of what Black theologians have traditionally argued, Black experience does not suggest teleological certainties. More accurately, Black struggle may suggest the presence of God working with humans to overcome evil; or, it may connote God's maliciousness and genocidal plans for the African-American population. Therefore:

> . . . in the face of human suffering, whatever its character, we must entertain the possibility that it is an expression of divine hostility. Moreover, if it is allowed that the general category of human suffering raises the possibility of a demonic deity, then the particular category of black suffering—and this is the crucial point for the argument—at least suggests the possibility of divine racism, a particular form of hostility.[9]

The notion of divine racism is premised upon a certain set of assumptions: (1) there is a hierarchy of human value instituted and orchestrated by God; (2) this hierarchy directly relates to levels of suffering ordained by God; and, (3) God favors the "in" group—the group with less suffering. As a note, this triadic system (particularly item three) is complicated by the potential for certain groups to serve a limited function which appears oppressive but is in reality a much-needed lesson. With respect to this, Jones argues that suffering is shrouded in complexity, and types of suffering are often indistinguishable. Suffering can be beneficial, harmful, or a combination of the two. Hence, it is difficult to determine whether it is a sign of divine "favor or disfavor."[10] In light of the possibility of both beneficial and harmful suffering, some type of structure for distinguishing them—ethnic or limited suffering—is needed. (Ethnic suffering entails the following elements: (1) maldistribution of suffering; (2) negative quality of suffering; (3) enormity of suffering; and, (4) suffering of long duration.[11]) This structure or proof can be nothing less than a full liberation event. Essentially, anything less than total liberation leaves questions concerning God's intent and does not preclude the possibility of divine racism. Underlying this assertion is the premise that God is the sum of God's actions. With regard to Black suffering then, God must want to remove it and cannot, or is able to remove it but desires not to. Jones asks, where is the liberation-exaltation event that suggests Blacks are God's "suffering servants" or that God is involved in their liberation? Many Black theologians, Jones acknowledges, point to the Christ event as proof of God's work towards the liberation of the oppressed.

James Cone certainly makes this argument in his texts and in his response to Jones's critique. His most explicit and forthright response to William Jones is contained in an extended footnote to chapter eight of *God of the Oppressed*.[12] Here, Cone argues for the Christ event as the ultimate proof positive of God's historical siding with the oppressed. Through the activities of Christ, God says "yes" to human freedom and fulfillment:

> The coming of God in Jesus breaks open history and thereby creates an experience of truth-encounter that makes us talk in ways often not understandable to those who have not had the experience. . . . [I]n the experience of the cross and resurrection, we know not only that black suffering is wrong but that it has been overcome in Jesus Christ. . . .[13]

The acceptance of this faith stance is an essential component of Cone's argument. Furthermore, Jones' failure to understand the importance of the Christ event for Black Christian faith-praxis keeps him from appreciating the nature of Black faith. Without this appreciation, Jones cannot, according to Cone, accurately respond to Cone's Christ-centered perspective. Consequently Jones provides an external critique:

> To do internal criticism is to think as another thinks and to criticize on the basis of another's presuppositions. In this case, Jones claimed to be thinking my thoughts [Cone's] on the basis of my frame of reference, and he concludes that my perspective on divine liberation of blacks from bondage demands that I produce the decisive liberating event. Apparently he has completely overlooked the *christological* orientation of my theology.[14]

Although an external critique—one outside the "tradition"—Cone believes that Jones deserves a reply:

> . . . Therefore, to William Jones's question, What is the decisive event of liberation? We respond: Jesus Christ![15]

Jones counters this evidence of God's liberative activity by first arguing that the Christ event is situated, in time, prior to the suffering of Black Americans; therefore, it cannot be used as a marker of God's concern for African-Americans:

> In point of fact, does not the continued suffering of blacks *after* the Resurrection raise the essential question all over again: Is God for blacks? We must not forget that black misery, slavery, and oppression—the very facts that make black liberation necessary—are all *post*-Resurrection events.[16]

Jones argues that Biblical stories such as the Exodus and Christ event merely point to God's favoring of the Hebrews and Children of Israel. Jones' counsel to Cone is to weigh the implications and ramifications of Cone's claim that:

> Divine truth is not an idea but an event breaking into the brokenness of history, bestowing wholeness in wretched places. Only one who has experienced and is experiencing the truth of divine liberation can tell the story of how God's people shall overcome.[17]

The resurrection does not speak directly—if at all—to Blacks.[18] Traditional Black theological formulation (based upon the Exodus and Christ event) is unable to adequately refute the charge of divine racism.

Having established traditional Black theology's relevant defects, Jones undertakes the constructive portion of his prolegomenon[19] by delineating a "theodicy" which addresses the question of divine racism. With this in mind, Jones suggests that the "rigid monolithic theism" of dominant Black theology must be reformulated in light of Black experience and the question of divine racism.[20] The doctrine of God corresponding to this "theodicy" is humanocentric theism. Jones argues that only this human centered theism or secular humanism can provide the necessary polemic regarding the presence of Black suffering. On this point, Jones chooses to only outline the former approach because of the dominance of theism (monotheism) within the Black religious tradition. Accordingly:

> [A] movement away from theism should come only if it is convincingly demonstrated that it is a hindrance to black liberation. Disregarding for the moment the issue of theological accuracy, the black theologian, for pragmatic reasons, should develop initially a theistic framework for theodicy.[21]

Any viable "theodicy," i.e., one resolving divine racism charges, must explain Black suffering in light of theological anthropology and a doctrine of God (e.g., character and activity of God). For Black theology, all of the above must support the human struggle for liberation and *confirm* Black experience.[22] Humanocentric theism alone (a hybrid of humanism and theism) fits the Black tradition of theism and meets the stated criteria.[23]

An essential element of humanocentric theism is human ultimacy which entails men and women freely determining the course of events within history. In a word, the human is supreme; even God's encounter with the world must be measured by human reaction to it. God is no longer the functional center. To clarify his argument, Jones distinguishes two types of ultimacy: (1) functional; and, (2) ontological. The former involves the human ability to operate freely. However, this freedom is not absolute because it was externally granted by the Creator who maintains ontological supremacy:

> Humanocentric theism does assign an exalted status to man, particularly to human freedom, but this status—and here we come to its theistic ground—is the consequence of God's will, and it conforms to His ultimate purpose and plan for humankind.[24]

God has, in giving humans free will, limited God's own range of activity within history. That is to say, God placed a restriction upon God's transforming contact with humanity. A consequence of this self-imposed limitation is the inability to assist humans through divine coercion. Rather, God involves God's self with humanity through the art of persuasion and in this way remains an integral and vital presence. Persuasion, borrowing from Howard Burkle and Harvey Cox, entails God's acting to influence (without force of any kind) humans to move toward the fulfillment of their best potentials:[25]

> ... God communicates, solicits, and tries by rational means to affect our choices. We are always responding to influences which are encouraging us to think, weigh and choose. Whenever a man seizes the possibilities of freedom and acts from within his own being, he is certifying the persuasive activity of God.[26]

To extend God's activity beyond persuasion would entail a form of omnipotence which allows for the divine racism charge. That is,

> the concept of divine persuasion and the functional ultimacy of man leads to a theory of human history in which the interplay of human power centers and alignment is decisive. In this context, racism is traced, causally, to human forces. Divine responsibility for the crimes of human history is thus eliminated.[27]

This self-imposed reduction in divine power makes it necessary for humans to serve as God's co-workers in the liberation struggle. Furthermore, humanocentric theism's emphasis on human freedom (of will) requires increased human accountability and responsibility for world conditions.[28] In other words, God is not accountable for oppression, it is the consequence of human misconduct—the perversion of human freedom.[29] Furthermore, Jones sees the pinning of human suffering on the activity of humans as a safeguard against quietism. He is convinced the oppressed will be more willing to fight humans for their freedom than to fight God. Albeit, passivity may occur, ". . .it is decidedly easier to validate the character of suffering vis-a-vis other men than vis-a-vis the divine."[30] In a word, Jones avoids charges of divine racism by removing God's responsibility for oppression. God is limited.

Although there are some notable differences, there are also similarities between this humanocentric theism and the positions held by other Black theologians. Regarding these similarities, Jones writes that:

> Only Washington's emphatic description of God's overruling sovereignty seems to oppose it at all points, though his theological development after *The Politics of God* may belie this conclusion.[31]

Theological similarities belie similar theodical dilemmas which relate to: (1) the continuing issue of divine racism; and, (2) the resulting possibility of redemptive suffering within humanocentric theism. Jones argues in his text that the divine racism charge is an ad absurdum argument. Therefore, he must simply demonstrate that traditional Black theology raises the issue of divine racism but cannot refute it. Maintaining this type of criterion for a functional "theodicy," Jones' humanocentric theism should raise and refute this charge in order to prove viable.

Does Jones in actuality challenge the assumed positive intentions of God? It appears humanocentric theism implicitly suggests good intentions on the part of God. One gleans this in Jones' use of supporting documents, during the construction of his "limited God" concept, which hold to this perspective. Some might argue that my remark is at best guilt by association. However, if Jones in fact constructs his notion of persuasion on works he disagrees with (i.e., those positing strictly good persuasive endeavors on the part of God) and fails to note this, his research is shoddy. Yet, the care he has taken in developing his agreement and disagreement with scholars/concepts in other areas of the text make this type of oversight hard to fathom. Within the materials taken from Burkle, notice that only positive forms of persuasion are attributable to God:

> God is the efficient cause of the world in that he is the agent, mover or source by which the world receives its being. There is no question of persuasion here; forbearance would mean nonexistence for the world. . . . Efficient causality, as the activity which grounds all being, must therefore be a sovereign or originating act. . . . Efficient causality . . . is the first step which the Persuader must take in order to have before Him someone to persuade. . . . Even though the creature exists whether or not he wishes to, . . . suicide is always possible. Also nihilism and other attitudes which deny the importance and reality of existence are possible. The creature retains a veto even though he had nothing to do with the determination that gave him being.[32]

Jones argues that humanocentric theism sufficiently resolves the issue of divine racism: God is good-intentioned but cannot act through coercive means. Therefore, questions concerning God's intentions surface because of faulty theologizing not because of God's actual movements in history.

What evidence does Jones provide for this other than the persistence of suffering and the visible role of humans in it? Such evidence is insufficient when one recalls that Jones does not believe suffering can do more than demonstrate the importance of the question; it cannot be used to refute divine racism because of the multievidential nature of experience.[33] Where then are the acts of persuasion which allow the reader to believe God is not malicious? Until these are presented, does not this self-limiting act of God betray the possibility of a well-masked racism? That is, for the good of humanity God has prevented divine intervention—is this respect for freedom or a back-handed form of racism? A reduction in God's authority out of respect for humanity does not suggest positive intentions on God's part. This is particularly true when one considers that this human freedom, granted by God, directly corresponds to human oppression and environmental destruction. Furthermore, divine malicious intentions are certainly a real possibility if one holds to Jones' premise of counterevidence.[34] In other words, the counterevidence and multievidentiality Jones argues for could just as easily suggest that God has determined to allow humans to do God's work—the destruction of unwanted groups. Perhaps God's self-limitation is the ultimate slight of hand, the supreme alibi—with human abusers of freedom as the fall guys. Perhaps evil is not the result of human misdeeds against divine persuasion. Rather, it is possible that God is persuading white Americans to act in oppressive ways.

If Jones is able to sense this type of trickery regarding the Christ event, why does this possibility elude him with respect to the self-limiting scenario? The words from Camus he refers to have relevance here:

> For as long as the Western world has been Christian, the Gospels have been the interpreter between heaven and earth. Each time a solitary cry of rebellion against human suffering was uttered, the answer came in the form of an even more terrible suffering. In that Christ had suffered and had suffered voluntarily, suffering was no longer unjust. . . . From this point of view the New Testament can be considered as an attempt to answer, in advance, every [rebel] by painting the figure of God in softer colors and by creating an intercessor between God and man.[35]

If there is any merit (or truth) to Camus' analysis of the Christ event as a divine cover-up, then it is possible that God has performed the same maneuver with respect to human freedom. That is, under the cover of human freedom, God condones the suffering of Black Americans without being held responsible for it. Granted, the actual acts are the result of human misconduct; yet, who made this misconduct possible? God. It must be noted that Jones argues for the neutrality of God with regard to coercive actions; but, he does not rule out the possibility of God taking sides with regard to persuasion: "The concept of God as for the oppressed must be relinquished if this means that the oppressed are the unique object of God's activity *in a manner that differs from persuasion*" [emphasis added].[36] This suggests God's evil designs worked out by willing human accomplices. In a word, the reduction of God's authority and the bolstering of human responsibility do not sufficiently alter the possibility of an evil (though limited) God or a God who persuades others to perform evil acts. If the latter is taken seriously, there is also the possibility of divinely approved and redemptive suffering.

When one rejects the possibility of an evil God as Jones seems to do, the possibility of redemptive suffering resurfaces. If a good-intentioned God limits God's self (in order to foster human freedom) even in light of the evil resulting from this freedom, there is something ultimately useful about suffering. That is, the existence of a benevolent God who allows suffering (through an act of restraint) suggests the possibility of the permitted suffering being redemptive. The biblical account of Job is an example of suffering permitted by God which serves to clarify my point. The book of Job is a theodical treatment[37] of a righteous man's seemingly unmerited sufferings. At the outset of this biblical story, the reasons for Job's loyalty to God are questioned on two occasions by Satan. With the first attack upon Job's integrity, Satan is allowed to take Job's possessions and family:

> And Jehovah said unto Satan, "Behold, all that he has is in your power; only upon himself do not put forth your hand. . . ."[38]

Notice that Jehovah does not *directly* inflict this suffering; yet, Jehovah does *indirectly* participate in it. Nonetheless, Job is not conquered by his pain; he remains faithful to God. Satan suggests that Job's loyalty is based on physical health. And so, Jehovah gives Satan permission to touch Job's body:

And the Lord said to Satan, "Behold, he [Job] is in your power; only spare his life."[39]

Over the course of the remaining chapters in the Book of Job, the possible reasons for Job's pain are outlined by his friends. Their reasons are incorrect. At the end of the story, Job realizes that the undeserved sufferings of the righteous do not bring into question the goodness of God. God's purpose for this suffering is eventually made clear and suffering is rendered beneficial:

And the Lord restored the fortunes of Job, when he had prayed for his friends; and the Lord gave Job twice as much as he had before.[40]

In short, the Book of Job suggests the possibility of a good-intentioned God indirectly participating in the affliction of suffering for justifiable reasons. Due to the presence of a situation similar to Job's—unmerited suffering—it is plausible to consider Black Americans modern Job figures. If this is correct, there are grounds for African-Americans perceiving suffering as redemptive. They must only wait for the restoration of all they have lost.

Finally, Jones argues that God does not take sides;[41] this alone can foster the quietism he seeks to avoid. Many choose passivity because God's role is uncertain, and so it is best to accept one's fate as divinely orchestrated. In this respect, humanocentric theism has the flaw citedin theocentric theism—uncertainty of divine intentionality resolved through unsubstantiated and psychologically comforting assertions:

This [commitment to the oppressed demonstrated through omnipotence] may seem like a lot to give up, but consider the other alternative: If the black theologians emphasize the theocentric side of their thought, if God's overruling sovereignty is affirmed, then they are forced to account for the maldistribution of black suffering in the face of His coercive sovereignty. They must answer these questions: Why has God not eliminated black suffering: Why are the oppressed always with us?[42]

According to Jones, it is better to have a limited God who attempts to work good through persuasion than a God whose goodness is brought into question by human suffering. Yet, neither position escapes the trappings of redemptive suffering.

Theology done by Black men fails to include the full spectrum of Black experience. And so, Black women have argued for its reformulation. Jacquelyn Grant gives voice to this task in one of her early publications (1979):

> Just as White women formerly had no place in white theology—except as the receptors of White men's theological interpretations, Black women have had no place in the development of Black theology. By self-appointment, or by the sinecure of a male-dominated society, Black men have deemed it proper to speak for the entire Black community, male and female.[43]

In addition to stating the problem, Grant suggests a resolution which serves to clarify the intellectual excavation she and other scholars seek to perform. In a word, Grant argues that theologizing must be sensitized to forgotten communities and their experiences. Through this conscientization, the patriarchal and sexist theological norms are debilitated, and theology is free to learn from the experiences of the larger community. In this respect, Black women theologians bring to the theological discussion alternative sources (e.g., Black women's literature) and objectives (e.g., freedom from sexism, racism, and classism) based upon the life of Black women.[44] According to Grant:

> There is a tradition which declares that God is at work in the experience of the Black woman. This tradition, in the context of the total Black experience, can provide data for the development of a wholistic Black theology. Such a theology will repudiate the God of classical theology who is presented as an absolute Patriarch, a deserting father who created Black men and women and then "walked out" in the face of responsibility. Such a theology will look at the meaning of the total Jesus Christ Event; it will consider not only how God through Jesus Christ is related to the oppressed men, but to women as well. . . . This theology will exercise its prophetic function, and serve as a "self test" in a church characterized by the sins of racism, sexism, and other forms of oppression.[45]

Black women involved in the restructuring of disciplines including theology have used the term womanist[46] as a description of their enterprise and its character. These scholars have taken upon

themselves the defining essentials of "womanish" behavior—
strength, daring, and hard questioning:

> 1. From *womanish* (opp. of "girlish," i.e., frivolous, irresponsi-
> ble, not serious) A black feminist of color. From the black folk
> expression of mother to female children, "you acting woman-
> ish," i.e., like a woman. Usually referring to outrageous, auda-
> cious, courageous or *willful* behavior. Wanting to know more
> and in greater depth than is considered "good" for one.
> Interested in grown-up doings. Acting grown up. Being grown
> up. Interchangeable with another black folk expression: You
> trying to be grown: Responsible. In charge. *Serious.* 2. Also: A
> woman who loves other women, sexually and/or nonsexually.
> Appreciates and prefers women's culture, women's emotional
> flexibility (values tears as natural counterbalance of laughter),
> and women's strength. Sometimes loves individual men, sexu-
> ally and/or nonsexually. Committed to revival and wholeness
> of entire people, male and female. Not a separatist, except
> periodically, for health. Traditionally universalist, as in:
> "Mama, why are we brown, pink, and yellow, and our cousins
> are white, beige, and black?" Ans.: "Well, you know the colored
> race is just like a flower garden, with every color flower repre-
> sented." Traditionally capable, as in: "Mama, I'm walking to
> Canada and I'm taking you and a bunch of other slaves with
> me." Reply: "It wouldn't be the first time."[47]

One of the best examples of womanist thought is found in the work of
Delores S. Williams.

In *Sisters in the Wilderness*,[48] Williams brings to Black theology
the forgotten experiences of Black women. With her "female identity
fixed firmly in her Consciousness," Williams recognizes that biblical
and other resources speak to a much larger perspective than that
presented by Black males. In other words, the "second tradition of
African-American Biblical appropriation" (the first being the norm of
God as liberator gleaned by Black men) points to the place of Black
women in this liberation tradition.[49] Fundamentally, such an appropriation requires rereading the Bible from the perspective of the most
oppressed—Black women and their religiosity.

Some argue that Black women's reliance upon religion is a problem. More precisely, male writers such as Richard Wright have
argued, according to Williams, that a strong reliance on religion fos-

ters a contentment with suffering (e.g., abuse and pain).[50] Williams refers to *Native Son*[51] in which Wright records a conversation between Bigger Thomas and Reverend Hammond which is rather revealing. Christians such as Bigger Thomas' mother find comfort, Wright suggests, in the words of ministers such as Reverend Hammond:

> Look son Ah'm holdin' in mah hands a wooden cross taken from a tree. A tree is the worl' son. 'N nailed t' this tree is a sufferin' man. Th's whut life is, son. Sufferin'. How kin yuh keep from b'levin' the word of Gawd when Ah'm, holdin' befo' yo' eyes the only thing tha' gives a meanin' t' yo' life?[52]

According to Wright, religiosity easily lends itself to resignation, the strength to gratefully accept life's hardships. It produces a martyr complex by which one's worth is measured in terms of pain endured. Williams notes that for writers such as Alice Walker, an important and powerful sense of self does not necessitate nor precipitate a rejection of religious devotion. Rather, a sense of self may entail a rethinking of religious images and a placing of them within the context of Black women's experience (particularly as care providers). One sees this in Alice Walker's characters Shug and Celie in *The Color Purple*.[53] Concerning these characters, Williams says: "Shug helps Celie to reexamine certain religious values Celie has held all her life—religious values supporting her bondage rather than her empowerment as a new, liberated woman. This reexamination centers on notions of God, man and church."[54] Celie establishes a constructive relationship with God once she no longer imagines God in the form of a man. With Shug's assistance, Celie begins to perceive God as connected to the environment—Celie, Shug, trees—life. And from this liberating doctrine of God, Celie forges a new love and respect for herself. This, in turn, transforms her familial relations. Williams writes,

> Celie's change of consciousness about "God-as-man" frees her psychologically from the fear of her husband, who was as stern as any God she had imagined. After years of silently suffering, Celie "enters into creation."[55]

In short, the map of Black women's religiosity is complex. It often contains markings left by abuse and manipulation; however, it points to liberative paths of faith and spiritual values carved out of wilderness.

Using Hagar's encounters with motherhood, surrogacy, and ethnicity (Genesis 16), Williams suggests the wilderness can be a place of both transformation and hardship which analogously speaks to Black life in America. On the one hand, the wilderness marks a state of rejection:

> And Sarai said to Abram, "May the wrong done to me be on You! I gave my maid to your embrace, and when she saw that she had conceived, she looked on me with contempt. May the Lord judge between you and me!" But Abram said to Sarai, "Behold, your maid is in your power; do to her as you please." Then Sarai dealt harshly with [Hagar], and she fled from her.[56]

On the other hand, the wilderness encompasses a place of divine—liberating—encounter. It is a place where one's faith in God is tested and rewarded:

> The angel of the Lord said to her [Hagar], "Return to your mistress, and submit to her. . . . I will so greatly multiply your descendants that they cannot be numbered for multitude."[57]

According to Williams, Hagar, like African-American women, navigates the world certain only of God's help. In examining the wilderness experience of Black women, Delores Williams provides surrogacy—forced and coerced—as an analogy for the economic, sexual, and caregiving forms of oppression historically encountered by Black women.

Williams begins her exploration of surrogacy in the article "Black Women's Surrogacy Experience and the Christian Notion of Redemption."[58] Here she defines surrogacy as the unique character of Black women's experience involving substitute labor. On one level, surrogacy (i.e., forced surrogacy) entails the roles Black women played as coerced care givers through domestic service, child care, physical field labor (man's work), and sexual exploitation. Within these antebellum roles, Black women were categorized as "jezebels," "mammies," or "work mules." This usurping of Black women's energy

> illustrate[s] a unique kind of oppression only black women experienced in the slavocracy. Only black women were mammies. Only black women were permanently assigned to field labor. Only black women permanently lost control of their bodies to the lust of white men. During slavery, black women were bound to a system that had respect for neither their bodies, their dignity,

their labor, nor their motherhood except as it was put to the service of securing the well-being of ruling class white families.[59]

The ending of slavery did not mean the demise of oppressive "substitute" labor situations. Regrettably, efforts by Black men and women to end surrogacy activities often fell victim to economic realities.[60] Furthermore, not all African-Americans worked toward the elimination of surrogacy roles. In order to demonstrate the strength of their familial structures, some African-American men attempted to mimic patriarchal patterns they observed in the homes of white Americans. The surrogacy role considered most appropriate for this emulation was that of the mammy, complete with child nurturing and household management skills.[61] While surrogacy activity transverses the Civil War, postbellum years mark changes associated with the mammy figure. Most noticeably, within Black families, female care givers were referred to as mother as opposed to the stereotype latent term mammy.[62] In addition, the protector role played by antebellum mammies with respect to white children was increasingly superceded by Black male protection of Black women and children.[63]

A consequence of continuing surrogacy has been the perpetuation of negative stereotypes which encourage and sustain abusive, sexist, and misogynistic attitudes. In many cases these stereotypes fostered the model of Black women as superwomen.[64] Status as superwomen entails Black women facing expectations—of labor and care—which extend beyond those held over other groups. The negative effect of surrogacy and superwoman status is tremendous. In short, these roles foster a subsumption of Black women's personality and worth under others they care for. This underexplored form of exploitation, "gives black women's oppression its unique character and raises challenging questions about the way redemption is imagined in a Christian context."[65]

Williams is forced by her use of scripture (the Hagar account) and the theological assumptions contained therein to address God's role in this surrogacy process. That is, what does one make of God's presence in the wilderness experience?

> The angel of the Lord found her by a spring of water in the wilderness. . . . And he said, "Hagar, maid of Sarai, where have you come and where are you going?" She said, "I am fleeing from my mistress Sarai." The angel of the Lord said to her, "Return to your mistress, and submit to her."[66]

Does this request suggest that God condones Hagar's oppression? Is there some inherently valuable lesson that Hagar can learn only through such an ordeal? Furthermore, is Black women's surrogacy an issue God is concerned with? Although these questions are legitimate in light of what scripture seemingly says, Williams vehemently opposes all suggestions that God approves of the oppressive surrogacy roles held by Black women. For Williams, God is on the side of the oppressed and such a God cannot orchestrate suffering. However, this is contradicted by traditional perceptions of the Christ event as an act of redemption through suffering. In Christ, the ultimate instance of suffering is elevated to its highest possible redemptive level: atonement resulting from pain and torture. Christians who emphasize death as the focal point of the Christ event implicitly suggest a strong connection between suffering and the will of God. It is then logical for Christians—imitators of Christ—to find divine approval in their hardships and sufferings. In this respect, an avenue is opened through which righteousness or closeness to God is measured by affliction endured; to be Christlike is to be in misery: "No Cross, No Crown." Williams rightly fears that the acceptance of suffering as Christlike will result in the oppressed supporting their oppression. Specifically, it entails Black women bolstering the surrogacy they face because Christ was also a surrogate.

Finding the traditional Christian interpretation inadequate and inaccurate, Williams recasts God's involvement in history:

> Perhaps not many people today can believe that evil and sin were overcome by Jesus' death on the cross; that is, that Jesus took human sin upon himself and therefore saved humankind. Rather, it seems more intelligent and more scriptural to understand that redemption had to do with God, through Jesus, giving humankind new vision to see the resources for positive, abundant relational life. Redemption had to do with God, through the *ministerial* vision, giving humankind the ethical thought and practice upon which to build positive, productive quality of life.[67]

The cross is separated from redemption, and the life and ministry of Jesus become the foci of liberative, salvific influence, and power. The victory over evil occurs in the wilderness when Jesus resists the tempter. In this refusal to surrender, and not in the shame of the crucifixion, Jesus defeats evil/sin through a radical commitment to life. That is to say:

> Jesus' own words in Luke 4 and his ministry of healing the human body, mind and spirit (described in Matthew, Mark, and Luke) suggest that Jesus did not come to redeem humans by showing them God's "love" manifested in the death of God's innocent child on the cross erected by cruel, imperialistic, patriarchal power. Rather, the texts suggest that the spirit of God in Jesus came to show humans life. . . .[68]

In this manner, the death of Christ illustrates what *not* to do. Emphatically put, "there is nothing divine in the blood of the Cross."[69] As with the Christ event, the importance of Black women's wilderness experience (as a time of temptation/pain and triumph) is its affirmation of life. God does not condone the abuse of Black women in the same way that God's actions through Christ did not glorify surrogacy.

The objective of the Christ event is a demonstration of life properly lived. However, there is another lesson: death indicates the depravity and misdeeds of humanity. It sums up the human tendency to destroy those persons who suggest an alternative to greed, fear, and oppressive relations. Therefore, to place emphasis upon death is to raise serious questions:

> Surrogacy, attached to this divine personage, thus takes on an aura of the sacred. It is therefore fitting and proper for black women to ask whether the image of a surrogate-God has salvific power for black women or whether this image supports and re-enforces the exploitation that has accompanied their experience with surrogacy. If black women accept this idea of redemption, can they not also passively accept the exploitation that surrogacy brings?[70]

And furthermore:

> Black women should never be encouraged to believe that they can be united with God through this kind of suffering. There are quite enough black women bearing the cross by rearing children alone, struggling on welfare, suffering through

poverty, experiencing inadequate health care, domestic violence and various forms of sexism and racism.[71]

Yet, is Williams implying that God sustains but humans must liberate? If God is working against surrogacy, what can be made of
continued oppression?

When one looks closely at the biblical story of Hagar and
expands it to include the experiences of women of color in general,
questions such as the one above are raised. In fact,

> when non-Jewish people—like many African-American women
> who now claim themselves to be economically enslaved—read
> the entire Hebrew testament from the point of view of the non-
> Hebrew slave, there is no clear identification that God is
> against their perpetual enslavement.[72]

Obviously, there is a tension between communal claims of liberation
and the biblical silence of God during certain cases of oppression.[73]
Williams suggests an interpretative tool capable of respecting the collective experiences of Black women—experience of pain, struggle, and
survival. When searching scripture, Williams suggests that thinkers
make use of a new hermeneutical approach—hermeneutic of identifi-
cation-ascertainment—which brings to the surface the hidden issues
of oppression. This hermeneutic entails a three-layered approach to
interpretation. First, a subjective reading, followed by a reading
geared toward the "faith journey of the Christian community with
which they are affliated." Finally, it entails an objective look at the
phenomena writers identify with and phenomena these same writers
ignore.[74] It takes account of the ways in which African-Americans
(particularly Black mothers) have traditionally read the Bible in light
of their existential realities of oppression and their efforts at survival.
By means of this interpretative process, a critical rethinking of scrip-
tural appropriations takes place. Using this new hermeneutic, one
can ask again an important question without damaging God's reputation: "What is God's word about survival and quality of life formation
for oppressed and quasi-free people struggling to build community in
the wilderness?"[75]

Williams believes God's relationship with humans is beneficial
for humans. She argues that God's involvement with oppressed
women corresponds to the development of needed "survival strate-
gies."[76] In a word, survival, not liberation, is what God promises the

oppressed. Therefore, God's reputation is secured in that God fosters the continued existence of those who are oppressed:[77]

> When they and their families get into serious social and economic straits, black Christian women have believed that God helps them make a way out of no way. This is precisely what God did for Hagar and Ishmael when they were expelled from Abraham's house and were wandering in the desert without food and water. God opened Hagar's eyes and she saw a well of water that she had not seen before. In the context of the survival struggle of poor African-American women this translates into God providing Hagar [read also African-American women] with *new vision* to see survival resources where she saw none before.[78]

Williams' position is questionable in part because of her reliance on the Hagar story. Firstly, it is not self-evident in the biblical story of Hagar that God does not enjoy or ordain the suffering of the oppressed. The survival of Ishmael and the fostering of a great nation through him is contingent upon Hagar's return to the suffering inflicted by Sarah. That is, God tells Hagar to go back to Sarah and thereby continue within an oppressive situation. Williams notes that, "God is clearly partial to Sarah. Regardless of the way one interprets God's command to Hagar to submit herself to Sarah, God does not liberate her."[79] Is this a sign of love for Hagar? To use Williams' terminology, it is through the "tragic" nature of the wilderness that ultimate "health" is achieved:

> Yet wilderness was a place where the slave underwent intense struggle before gaining a spiritual/religious identity, for example, as a Christian. But the struggle itself was regarded as positive, leading to a greater good than the slave ordinarily realized.[80]

This certainly is reminiscent of earlier arguments concerning redemptive suffering; in a word, good things occur as a consequence of unmerited suffering. That is to say, if God is good and on the side of the oppressed, their continued oppression must have a divine reason. As a result, unmerited and intrinsically evil suffering is transmuted into something good. This is the case when one considers Williams' claim that God is concerned with the survival of the oppressed rather than their liberation. If their suffering was ultimately useless, would not a concerned and able God work toward their liberation rather

than survival? Williams apparently answers "no" to this and consequently raises the possibility of redemptive suffering.

Delores Williams would disagree with my assessment of her
position. In fact, she ideologically separates herself from the redemptive suffering philosophies. Lining up with feminists who also reject
this thought, she writes:

> Brown and Parker claim, as I do, that most of the history of
> atonement theory in Christian theology supports violence, vic-
> timization and undeserved suffering. The earlier discussion of
> atonement in chapter 6 [of *Sisters in the Wilderness*] above
> agrees with Brown and Parker's assertion that "the central
> image of Christ on the cross as the savior of the world commu-
> nicates the message that suffering is redemptive."[81]

Williams is careful to note the possibility of Black thought leading to
passivity in the face of suffering. She does not want this opinion to be
connected with her work on Hagar and surrogacy. To prevent this,
Williams voices her disagreement with Black leaders such as King in
that his opinions on Black experience require an oppressive interpretation of Black suffering. Once again, with reference to Brown and
Parker she says:

> Their critique of Martin Luther King, Jr.'s idea of the value of
> the suffering of the oppressed in oppressed-oppressor confronta-
> tions accords with my assumption that African-American
> Christian women can, through their religion and its leaders, be
> led passively to accept their own oppression and suffering—if
> the women are taught that suffering is redemptive.[82]

Even in light of the above considerations, Black women's surrogacy experiences do not call into question the intentions of God. The
focus of blame for evil rests with human misconduct. Jones suggests
that the divine racism dilemma is rectified by rethinking the divine-
human makeup of liberative activity. And reminiscent of this,
Williams argues for a rereading or a new vision regarding Christ's
purpose and God's agenda for the oppressed. Hagar and Black
women's experiences teach that God provides the oppressed with survival skills and improved life options, *not* liberation. If one follows
Williams' reasoning, "theodicy" is only an issue for those who misun-
derstand God's intentions and assume liberation is God's objective.
Otherwise, the suffering of the oppressed does not require a question-

ing of God because the measuring stick of God's worth is no longer liberation. It is survival—the basic necessities such as sustenance, shelter, and hope. Hence, to the extent the oppressed survive, workings of God are confirmed. With survival granted, it becomes the responsibility of the oppressed to seek their liberation.[83] The continuing question is this: should Christians devote their time and worship to a God who merely points out the already present elements of survival? Is this position substantially better than explicit redemptive suffering arguments? Although Williams attributes survival to contact with the divine, cannot survival just as easily point to humanly fostered tenacity of spirit?

It turns out, then, that even the two thinkers—Jones and Williams—who question traditional theological assumptions in actuality maintain them: the activity and responsibilities of God are given new packaging. Things required of God are adjusted so as not to contradict an unchanging reality of Black oppression. That is, Jones resolves the problem of evil by limiting God and making humans responsible for evil. Williams manages the same effect by limiting God's responsibility to the area of survival. In both cases suffering persists while God's intentions remain good, and this allows for the continuing feasibility of redemptive suffering.

Once again, the problem of evil can be resolved in four ways: (1) rethinking the nature of evil; (2) rethinking the power of God (humans become God's coworkers); (3) questioning of God's goodness/ righteousness; (4) questioning/denial of God's existence. To this point, the arguments examined reveal the use of the first two resolutions to Black suffering (i.e., rethinking the nature of evil and rethinking the power of God), with some limited use (by Jones) of option three. However, dialogue concerning the problem of evil within the Black community should extend itself to a full exploration of all four resolutions. I initiate this type of dialogue by outlining a resource (i.e., Black humanism) in Black thought for the questioning/ denial of God's existence as a response to the problem of evil. Furthermore, I begin the exploration of a method beyond "theodicy" by which to adequately explore the resolution offered by Black humanism as a religious option. I label this alternative methodology nitty-gritty hermeneutics.

5

BLUES, RAP, AND
NITTY-GRITTY HERMENEUTICS

---

errence Tilley in the essay "The Uses and Abuses of Theodicy" and later in *The Evils of Theodicy*,[1] suggests that "theodicy" creates hardships. That is to say, when theologians attempt to
respond to the question "Why does evil exist in God's good world?,"
they inevitably damage the faith they seek to secure:

> These attempts to explain evil founded in the fact that the
> theodicists' answers to the atheologians' challenge . . . either
> entail a denial of divine goodness, divine power, or the reality
> of evil. . . . In short, contemporary theologians should not play
> the theodical game on the terms constructed by the atheolo-
> gians both because there is no compelling reason to play their
> game and because when theists do play it, they either lose or
> misrepresent the faith they seek to defend.[2]

Tilley concludes that "theodicy" fails to explain evil because of its
need to maintain the attributes of God, irrespective of evidence to the
contrary. Therefore:

> . . . to write a theodicy is not merely to express a wish. Such
> writing is an illocutionary act which is not merely an expres-
> sive act, but a declarative act which makes "true" what is only
> a wish. One of the evils of theodicy is that it effaces the differ-
> ences between the world that theodicists wish to be (a world
> wherein God reigns) and the world that is.[3]

It increases the chasm between the practical and theoretical—a gap which should be closed. In this manner, "theodicy" does not allow the theological space for primary and critical thought regarding an a priori theological system of assumptions. Hence, "theodicy" has functioned as a safeguard against assaults upon the substance of religious belief and structures. In this manner, it guards theological houses from the housecleaning horrific human experience periodically demands. That is, ". . . theodicies do falsify the picture and construct consoling dreams to distract our gaze from real evils." Sadly enough, it virtually silences those who suffer, because their suffering is seen as good.[4] In essence "theodicy" is an "impractical practice" which must not be forgotten but *never* used.[5]

Having this theodical game in mind, I reject "theodicy" as a useful tool. It does not exhibit the ability or a willingness to entertain *all* the questions and responses forced to the surface by the paradox of faith and existential reality. I argue that religious thought concerned with alleviating the human existential condition must expose its questions and assumptions to the full spectrum of religious responses. However, this can only be achieved by a methodology free inherent restrictions of "theodicy," a methodology capable of addressing a complete range of perspectives.

Consequently, I argue that a method involving what Peter Hodgson calls "hard labor"[6] (strong and aggressive inquiry) must be utilized. Such a method must have the capacity to appreciate and respond to the hard facts of African-American life. Regarding this, the words of Lerone Bennett are revealing:

> The overriding need for the movement is for us to think with our own eyes. . . . We cannot think now because we have no intellectual instrument save those which were designed expressly to keep us from seeing. It is necessary for us to develop a new frame of reference which transcends the limits of the oppressor's concepts. . . . The initial steps towards liberation is [sic] to abandon the partial frame of reference of our oppressor and to create new concepts which [rely on] our reality.[7]

Only the broadened frame of reference implied by Bennett will allow for a full explanation of all vital materials relevant to the problem of evil. For this task, I suggest an approach I have labelled nitty-gritty hermeneutics.[8]

The term hermeneutics is etymologically derived from the name Hermes, the messenger of the Greek gods. It was his task to take information directly from immortals to mortals, in the process making the words of the gods understandable for humans. In essence he interpreted. Thus, hermeneutics denotes interpretation of the meaning submerged in events, texts, etc. That is, words and texts contain valuable information that must be recognized and processed within one's system of values and concerns. Hermeneutics makes this possible.

Interpretation of events and texts has occurred throughout history; however, it is not until after the Renaissance that hermeneutics becomes a discipline. Debate between Catholic officials and reformers over the nature of scripture combined with developments in philosophy, linguistics, and the study of law faciliated the emergence of modern hermeneutics and its eventual association with philosophy.[9] The nineteenth and twentieth century use and complex expansion of hermeneutics has been marked by figures such as Schleiermacher, Bultmann, Heidegger, Gadamer, and Ricoeur.

Although hermeneutics proves invaluable in the assessment of important documents, interpretation is far from problem-free: how is meaning made objective when it must be filtered through subjective interpretators? How is the meaning of a text (and therefore application) rendered universal when it is the product of a contextually bound human? This dilemma shapes the content and nature of contemporary hermeneutics.

Many groups who believe dominant interpretations of sacred texts support their oppression have developed alternative approaches. For example, Black theology looks at scripture, tradition, history, and contemporary (white) theology using what can be categorized as a hermeneutic of liberative suspicion. The universalization of experience is rejected as oppressive and exclusive of the concerns and history of oppressed people. Subordinating of particulars (context) in favor of illusionary universals supports the status quo. What, then, is God's message to those suffering from discrimination? Black theologians look at theological sources through the experiences of African-Americans and reject interpretations and principles failing to recognize and highlight the demand for full liberation. The hermeneutic of liberative suspicion centralizes theological investigation around the oppressed and their perspective. A consequence of this hermeneutic is the rethinking of God and God's role in history. Black theology interprets scripture and history as the concrete evidence of God's commitment to the oppressed; God is in human history (as evidenced through Jesus

Christ), fighting for the deliverance of the victimized. Hermeneutics, according to Black theology, must provide for praxis. In short:

> The norm [hermeneutic] of all God-talk which seeks to be black-talk is the manifestation of Jesus as the black Christ who provides the necessary soul for black liberation. This is the hermeneutical principle for black theology which guides its interpretation of the meaning of contemporary Christianity.[10]

As was demonstrated in the previous chapter, the efforts of Black theologians such as James Cone to provide a theological platform responsive to the needs of Black Americans falters on the problem of evil. That is, this hermeneutic of liberative suspicion does not render an interpretation of the gospel and Black suffering free of damaging redemptive suffering arguments. The hermeneutic of liberative suspicion unknowingly compromises Black experience by forcing it to conform to Christian principles and values, thereby softening Black experience's "rough" edges. Nitty-gritty hermeneutics is not restricted by this theodical quagmire.

The exploration of nitty-gritty hermeneutics is an exercise which, through additional discourse and exploration, promises a deeper understanding of Black religious thought and its various responses to suffering—the problem of evil. Nitty-gritty hermeneutics and its interpretative roughness free inquiry from the restrictions posed by "theodicy." This hermeneutic differs from the hermeneutic of liberative suspicion in that it is not wed to the same doctrinal or theological presuppositions, thereby freeing inquiry to critique these presuppositions. Its guiding criterion is the presentation of Black life with its full complexity, untainted by static tradition.

Although the etymology of the term nitty-gritty is uncertain, it is apparently (based upon usage) couched in Black expressivity and linguistic creativity of the mid-twentieth century. The term nitty-gritty denotes a hard and concrete orientation in which the "raw natural facts" are of tremendous importance, irrespective of their ramifications. While serving to confine vision and orientation to certain parameters of roughness, it also expands the meaning and possibility of life to its uncompromising and endemic limits. Therefore, nitty-gritty hermeneutics seeks a clear and unromanticized understanding of a hostile world. In a word, nitty-gritty hermeneutics entails "telling it like it is" and taking risks.

Aspects of this hermeneutic include a sense of heuristic rebelliousness as well as raw and uncompromised insight. This hermeneutical approach takes the material of life that goes unspoken and hidden, and expresses it. In Foucault's terms, this hermeneutic ruptures American dialogue by both surfacing subjugated knowledge which dismantles false perceptions and harmful practices, and by altering popular perceptions and life values.

Defined by its nitty-gritty character, nitty-gritty hermeneutics exhibits a sense of nonconformity. It ridicules interpretations and interpretors who seek to inhibit or restrict liberative movement and hard inquiries into the problems of life. The nitty-gritty "thang," so to speak, forces a confrontation with the "funky stuff" of life and oddly enough, finds strength in the challenge posed. One finds these two principles, which give shape to this hermeneutic (i.e., roots in rebelliousness and raw/uncompromising insight), exercised within cultural expressions such as the blues. That is to say, the blues illustrates and helps to clarify the nature and function of nitty-gritty hermeneutics.[11] As a note of importance, this does not suggest an endorsement of the oppressive opinions held within the blues or other forms of musical expression such as rap. However, I am not willing to reject these musical forms of expression simply because they contain some of the misguided tendencies of the larger society. Rather I am suggesting that the positive expressions of this music (i.e., the examples of this music which have a constructive intention) suggest a hermeneutic which is worthy of investigation and implementation.

As a musical form, the blues' historical origin is virtually impossible to pinpoint. It is, however, safe to say that blues songs took form long before their actual recording and likely developed alongside spirituals and secular work songs. Consequently, existential and musical contexts informing work songs and spirituals determined the content, shape, and sound of the blues. Country or Southern blues, as early forms of blues are commonly called, relate to spirituals in that both make use of an eight- or sixteen-bar form.[12] Yet, whereas the spirituals tell the story of Black life in terms of a collective reality, blues songs connote a shift to an individualized and personal accounting of existence within a hostile society. Ontological shifts in the music mirror epistemological shifts in that the blues highlight the role of humans in the redressing of societal wrongs.[13]

The use of blues tones by vaudville artists demarcates the emergence of classical blues—blues for entertainment beyond the immediate community of origin. Classical blues, in turn, stands between country and urban blues which is marked by movement to Northern cities (e.g., Chicago and New York) and the blending of styles such as New Orleans honky tonk (strong piano use) and country guitar-dominanted blues.

Until the occurence of changes in the blues fostered by geographical movement of artists (early twentieth century migration patterns) and the proliferation of "race records" (beginning in the 1920s with singers such as Mamie Smith), the blues functioned within definable and local settings such as the entertainment of friends and relatives, and the pleasure of small local tavern audiences.[14] No one envisioned the mass appeal the blues could have and the volume of people who would pay to hear these songs performed. The musically expressed plight of individual Black Americans was of interest to other Black Americans with similar experiences, and of interest to white Americans. The mass marketing of blues records and the subsequent play, after the Depression, on radio stations allowed the diversification of style. Blues performers were no longer restricted to the instrument and voice use popular in their region; blues figures were free to vary their sound through imitation. The production of blues changed as a result of recording and migration patterns but the existential content of the blues remained the same. Whether in the country, New Orleans, or Northern cities, the blues continued to explore the pressing issues of Black life.

Within these songs, the promises of the spirituals were weighed and tested in light of life's controlling hardships, and utopian ideals were found wanting. Hence, the blues as a musical form is concerned with truth as it arises out of experience. That is, for blues artists: "truth is experience and experience is the truth."[15]

The blues' commitment to the unpolished expression of Black life made some segments of the Black community uncomfortable. For example, the blues met with the disapproval of Black churches because the lyrical content and "seductive" nature of the music fell outside of the norms, values, and morality advocated by Black church tradition.

> The old-time religion of the southern churches did not permit the singing of "devil songs" and "jump-up" songs as the blues were commonly termed, and it is not an expression that is natural to the church member. . . . Lower class Blacks often had to decide whether to accept with meekness the cross they had to

bear in this world and to join the church with the promise of "Eternal Peace in the Promised Land" or whether to attempt to meet the present world on its own terms, come what may.[16]

The raw or "gutbucket," so to speak, experiences were poetically presented, critiqued, and synthesized; yet, understood as unapologetically real and unavoidable. No subject was taboo—although most were shrouded in metaphorical language. The rejection of the blues stems from the hard living and hard questioning noted within the lyrics. In this manner, blues performers openly discussed aspects of life that church folk would just as soon keep hidden and brought into question basic premises of religiosity.[17]

James H. Cone considers the blues "secular spirituals" because they, like spirituals, affirm Black identity. They are distinctive in that they seek to understand the world strictly in light of temporal concerns and possibilities. Why do the blues restrict themselves to this material and perspective? This is done because blues artists find traditionally religious interpretations of life fundamentally flawed and unproductive. The blues critiqued the hypocrisy and inactivity of Black churches and used this as fuel for significations and sarcasm. J. T. "Funny Paper" Smith hits upon this point when singing the following lines:

> Some of the good Lawd's children, some of them
>   ain't no good. (2x)
> Some of them are the devil, ooh, well, well,
>   and won't help you if they could.
> Some of the good Lawd's children kneel upon
>   their knees and pray. (2x)
> You serve the devil in the night, ooh, well
>   and serve the Lawd in the day.[18]

The blues unremittingly question banal theological formulations and treat hyperoptimistic religiosity with sarcasm. Smith provides an example of this when questioning the traditional notion of a good God held by Black Christian religion. He sings:

> I used to ask God questions, then answer that
>   question my self, (2x)
> 'Bout when I was born, wonder was there any
>   mercy left?

> You know it must be the devil I'm servin',
>> I know it can't be Jesus Christ, (2x)
> 'Cause I ask him to save me and look like he
> tryin' to take my life.[19]

Looking over the course of his life, Smith is unable to accept traditional conceptions of God (as compassionate and involved in human history) nor is he willing to explain his continual hardship through divine mystery. Taking a hard look at his condition and Christian faith, Smith asserts that God's activity either has a benign effect on history or is geared towards his demise.

The blues forces a rethinking of what religion is and what it means to be religious. In this way, blues players expanded the narrow perceptions of religiosity beyond the confines of mainstream Black traditional approaches. Hence, with respect to the blues, it is unacceptable to limit religion/religiosity to Black traditional Christian (or theistic) models. Consider the following lines:

> Yes I went out on the mountain, looked over in
>> Jerusalem, (2x)
> Well, I see them hoodoo women, ooh Lord, makin'
>> up in their low-down tents.

> Well I'm going to Newport to see Aunt Caroline
>> Dye, (2x)
> She's a fortune-teller, oh Lord, she sure don't
>> tell no lie.[20]

Productive religiosity becomes religiosity whose principles have *felt* consequences for daily life. Doctrinal and theological purity pale in comparison to existential need. Usable religion must not place abstraction and neat theological categories above human experience. Only that which is proven by experience holds value. Religious expression is here defined by its commitment to human accountability and responsibility. To a large extent, productive religiosity is fluidlike in that its dynamics alter with the existential situation; in this way, it avoids applicability dilemmas resulting from the rigid demands and dictates of tradition. Black Christianity ultimately falls short in that it retains a commitment to theological assertions (such as theodical resolutions) that are not aligned with existential reality and experience. This is not necessarily a denial of God. I am not arguing that the

blues, in general, is humanistic in orientation. The blues leaves open
the possibility of God's existence, but God's nature and activities are
not as certain. (Here the blues differ from the spirituals.)

In response to this, the blues promotes a raw religiosity which
includes African practices in various forms—hoodoo, voodoo, and con-
jure. Along these lines, Muddy Waters (born McKinley Morganfield)
declares the power of his "mojo" while singing "Hoochie Coochie
Man" (written by Willie Dixon). In this piece, the merit of hoodoo as a
system responsive to existential need is highlighed. And in this way,
an alternative to mainstream Black Christianity is offered. "Hoochie
Coochie Man" and similar songs suggest a form of religion that is
centered around human needs and is responsive to the material concerns fostered by physical hardship without reliance on theological
ghosts and unsubstantiated religious guarantees. Nitty-gritty
hermeneutics surfacing in the blues interprets religion, based upon
complex Black life, as a tool by which humans are encouraged to
remove pyschologically comforting theological crutches and develop
themselves as liberators. Ralph Ellison captures this meaning in
"Richard Wright's Blues":

> The blues is an impulse to keep the painful details and
> episodes of a brutal experience alive in one's aching conscious-
> ness, to finger its jagged edge and to transcend it, not by the
> consolation of philosophy [or religious constructs] but by
> squeezing from it a near-tragic, near-cosmic lyricism. As a
> form, the blues is an autobiographical chronicle of personal
> catastrophe expressed lyrically. . . .
>
> . . . Their attraction lies in this, that they at once express
> both the agony of life and the possibility of conquering it
> through sheer toughness of spirit. They fall short of tragedy
> only in that they provide no solution, offer no scapegoat but
> the self.[21]

Blues songs make use of the same creative and existential materials as the spirituals, thereby creating a continuum of musical
expression. In like manner, the prevalence of continued hardship and
the need to creatively respond has resulted in the development of a
musical exploration in keeping with current conditions and contexts—rap music. The link between earlier forms of musical expression, necessitiated by common existential hardships and cultural
tools is, once again, forged; this time, the continuity is between blues

and rap. Consequently, one can further locate the substance of this nascent method of interpretation—nitty-gritty hermeneutics—within the recent form of musical expression known as rap.[22]

An accurate history of rap music must understand it in connection to the larger development of hip-hop culture. Hip-hop first emerges as a cultural and creative response to the matrix of industrial decline, social isolation, and political decay endemic to New York City's Bronx section.[23] Faced with declining opportunities for socioeconomic mobility and accompanying marginality, young artists made use of their creative resources to establish an alternative "way of being" in the world. This development was complete with a vocabulary, style of dress, visual artistic expression (graffiti art emerges as early as 1971), and dance (break dancing present as early as 1973) uniquely their own.[24]

In essence, hip-hop culture and its musical voice—rap—signal cultural resistance. The music behind rap lyrics, with its sampling and strong beats, rethinks traditional understandings of proper musical formation, and finds pleasure in the sounds the music industry labelled undesirable. As Tricia Rose insightfully points out:

> Although famous rock musicians have used recognizable samples from other prominent musicians as part of their album material, for the most part, samples were used to "flesh out" or accent. . . . Rap producers have inverted this logic, using samples as a point of reference, as a means by which the process of repetition and recontextualization can be highlighted and privileged.[25]

On another level, rap lyrics present a postmodern articulation of themes, lifestyles, and behaviors found in Black oral tradition: for example, heroes such as "Bad Niggers," Brer Rabbit, Signifying Monkey, Stagolee, and Dolemite. Using these figures and their adventures as a model, rap music develops ways of circumventing powerlessness, outsmarting and temporarily gaining the upper hand over the dominant society. Hip-hop's verbal expression provides invaluable affirmation of identity and critique of the larger society while rehearsing the realities of Black urban life. The musical component of this larger development—rap music—has roots in African musical techniques and African-influenced oral practices. However, more recent influence is traceable to storytellers such as the Last Poets and Gil Scott-Heron as well as mid-century radio personalities such as

Douglas "Jocko" Henderson who used lines such as the following during his Philadelphia radio show:

> Bebop, this is Jock, back on the scene with a record
>   machine.
> Saying, hoo-popsie-do, how do you do?
> When you up, you up, and when you down, you down,
> And when you mess with Jocko, you upside down.[26]

Rap music effectively combines musical and oral practices with the
possibilities offered by electronic advances.

Most rap music afficinados mark the emergence of what became
contemporary rap with the arrival of DJ Kool Herc to New York City,
from Jamaica, in 1972. DJ Kool Herc used the Jamaican tradition of
toasting or speaking over extended beats and, like Afrika Bambaataa
and Grand Master Flash, began holding open air parties in the
Bronx. DJs, following Kool Herc's lead, would talk over the music in
order to keep the crowd moving while records were being adjusted
and changed. Out of this practice, the MC developed as the one who
perfected the style and content of this in-between-the-music talk.
However, rap at this point was an "underground" form of expression,
acknowledged only by those who attended street parties, frequented
the clubs, or gained access to home-made tapes.

In 1979 "Rapper's Delight" was recorded by the Sugar Hill Gang
(on Sugar Hill Records) and sold millions of copies.[27] The Sugar Hill
Gang, from New Jersey, brought rap to a larger audience by making
it available to groups outside New York's select circles. Prior to this,
MCs and DJs distributed their goods using dubbing devices and cas-
sette players known as boom boxes. With the success of "Rapper's
Delight," the commercilization of rap music was underway. Others to
obtain status on the East Coast include Kurtis Blow ("These are the
Breaks"), Soul Sonic Force ("Planet Rock"), Run DMC ("Walk This
Way"), UTFO ("Roxanne Roxanne"), and Grand Master Flash and the
Furious Five ("The Message").[28] More recent East Coast rap stars
include Salt-n-Pepa, Public Enemy, KRS-One, Eric B. and Rakim, and
De La Soul.

In the early 1980s East Coast hip-hop made its way to the
West Coast where Soul Sonic Force and Afrika Bambaataa toured
in 1980. (Break dancing arrived in 1982 only to be met by a West
Coast style of dance referred to as "popping and locking" and associated with gangs.) Captured by the rap music craze, Los Angeles res-

idents used two skating rinks, World on Wheels and Skateland, as rapper training camps where contests sponsored by radio station KDAY were held. This station also devoted air time to the playing of local rap talent.[29]

Although indebted to the East Coast, Los Angeles artists emphasized an electronic sound which distinguished it from the East Coast sound. (One reason for the creation of this distinctive beat was the difficulty with which East Coast materials were obtained.) An example of this early West Coast sound is the World Class Wreckin' Crew's "Cabbage Patch." This style gave way to the creativity of Eazy E, Dr. Dre (formily of the World Class Wreckin' Crew), Ice Cube and the other members of N.W.A. (Niggaz With Attitude). Although the success of Young MC ("Bust a Move") and Tone Lōc's "Wild Thing" are important, N.W.A. firmly established a style of rap based upon the hard facts of L.A. gang and hustler life. Granted, this hard-life form of rap music had been presented by Schooly D and KRS-One (with Scott La Rock) on the East Coast and Ice-T ("Six in the Morning" and "Colors") on the West Coast. Yet, it was not until N.W.A. recorded (as a Macola Company/Ruthless Record production for sale out of car trunks) "Straight Outta Compton" that this style gained a large audience:

> Although the myth of gangsterism was already used as an image to titillate the masses of hip-hop culture (Big Daddy Kane and Ice-T, to cite two examples), the signal was that these rappers were catering to America's romance with cartoon violence. With Ice Cube and the rest of N.W.A., the gritty tone of their voices informs that these boyz in da hood were not merely posing with their black jeans and loaded Uzis. Without a doubt, this was just a continuation of the "badder than you" stance favored by the hip-hop nation, but for the first time the myth was flavored with a sense of reality.[30]

The raw agression and reckless lifestyle caught the attention of rap fans and secured the West Coast as the center of "realism" rap or "gangsta" rap.[31] New York's rap was flavored by the dymanics of hip-hop culture and West Coast rap highlighted, in response, its defining features—the most prominent being gang culture. Compton was in direct competition with the Bronx.[32] The reputation of West Coast rap has been enhanced, in recent years, by the work of Cypress Hill, Snoop Doggy Dogg, Dr. Dre, Warren G., Ice Cube, and Yo-Yo.

The above history, although brief, presents the social and cultural context, creative dynamics, and scope—East Coast and West Coast—of rap music's development. What is needed at this point is a typology to clarify the thematic structure of rap's lyrical content. I argue that there are three major (at times overlapping) categories of rap music: (1) "status" rap; (2) "gangsta"[33] rap; and, (3) "progressive" rap. Others have presented typologies including categories such as "dis" rap, "political" rap, "message" rap, etc; the triadic typology presented here easily incorporates these other categories within its framework. So, for example, "dis" rap style is a major element within "status" rap. And "political" rap style and "message" rap exemplify a component of "progressive" rap's agenda.

One first sees the "status" strand of rap in the Sugar Hill Gang's "Rapper's Delight." This cut consists of braggadocio and mild signification, which denote a strong concern with status and social prowess. At one point in this rap, "Big Bank Hank" outlines his superior skills and sexual attractiveness. He boasts that a:

Reporter stopped me for an interview
She said, she's heard stories and she's heard fables
That I'm vicious on the mike and the turntables.
This young reporter I did adore,
So I rocked the mike like I never did before,
She said damn fly-guy I'm in love with you,
the casanova legend must have been true.
I said by the way baby what's your name,
She said I go by the name of Lois Lane.
She said you can be my boyfriend, you surely can,
Just let me quit my boyfriend called Superman.[34]

This style of rap music, emerging early, is concerned with distinguishing artists from their competitors. As Tricia Rose points out, the early hip-hop community was subdivided into territorial groups of rappers and dancers and an effort was made, during artistic battles, to gain respect and control of neighborhoods. "Status" rap, combined with break dance movements, served as the major tool within this struggle for artistic dominance. Both cultural expressions—rap and dance—highlighted competitors' flaws and shortcomings while emphasizing the rapper's/dancer's prowess.

The sense of social critique offered in this brand of rap is usually limited to the asserting of self in opposition to a society seeking

Black nonbeing. This ontological rupture is often sexually expressed and overt in the lyrics. One sees this in the lyrics of New Yorker Heavy D (born Dwight Myers). The following lines are from "Mr. Big Stuff" (1990):

> I'm a fly girl lover and a woman pleaser
> Girls say, "Heavy, let me squeeze you"
> An incredible
> Overweight, huggable
> Prince of poetry
> That's why I'm so lovable.[35]

Without directly challenging the existing political order, this form of rap music, at its best, is still political in nature. That is to say, it argues for the inclusion of African-Americans in the exercise of material benefits associated with the "best" of American life. The affirmation of self-worth in opposition to societal norms is not limited to Black men. Salt-n-Pepa[36] argue for self-appreciation—the creation of strong and assertive individuals. In so doing they promote the value of human personality as in "It's About Expression" (1991):

> You know life is all about expression
> You only live once, you're not coming back
> So express yourself
> . . . .
> Express yourself
> You gotta be you and only you, baby
> Express yourself
> Let me be me
> Express yourself
> Don't tell me what I cannot do, baby
> Express yourself.[37]

Groups such as Salt-n-Pepa effectively brought Black women into the rap world beyond roles as sexual objects and targets for male aggression and distrust. The personal value and strength of Black women are highlighted by such artists.

Although "status" rap contains an underlying political agenda, it explicitly discusses the social living of life. As Michael Dyson recounts, rap of this nature allows rappers and, by extension, their listeners to momentarily move beyond physical demise and enjoy the material benefits of the American Dream.[38] Unfortunately, this struggle for individual, ontological, and material "space" often results in counterproductive and oppressive tendencies. This is seen in the sexism, patriarchal ideals, and problematic consumerism expressed in much "status" rap. On one level, this brand of rap strikes at the dehumanizing tendencies of American society; yet, on another level, it buys into the structures and attitudes fostering dehumanizing practices. "Gangsta" rap presents this dual message in even stronger terms. (This is a major distinction between "status" and "gangsta" rap.) The dehumanizing effects of life in the United States are known to both sets of artists; yet, it does not promote the same type of overt intracommunal and extracommunal aggression in "status" rap that it does in "gangsta" rap.

"Gangsta" rap provides a mild critique of society by demonstrating the destruction done to humans by market-driven goals. The first major gangsta group, N.W.A. (Niggaz With Attitude), consciously plays out America's nightmare—depicting itself as ruthlessly dominating its environment. However, one notices an implied critique of American racism. Take, for example, NWA's controversial rap "Fuck tha Police" (1989):

> Fuck the police, comin' straight from the
>   underground
> A young nigger got it bad because I'm
>   brown
> And not the other color. Some police
>   think
> They have the authority to kill a
>   minority
> Fuck that shit 'cause I ain't the one
> For a punk motherfucker with a badge
>   and a gun.[39]

The members of this group point out the manner in which "law and order" operates on principles that encourage the victimizing of young people based upon style of dress and skin color. Whereas some acquiesce to this treatment, N.W.A. promotes resistance of such practices in order to maintain a sense of self-worth and importance: "I ain't the one for a punk motherfucker with a badge / and a gun."

If N.W.A. is correct in its analysis, the anger and violence expressed in "gangsta" rap is reflective of American society in general.

(Eldridge Cleaver makes a similar claim concerning the violent nature of America when discussing "law and order."[40]) In other words, violence and crime do not originate with rap music. To the contrary, this activity is part of the American fabric and is merely magnified by musical expression:

> We ain't the problems, we ain't the villians
> Its the suckers deprivin' the truth from our
>   children
> You can't hide the fact, Jack
> There's violence in the streets everyday
> Any fool can recognize that
> But you try to lie and lie
> And say America's some motherfuckin'
>   apple pie.[41]

The "American-ness" of "gangsta" rap's lyrics is used by Dr. Dre to justify the violent nature of his album, *The Chronic* (1993). In an interview with *Rolling Stone*, Dr. Dre says:

> People are always telling me my records are violent . . . that they say bad things about women, but those are the topics they bring up themselves. . . . They don't want to talk about the good shit because that doesn't interest them, and it's not going to interest their readers. . . . If I'm promoting violence, they're doing it just as much as I am by focusing on it in the article. That really bugs me out—you know, if it weren't going on, I couldn't talk about it.[42]

In addition to pointing out the oppressive nature of American society, "gangsta" rap outlines the practices within the "hood" allowing for survival. That is to say, "gangsta" rap, with literary license, chronicles the "gangsta" lifestyle. It tells the story of drug deals, murder, and paranoia marking life as a "G". As with "status" rap, "gangsta" rap often entails using counterproductive tools in order to achieve identity and material comfort.

A consequence of this is the sexist and misogynistic attitude glorified in the music. Women are often viewed as the enemy, the ones who destroy Black manhood and thereby bring into question the "gangsta's" survival. As a result of this assumed threat, women are dealt with harshly; they are stopped at all cost from ending the "G's" quest for success. Interaction with women is effectively limited to sexual contact whereby men maintain the upper hand through violence and physical domination. (The penis is often referred to using gun imagery.) Violent sexual encounters are also used as a tool of control, a method of belittling exercised between men. That is, male "gangsta" rappers often rap about sexually violating their male competitors as an indication of their "gangsta" status and their dominance over that individual and the rap game. In this way, sexual contact is used to demoralize and demean. In addition, the techniques of material acquisition mirror the practices rappers often complain about. "Gangsta" rappers are often guilty of exercising the agenda of capitalistic acquisition, the very concern for profit above human value that fosters the living conditions they rebel against.

Rappers, without question, must be held responsible for the oppression supported in their music. At the same time, however, critics and fans must recognize that "gangsta" rap echoes oppressive precepts acknowledged and encouraged by the larger society. This is why "gangsta" rap sells millions. As bell hooks has voiced, the troublesome code of conduct voiced in "gangsta" rap mirrors business practices and relational patterns embraced by and endemic to the society in which these rappers live: "More than anything, gangsta rap celebrates the world of the material, the dog-eat-dog world where you do what you gotta do to make it even if it means fucking over folks and taking them out."[43] Even with these flaws, "gangsta" rap (and to a lesser extent "status" rap) provides a brief glimpse of the interpretative honesty, roughness, and concern for personal identity inherent in nitty-gritty hermeneutics. The appeal to reality at all cost, and despite the possibility of more comfortable agendas, is decipherable in these two forms of rap:

> . . . Rap music is a contemporary stage for the theater of the powerless. On this stage, rappers act out inversions of status hierarchies, tell alternative stories of contact with police and the education process, and draw portraits of contact with dominant groups in which the hidden transcript inverts/subverts the public, dominant transcript. Often rendering a nagging critique of various manifestations of power via jokes, stories, gestures, and song, rap's social commentary enacts ideological insubordination.[44]

Although somewhat present in "status" and "gangsta" rap, this critical insight is most forcefully presented in "progressive" rap.

Aware of the same existential hardships and contradictions as "gangsta" rap, "progressive" rap seeks to address these concerns outside of intracommunal aggression and in terms of political and cultural education. It is also within "progressive" rap that one encounters a more consistently present interpretation of Black religiosity.[45]

Nascent "progressive" rap gains popular attention with "The Message" (1982) by New York rappers Grand Master Flash and the Furious Five. Using a portrait of life amid industrial decline, social alienation, and political corruption, this rap interprets the cycle of poverty and dehumanization producing limited life options and despair. It speaks to the destructiveness of systemically imposed ghetto existence:

> A child is born with no state of mind
> Blind to the ways of mankind
> God is smiling on you, but he's frowning
>   too
> Because only God knows what you'll go through
> . . . .
> You'll grow in the ghetto living second-rate
> And your eyes will sing a song of deep hate
> The places you play and where you stay
> Looks like one great big alleyway.
> You'll admire all the number-book takers
> Thugs, pimps, pushers, and the big money-
>   makers
> Driving big cars, spending twenties and tens
> And you wanna grow up to be just like them, hah![46]

This strand of rap provides an interpretation of American society and a constructive agenda (e.g., self respect, knowledge, pride, and unity) for the uplift of Black America.

"Progressive" rap first seeks to change the system by changing the perspective held by its victims. It uses Black history and cultural developments as well as a critique of social structures to point out the intrinsic value of Black life in order to increase positive Black self-expression. Two classic expressions of this agenda are KRS-One (of Boogie Down Productions) and Public Enemy. KRS-One and Chuck D (of Public Enemy) understand rap music as an arena for the exchange of vital information. In pieces such as "Who Protects Us from You?", KRS-One (Knowledge Reigns Supreme Over Nearly

Everyone) decodes the hypocrisy inherent in a legal system that brutalizes those who need protection the most. Furthermore, "Why Is That" interprets scripture and race identity in light of Black oppression: KRS-One locates the fundamental flaw in current interpretation of scripture in the failure to mention the physical Blackness of biblical patriarchs. This oversight translates into the negation of Black bodies and their importance; as a result, Black children are trained to downplay the role of Black people in history and the significance of their culture and their personal value. KRS-One views this as an intricate plot to destroy the ontological and epistemological bearings of African-Americans.

According to Chuck D, rap music is the Black community's CNN. It is the popular medium for information on Black history, culture, and politics. It deciphers the muddled ideologies of political, economic, and social institutions and makes listeners aware of necessary steps leading to self determination. As the self-proclaimed "prophet of rage," Chuck D sees meaning within American society centering around the control and destruction of Black minds and bodies. And through raps such as "Fight the Power," "Bring the Noise," "Shut Em Down," "Party for Your Right to Fight," and "White Heaven/Black Hell," Public Enemy outlines this control and the methods for breaking its grip. Public Enemy's interpretive eye is not focused soley upon the larger society and its flaws; this group also chastises African-Americans for the role they play in their own destruction. One sees this, for example, in Chuck D's denouncement of Black drug use presented in "Night of the Living Baseheads."

Of more direct interest is Chuck D's insight into Black religion. He argues that Black religion should contribute to the liberation of Black people. The meaning of Black religion is found in its support of Black identity and consciousness, and its rejection of status quo politics, economics, and social relations. Chuck D's support of the Nation of Islam suggests that Black churches, as representative of majority Black religious expression, are not in line with religion's ultimate purpose and that the Nation's praxis better fulfills the meaning of religion. Public Enemy clearly understands the Nation of Islam as redemptive because it provides the quest for African-American progress with a vivifying spiritual base. The album *Fear of a Black Planet* presents a musical interpretation of the Nation of Islam, inspiring comments such as this: Public Enemy "has become the spokesperson for a new wave of African-American consciousness shaped in the tradition of Elijah Muhammad, Malcolm X, and Louis

Farrakhan. [It] is not the only rap group influenced by the symbols and rhetoric of the Nation of Islam, they are [sic] by far its most significant and most consistent proponents."[47]

Although Public Enemy and KRS-One, among others, have defined the nature and content of "progressive" rap, it is my opinion that in recent years the best "progressive" rap has been produced by Arrested Development—notwithstanding the lack of attention given the group within academic treatments. AD (from Atlanta) as the group is commonly called, exhibits a hybridization of Afrocentrism and the 1960s Black aesthetic. In keeping with the interpretation of American society provided by Public Enemy, AD sees the base meaning behind U.S. institutions and ideologies demarcated by the ontological and epistemological demise of Black individuals and communities. Through raps such as "People Everday" and "Ache'n for Acres," Arrested Development illustrates the self-destructive and community-erosive effects of consumerism and sociopolitical alienation. Seeing through ideological platforms aimed at the extirpation of Black life, Arrested Development offers a regenerative program based upon pan-African cultural nationalism, social cohesion, economic cooperation, and proactive politics.

In stronger terms than the other groups mentioned, AD provides a critique of religiosity which demonstrates the tenacity of nitty-gritty hermeneutics. A clear example of this is the rap "Fishin' 4 Religion."[48] In this rap, AD critiques Black ministers' promotion of passivity—as a sign of righteousness—as well as the lack of sustained and direct community involvement by Black churches. In part, this involves an attack upon the symbolic and imagistic grounding of Black religion by critiquing the inconsistencies between the demands for liberation and the conception of God peddled by Black Christian churches. Using liberation as a theological norm, AD determines that many Black churches do not embody the true nature and meaning of Black religion's objective. Black religion must promote ontological and epistomological Blackness and thereby encourage the wholistic survival of the Black community. Unfortunately, however, Black churches are

> praising a God that watches you weep, and doesn't want you to do a damn thing about it.[49]

The activism suggested by Black religion is actually counterproductive because it does not extend beyond emotional outburst and spiritual platitudes. Resolutions of this nature have no relationship to temporal and proactive plans for social transformation; they are far too spiritualized to be of any worldly good:

> When they want change the preacher says shout it,
> Does shoutin' bring about the change, I doubt it.
> All shoutin' does is make you lose your voice.[50]

In the words of MC Speech (the group's leader), Black churches fail to nurture African-Americans and instead enslave them within a web of opiatic eschatology and debilitating consternation. In this way, the essence or genuine meaning of religion is transmuted into a plea for religiously coded banality and "turn-the-other-cheek" benignancy. AD expresses this while relaying a particular church scene:

> . . . sitting in church hearing legitimate woes.
> Pastor tells the lady it'll be alright,
> Just pray so you can see the pearly gates so white.
> The Lady prays and prays, prays, prays, it's
>   everlasting.
> There's nothing wrong with prayin', it's what
>   she's askin'[51]

According to this critique, many Black churches are unwilling to address the hard issues of life. Therefore, in Marxist terms, they are the opiate of the people. Individualistic and indolent religiosity promoted by churches is a major factor in the underdevelopment of Black America.

Arrested Development musically outlines religiosity committed to the hands-on deliverance of Black people from a profusion of existential dilemmas, without respect to traditional theology and doctrine. In this—AD's constructive project—one sees another aspect of nitty-gritty hermeneutics: the uncovering and revitalizing of religion outside the confines of long-standing but ineffectual theological tradition. It is a project steeped in realism, in the primacy of experience over doctrine. For example, in keeping with traditional African religions,[52] Arrested Development extols the value of the earth and union with the earth as a divine source of power and a chief objective of any vibrant religious system. The pieces of a religious system are amassed, for example, from the rudimentary and rather Manichean treatment of certain life principles and pinnacles found in the rap

"Washed Away." Herein the delusion of righteousness and goodness is metaphorically depicted as the destruction of a seashore by demonic forces. AD urges humans to fight the trickster serpent's efforts to destroy the seashore:

> Why do we let them wash it away
> Why are we allowing them to take what's
>   good
> Why won't we teach our children what is
>   real
> Why don't we collect & save what is real
> Look very hard & swim the ocean
> We must find what needs to be found.
> Look all around & find a wise man
> To feed us the truth & keep us sound
> . . . .
> My one purpose it to swim the seas
> Find the Truth & spread it around
> Give it to the children that know how
>   to listen.
> So they can pass it after I drown
> We can stop being washed away.[53]

From this sense of connectedness to a scene much larger than oneself, comes the inspiration for transformation. That is, the proper working of a religion must involve collective efforts to identify the sources of oppression and the storehousing (and sharing) of vital, self-affirming cultural information. Only a religiosity that participates in and affirms the cultural life of the community and speaks plainly to pressing issues without paying tribute to unproven theological assertions—no new wine in old skins—is in keeping with the meaning of religion. For Public Enemy, the Nation of Islam is a religious fit. Arrested Development finds affirmation of religion's true objective in traditional African appeals to the dignity of the individual, the sanctity of communal harmony, and the spiritual significance of creation's interconnectedness.

What rap artists and their predecessors—the blues singers—seek is not couched in psychologically comforting language. Rather, their interpretation or perceptions are raw and unpolished. In this way, they illustrate the intent, function, and operation of nitty-gritty hermeneutics. Those who listen must prepare themselves to deal with a reality which cuts past catchy doctrinal slogans and, without apology, "drops the science."[54]

Furthermore, as presented in this rudimentary exploration of the blues-rap musical continuum, nitty-gritty hermeneutics urges a rethinking of Black religion beyond the confines of theological conformity and strict theistic expression. The blues, rap, and religionists such as Charles Long lament the narrowness with which religion is commonly defined. Long, in his text *Significations: Signs, Symbols, and Images in the Interpretation of Religion*,[55] argues that religion is, so to speak, where you find it. That is, since Black American life and identity have been shaped by European contact and conquest (i.e., post-Enlightenment oppressive realities and interactions), to conclude that only monolithic and obvious forms of expressivity resulted is misguided. Regarding this, Long writes:

> The church was not the only context for the meaning of religion. . . . The Christian faith provided a language for the meaning of religion, but not all the religious meanings of the black communities were encompassed by the Christian forms of religion. . . . The religion of any people is more than a structure of thought; it is experience, expression, motivations, intentions, behaviors, styles, and rhythms.[56]

Scholars such as George Cummings and Dwight Hopkins implicitly argue against this expansion, countering Long's typology with apologetic assertions of theistic (if not Christian) normality. For example, Cummings views Black expression through a Christocentric lens which narrows the scope of both religiously expressed *communitas* and Black theology. Cummings writes:

> Contemporary black theology from its inception has identified itself as a black Christian theology of liberation. While the debate concerning the specific character of the black religious experience, or the function of theological categories, may continue, black theologians must continue to insist that black theology is Christian. While black theologians may acknowledge the diverse religio-cultural sources and the ambivalence and ambiguity of the black witness, it is nevertheless the task of the black Christian theologians of liberation to explicate the meaning of the gospel of Jesus Christ from the perspective of the experiences of black oppressed people.[57]

The ambiguous nature of "black witness" mentioned by Cummings ofttimes denotes the use of non-Christian resources. In using these sources, theologians such as Dwight Hopkins acknowledge that Black religion is at least two dimensional—Christian and non-Christian.

However, a tension is obvious in this confession; how does one maintain a particular faith stance as the filter for exploration while fully acknowledging the multidimensional nature of Black religious expression? All too often this strain culminates in a particular faith stance as normative and in lip service to Black religious diversity; non-Christian resources are forced into the parameters of theistic expression. And so, even non-Christian expression must point to the workings of God.

Dwight Hopkins demonstrates this tendency when discussing trickster figures (e.g., "savior intermediaries") in Black literature. Hopkins does not entertain the possibility that these figures represent human efforts at liberation owing to the nonexistence of God. Rather, he asserts that "savior intermediaries" point to God working with humans and nature, and thereby confirm the strict theistic nature of Black religion:

> ... The image of God planted in all creation, Christian and non-Christian, means a reflection of divine co-laborer and co-creator. In other words, God does not work alone. . . . Moreover, the Way Maker [a foundational being appealed to for assistance in Black culture] extends the created co-laboring power beyond human beings to the entire cosmos and ecological sphere. Nature can also serve as a co-worker with God or God's Spirit.[58]

In this way, Hopkins effectively excludes from the realm of Black religion any position not theistically oriented. In a word, Black religion can be Christian or non-Christian; but it must be theistic. Such thinking is myopic and therefore dangerously misguided. It leaves a wealth of Black expression untapped as religious insight. Hence, in considering what the Black community says about Black suffering, it is irresponsible to limit the investigation to theistic responses—irrespective of the relative volume and majority status of theistic responses. This epistomologically based expansion must, I admit, eventually include a conversation with other nonmajority Black religious traditions (such as the Nation of Islam, Spiritual churches, and Voodoo). Only a complex discussion of this nature can provide a final understanding of BLACK RELIGION. This book, however, is an initial effort on this front.

In order to genuinely explore the complexities of Black religious expression/experience, one must rethink what Black religion entails; that is, what it means to be Black and religious. Along this line, I agree with Charles Long who argues:

> Religion will mean orientation—orientation in the ultimate sense, that is, how one comes to terms with the ultimate significance of one's place in the world.[59]

With respect to the expanded corpus of Black religion fostered by Long's definition, I offer Black humanism as an important aspect of Black religious reflection which resolves the problem of evil (i.e., Black suffering) without collapsing into redemptive suffering argumentation. What follows in chapter six is the tracing of humanism within Black cultural production. In this way, the historical presence of Black humanism is affirmed; its philosophical framework is provided; and, its theological-ethical premises are explored.

6

BLACK HUMANISM AND BLACK RELIGION

The term *humanism* has been used as a descriptive term for Black self-control, self-assertion, and concern for the human family. This is illustrated in Patricia Hill Collins' text *Black Feminist Thought*:

> . . . African-American women intellectuals repeatedly identify political actions such as these as a means for human empowerment rather than ends in and of themselves. Thus the primary guiding principle of Black feminism is a recurring humanist vision.[1]

According to Collins, humanism is suggestive of a certain "vision" of mutuality,[2] often related to the global community—e.g., collective international health. In this context, humanism is a statement of humanity's connectedness/oneness and need for self-determination, without a conscious discussion of this assertion's impact on traditional conceptions of divinity or ultimate reality. Margaret Walker, one of the few Black writers to deliberately label herself a humanist, also understands humanism in this manner. For her, it entails enlarging the self in order to connect to the whole of humanity:

> I think it is more important now to emphasize humanism in a technological age than ever before, because it is only in terms of humanism that the society can redeem itself. Even the highest peaks of religion's understanding must come in a humanistic understanding—the appreciation of every human being for his own spiritual way.[3]

The popularized understanding of humanism presented by Collins and Margaret Walker is also found in Cornel West's analysis of the African-American humanist response to modernity. Within "Philosophy and the Afro-American Experience," West outlines the four basic African-American responses to modernity: vitalist, rationalist, existentialist, and humanist. Within *Prophesy Deliverance* three of the four traditions are renamed in accordance with the American intellectual and racial climate which serves as their context (i.e., vitalist becomes exceptionalist; rationalist becomes assimilationist; existentialist becomes marginalist). Nonetheless, the content of these traditions is unaltered. In response to modern race theory depicting African-Americans as intrinsically inferior, vitalists/exceptionalists assert the superiority of Blacks over other groups. Rationalists/assimilationists argue the cultural inferiority of Blacks. And existentialists/marginalists confront modernity by seeking to live between the Black world and the dominant society.[4] West finds the humanist tradition most helpful and endorses it as the most viable means of Black progress, despite the tide of modern racism. The humanist tradition seeks to intimately connect Black Americans to the larger web of human existence. Herein, self-esteem and importance are derived from being a functioning and unique part of the whole. As Spike Lee remarks in a Nike commercial: "the mo' colors, the mo' betta!"

Notably, beauty and value are not attached to the absence of shortcomings; both flaws and strengths are unashamedly considered essential components of being in the world. Tempered goodness is not a blemish; rather, it is the mark of humanity. An example of this tradition is found in Black cultural expression which finds value in both sorrow and joy, strength and weakness. That is:

> [T]hese distinct art forms [e.g., spirituals], which stem from the deeply entrenched oral and musical tradition of African culture and evolve out of Afro-American experience, express what it is like to be human under black skin in America.[5]

The manner in which West likens his project to the "prophetic spirit" of the gospel intimates that he does not consider the humanist tradition a direct challenge to the major theological assumptions framed by Black Christianity. He fundamentally sees humanism in sociopolitical terms:

> Revolutionary Christian perspective and praxis must remain anchored in the prophetic Christian tradition in the Afro-

American experience which provides the norms of individual-
ity and democracy; guided by the cultural outlook of the Afro-
American humanist tradition which promotes the vitality and
vigor of black life. . . .[6]

In opposition to West's perception of humanism as compatible
with Christianity, other African-Americans note conflict between the
two. For these African-Americans and myself, the increased status
and worth of humanity rightly requires a questioning of God's status. Tension along this line portends two manifestations of humanism within Black thought: weak humanism and strong humanism.
The former entails an increased sense of self and one's place in the
human family. This position does not call God's existence into question. Anxiety arises, for weak humanists, when reflecting upon the
realm of God's activity in the world; not over the very existence of
God. It sees enough evidence of divine activity to leave unchallenged
God's place in the universe. But there is not enough evidence for the
weak humanist to confidently proclaim divine activity as the sole
factor in historical happenings. World affairs seem the result of joint
effort—God and humanity. Furthermore, God's existence is not questioned because weak humanism seeks—in response to oppressive
conditions—the increased status of Black humanity relative to that
of white humanity. It is a matter of humans seeking parity with
other humans. The goal is to prevent the oppressed from underesti-
mating their humanity and oppressors from overestimating their
humanity. Collins, Margaret Walker, and West understand humanism in this way.
    For strong humanism, relatively sustained and oppressive world
conditions bring into question the presence of any Being outside of
the human realm. The record of temporal developments does not bear
the noticeable imprint of any One beyond humanity; moments of
achievement are far too serendipitous to promote a teleological perspective and conviction that there is cosmic companionship.
Consequently, humanity has no one to turn to for assistance.
Furthermore, oppressive circumstances do not point to a level of
activity beyond the scope of human capability. That is, moral evil in
the world is easily understood as the result of misguided "will to
power" and nothing more. As a result, strong humanism also denies
the existence of an evil God who is responsible for human suffering.
Hence, strong humanism seeks to combat oppression through radical
human commitment to life and corresponding activity. Trudier

Harris' remarks concerning the words of literary figures and their correspondence to the beliefs of "folks" are appropriate here:

> When the choice is between Christian resignation or faith and humanistic actions or reason, literary characters, like their folk counterparts, often rejected Christianity in favor of a more exacting and humanistic idealism. They reject the easy way out in favor of more challenging solutions. . . . the goals they set for themselves, their aspirations for peace, freedom, and happiness, go beyond Christianity. Instead of an externally imposed God, they look to their similar heritages in folk tradition and to their inner selves for guidance in their actions.[7]

Part of this platform involves an increase in humanity's importance which makes impossible the location of a space for God. Strong humanism operates according to an "ethic of risk" (to use Sharon Welch's terminology)[8] and pragmatic principles: it would rather lose God than human value. There is no evidence of God's existence (no progress humans cannot easily take credit for and no suffering they are incapable of fostering), but on the other hand, there is no doubt that humans exist (ironically, moral evil and suffering scream this existence). Strong humanism considers theistic answers to existential questions simplistic and geared toward pyschological comfort without respect for the complex nature of the human condition.

An example from Brer Rabbit folk wisdom serves to clarify the way in which I understand the distinction between weak and strong humanism. Riggin Earl relates a Brer Rabbit story ("Brer Rabbit's Hankering for a Long Tail") in which Brer Rabbit goes to God requesting a long tail:

> Brer Rabbit worked himself into a state of dissatisfaction over the way that God had made him for several reasons including the aggravation of pesky insects such as fleas and gnats in hot weather, and the aggravation over the thought that long-tail animals had a functional and an aesthetic advantage over short-tail animals. Perennial displeasure with himself provoked Brer Rabbit to go before God in person and petition for a long tail.[9]

God is annoyed by the request:

You are made like you are made. You have been contrary
about that tail from the first day. . . . Even with all of the
blessing you already have you come here to me to get a tail like
the very best of creatures have. Hmm you are mighty little to
have a long tail. . . . You can jump around in the grass to keep
those flies off.[10]

Brer Rabbit is most persistent, and although God believes that the
rabbit only wants the tail in order to "be high fashion," God offers to
grant the request if Brer Rabbit can complete a most difficult assign-
ment. God does not think that Brer Rabbit will fulfill the assigned
task, and certainly not as quickly as he does. God is angered by Brer
Rabbit's return with the three required items (tooth from Brer
Crocodile; tears from Brer Deer; and blackbirds in a sack). And, upon
seeing Brer Rabbit again, God slams the door of the "Big House" and
ignores Brer Rabbit. Frightened by God's reaction, Brer Rabbit
retires under a tree only to have God strike the tree with lightning.
Brer Rabbit runs off and hears in the distance the voice of God: "You
are so smart get your own long tail."[11]

Earl interprets this story as suggesting an awareness of God having provided all humans could possibly need (weak humanism, at
best). Slaves need not request additions because "God in the primal
act of Creation had given the oppressed the necessary intelligence for
its own preservation."[12] Seen this way, oppression does not call into
question theological assumptions concerning the good intentions of
God. Quite the opposite, if one does not have needed resources, one
has failed to discover the "blessings" God has already provided. That is
to say, "it was the responsibility of the oppressed to utilize the knowledge that God had already given them for their own liberation."[13]

My strong humanistic interpretation highlights the implied critique of God which is in line with both the third and fourth resolutions to Black suffering (i.e., questioning God's righteousness/
goodness and questioning God's existence). First, the compassion (or
goodness) of God is called into question by God's harsh response
to/treatment of Brer Rabbit. Furthermore, God's imposed treasure
hunt prior to granting the request, reveals a sadistic side. This
implies a questioning of God's righteousness. Did God know that Brer
Rabbit would not be granted his request? Is this run-around the
actions of a just/righteous God? This story calls into question the
use/need for a God who cannot be relied upon. If we "must get our

own tail" what need we of this God? The rabbit in this case represents African-Americans and their search for completeness/freedom; and so, like Brer Rabbit, African-Americans are smart and want great things. Like Brer Rabbit, they must seek and obtain desired items on their own. So much for God!

A great deal of folklore, traceable to slavery, promotes weak humanism in that it suggests a necessary partnership between God and humanity because there are functional limitations to God's power on earth.[14] An example of this limited God is seen in an account of a slave (John) who prays to go to heaven and is the object of his master's questionable sense of humor. According to the story, it was not uncommon for John to pray for release from his hard work:

> Come Lawd, you know Ah have such a hard time. Old Massa works me so hard, and don't gimme no time to rest. So come, Lawd wid peace in one hand and pardon in de other and take me away from this sin-sorrowing world. Ah'm tired and Ah want to go home.[15]

One evening, the slaveholder approached John's cabin and heard him praying for the Lord to take him to heaven. The slaveholder decides to teach John a lesson; placing a sheet over himself and pretending to be God, the slaveholder knocks on the door and says,

> It's me John, de Lawd, done come wid . . . fiery chariot to take you away from this sin-sick world.[16]

Upon hearing the voice of "God," John thinks of ways to delay "God" taking him. Finally, John asks "God" to step back from the door so that he can withstand God's countenance and come out to join "God."

> Ole Massa stepped back a step or two mo' and out dat door John come like a streak of lightning. All across de punkin patch, thru de cotton over de pasture—John wid Ole Massa right behind him. By de time dey hit de cornfield John was way ahead of Ole Massa.[17]

It is here that we see the limits to God's power in relationship to human effort:

> Back in de shack one of de children was cryin' and she ast Liza [John's wife]: "Mama, you reckon God's gointer ketch papa and

carry him to Heben wid Him?" "Shut you' mouf, talkin' foolish-
ness!" Liza clashed at de chile. "You know de Lawd can't out-
run yo' pappy—specially when he's barefooted at dat."[18]

As Liza's comment indicates, God does exist but not without limitations to divine power and domain. Some might argue that the limitation is actually upon humans who play God rather than upon God.
However, I suggest that this story signifies God. That is, this story
questions the abilities of God, irrespective of how the conception of
God is constructed.

Undoubtedly, others will argue that Black oral tradition's humor
regarding Black religious beliefs, practices, and institutions does not
indicate a rejection of said elements. In fact, some suggest, these stories are provided by devout Christians and are, therefore, free of the
critical edge I see in them.[19] However, this perspective betrays a
denial of Black humor's multidimensional nature. Folklore often
entails the use of "comic vision" as a means by which to explore and
address the sociopolitical complexities of life, and on some occassions,
this allowed African-Americans to "turn the joke," through double
meanings and irony, on the racists they encountered. In this way,
folklore and the humor it provides (with an element of realism) forms
a critique of existing structures and ideologies. Hence, Black humor—
regardless of academic objections—has an underlying function by
which powerless African-Americans express actual complaints over
questionable thought and conduct:[20]

> . . . Black's humor is most often not predicated on fabricated
> scenarios intended merely to entertain or symbolically to
> expose absurdity, much black humor derives from a candid,
> unflinching view of everyday life.[21]

It follows, then, that my reading of Black folklore is accurate because
folklore has the capacity to function as a not-so-subtle critique of religious belief. Those who miss this aspect of Black humor will overlook
the lampooning of religion and, therefore, be bothered by claims I
attach to it.

Contemporary proponents of Black theology such as James
Cone, William Jones, and Delores Williams can be described as weak
humanists. Jones attempts to distinguish himself, as was discussed
in chapter four, through his humanocentric theism. However, as
Jones acknowledges, his theistic stance is fundamentally in keeping
with the position of those he critiques. Jones and these other theolo-

gians assert a coworker relationship between God and humanity; both must work toward liberation. Weak humanism as presented here makes this same claim. Granted, Jones, unlike the others mentioned, seeks to question God's goodness and righteousness. Yet, his argument ultimately turns on a rethinking of God's power as persuasion. Ultimately, contemporary Black theologians, in exploring the nature of Black suffering, fail to hold in tension or effectively question the goodness of God. And as a result, the theodical dilemma—the labeling of suffering as redemptive—is unavoidable.

Why is genuine debate on the goodness of God taboo? Major Jones provides an answer based upon biblical precedence, Black Christian tradition, and existential need.[22] He argues that scripture depicts God as concerned with and fundamentally committed to bringing about the good of creation. God's very being is in harmony with progress and is opposed to moral evil. According to scripture, one cannot think and speak of God without reference to God's goodness. Therefore, Black theology, which has used scripture as a source, cannot maintain a connection to the Christian tradition and the theology of the Hebrew Bible without affirming the goodness of God.Because of Black religion's historical commitment to this position, belief in a good and righteous God has become a reified element in its thought structure. In turn, those who fail to maintain this position are ostracized from the Black tradition.[23]

Finally, Major Jones argues that the goodness of God must be maintained in order to preserve the pyschological health of the battered Black community. Accordingly, the maintenance of hope in the face of an oppression-fostered nihilism results in an adherence to the concept of a powerful God. And for Major Jones: "What weak, oppressed people could afford to worship a weak God?"[24] This Black need also demands an affirmation of God's goodness because the questioning of God's goodness must ultimately result in a questioning of God's relevance: "If God is not a personal, consciously caring being, who knows each one of us intimately enough to be concerned about what happens to every one of us, then God has no relevancy for our individual faith."[25] By extension, faith is premised upon the sustenance of hope, a hope that cannot exist without the theological underpinnings of a concerned and good God.[26] Relief from the pressures of existential hardship comes only through a good and powerful God.[27] To think about God in terms other than these raises questions concerning evil's ability to triumph over good. Those with a defeatist attitude will question the merit in waging a war they are not guaranteed to win. Yet Major Jones responds:

> But to this defeatist attitude, one must answer morally to the contrary: unless one fears diminishing God's majesty by denying God's infinity, it is far more degrading to God's divine nature to believe that God could eliminate evil but does not care enough for good to do so. Stated differently: better a limited God than one who is morally neutral towards pain and the purpose and end of his creation. . . . God must be a God of absolute goodness. . . .[28]

Major Jones is able to ignore challenges to God's goodness (and existence) through appeal to "epistemological humility." That is, Jones is content to wait for divine signs, for God to "say" God is good. Anything else amounts to theological arrogance. [29]

As has been demonstrated, approaches to Black suffering that leave intact God's goodness and existence are doomed to collapse into redemptive suffering apologetics. Theistic approaches to this question are inherently trapped within a theodical game. (i.e., a compromise with evil/suffering). Only a questioning of God's existence provides a working resolution (i.e., a full rejection of redemptive suffering). Many Black folktales acknowledge this.

Mel Watkins provides an interesting account regarding a slave named John whose owner discovers John's prayer habits. It comes to "Ol' Marster's" attention that John prays underneath an oak tree every day. In order to have fun at John's expense, "Ol Marster" puts his two sons in the tree with a bag of stones. During his prayer, John asks God to give him religion and to prove John has it by dropping something on him. In response, the two boys drop a stone on his head. John feels this but asks God to drop something with a little more force. With this said, the two boys drop a stone on John and knock him out. When he comes to, John says:

> Jesus that the way you got to give me religion? Knock me out? Take your religion on back to heaven. I'm gonna stay down here and do the best I can do. Please now.[30]

While this tale does not indicate a rejection of God, it does express an unwillingness to accept a tradition that simply intensifies pain. John is opposed to religion that provides benefits (or suffering) human effort alone can achieve. This hints at a strong humanist position—reliance on human effort—that other accounts more forcefully promote.

The alternative nontheistic position of strong humanism first emerges in antebellum slave communities' cyncism toward God, and has these characteristics: (1) it gives historical reign to humans; (2) it makes humanity the measure for all proofs; (3) it signifies or denies God's existence; (4) it operates according to an ethic of risk and is pragmatic in nature; and, (5) it provides an ultimate concern related to community or human life. These points are essential because they mark the defining character of strong humanism: that it entails an atheistic outlook which places humanity at the center of interest and activity.

Strong humanism is presented humorously in the folk story entitled "Sister Sadie Washington's Littlest Boy." In this story, Sister Sadie—a God-fearing woman—is concerned about the spiritual condition of her son (Pete) who does not like church and has never "jine de chu'ch an' come to be a Chistun."[31] Pete is, it appears, representative of folks such as ex-slave Jess Davis who did not particularly care for church. In fact, "'On Sundays', [Jess] says, 'we didn't do anything but lay 'roun' n' sleep, 'case we didn' lack to go to church."[32]

During a revival service that Pete is apparently coerced into attending, the physically large preacher's energetic sermon shakes the church. This scares Pete; and as a result—not as a matter of "heart knowledge"[33]—he joins the church. When baptized, Pete does not come out of the water exclaiming his faith. This disturbs the preacher who dunks Pete two additional times. After the last push into the water, Pete exclaims: "Ah b'lieves! Oh! Ah b'lieves!" When asked by his mother what he believes Pete responds: "Ah b'lieve . . . dat dis damn preachuh tryin' to drown me; dat's what Ah b'lieve."[34] This story sarcastically presents religion as illusion—based upon fear or human actions mistaken as divine. The faithful are easily misled. That is, the cause of what Pete initially perceives as the movement of the spirit— the floor shaking—had human authorship. Recall Pete's amazement:

> Dis de fuss time in his life he done evih seed a preachuh dis big
> what him shake de flu', so he thinks hit's de Lawd . . . an 'he
> goes up to de mornnah's bench.[35]

The bottom line: humans, not God, are the cause of what we encounter even in the church. Pete teaches that humanity is the true measure of reality and that adherence to a God concept results in harmful illusions.

The critique of God as fundamentally unimportant is also evident in the folktale entitled "The Preacher and His Farmer

Brother." Like Pete, the farmer provides a glimpse of a churchless/nontheistic Black community. The narrator of this story recognizes this: "In de same fam'ly you kin fin' some of de bestes' preachus dat done evuh grace a pulpit, an' a brothuh or a sistuh what ain't nevuh set foot in de ch'ch ez long ez dey live."[36] This is certainly true for the brothers in the tale—Sid and 'Revun Jeremiah Sol'mon.

The account states that after a twenty year absence, the "Revun" paid Sid a visit. During their time together, he observed Sid's farm and commented concerning its productivity in this manner: "Sid yourse got a pretty good cane patch by de he'p of de Lawd." Sid, in response, suggests the hard human labor involved in all human achievements: "Yeah, but you oughta seed hit when de Lawd had it by Hisse'f."[37] Sid betrays a certain lack of concern with divine assistance and presence. For him, his human sweat and pain had produced the land and its yield, and so Sid looked no further than himself for his and his family's sustenance. Sid's position corresponds with strong humanism's signifying of God, making human effort the measure of reality, and the limiting of ultimate concern to what humans are able to do for self and community.

Many African-Americans live out a similar call to experience life without thought of God—to be human, fully human. This is certainly the thrust of John Junior's comments concerning his life ("Experiences of a Chimney Sweeper"). John proudly acknowledges his family's freedom from the constraints of Christianity. "No, indeed! There never was a Christian in my family, we don't believe in that stuff."[38] According to John Junior, humanity must concentrate on itself—making enjoyment of life central. He does not depend on a God concept for security and motivation. Interestingly enough, John does not lose hope, nor become nihilistic as a result of this anthropocentric orientation. Rather:

> I strictly have my fun. No, I ain't tendin' been' no Christian. That's the trouble with niggers now. They pray too damn much. Everytine you look around you see some nigger on his knees and the white man figurin' at his desk. What in the world is they prayin' fo'? Tryin' to get to heaven? They is goin' to get there anyhow. There ain't no other hell but this one down here. Look at me. I'm catchin' hell right now.[39]

Dwight Hopkins argues, falsely I believe, that John's remarks suggest a critique of nonliberative and hypocritical white Christianity rather than a rejection of authentic Black religion.

> At least one reason why Junior chooses having fun as practical
> faith is because his life experiences have shown that Christian-
> ity is the white man's religion.[40]

Hopkins does not provide documentation to support the notion that
Junior is critiquing white Christianity as opposed to Black religion.
He simply infers this. Junior does not, in his remarks, distinguish the
Christianity he condemns as being within white churches; nor does
Junior appear to be merely concerned with Black Christians imitat-
ing white Christians. Without qualification, he squarely criticizes the
false beliefs and activities of Black Christians.

Strong humanism in more recent Black thought is exemplified
within Black literature during the twentieth century. Figures such as
Richard Wright and Nella Larsen provide commentary concerning
the lack of existential evidence for the divine. Their writings, all
somewhat autobiographical, demonstrate the continued existence of
strong humanism within the African-American community.[41]

Larsen's novel *Quicksand* outlines the pyschological, emotional,
and geographical journeys of Helga Crane, framed by issues of racial
identity and alienation. In keeping with the "tragic mulatto" literary
tradition, Crane journeys from the Tuskegee-like Naxos school in the
South to the North in search of identity and escape from the counterproductive accomodationism of white-supported Black education. Reflecting
upon a chapel service, at Naxos, during which a white preacher gave a
sermon, Helga comments on the nature of Black people at Naxos:

> Naxos Negroes knew what was expected of them. They had
> good sense and they had good taste. They knew enough to stay
> in their places and that, said the preacher, showed good taste.[42]

She could no longer stand the complacency and homogeneity of
Naxos, and so she decides to leave and move North to Chicago where
her bright clothing and independent thinking could find expression.[43]
Finding a job in Chicago is difficult until she is connected with a "race
woman," Mrs. Hayes-Rore, who hires Helga to travel to New York as
her secretary. Mrs. Hayes-Rore puts Helga in touch with her
daugher-in-law (Anne Grey), and Helga decides to remain in New
York and bask in the progressive atmosphere of a Harlem that rejects
the self- denying mode of Naxos-like attitudes.

Helga's contentment does not last. Once again she becomes com-
pletely restless: "Somewhere, within her, in a deep recess, crouched

discontent. She began to lose confidence in the fullness of her life, the glow began to fade from her conception of it."[44] Part of Helga's discontent rises from the discomfort created by Anne and others who constantly espouse race-based platitudes in front of Helga. While initially intrigued by Anne's analysis of injustice, Helga grows tired and decides to abandon Harlem. Unexpected financial help from Uncle Peter in the amount of five thousand dollars makes this flight possible. With Uncle Peter's encouragement, Helga decides on Denmark; she will visit the aunt (Katrina and uncle Poul Dahl) who had shown her favor as a child.

In Copenhagen, the attention and treatment Helga receives in consequence of her uniqueness—read Blackness—appeals to her. She was convinced that Denmark would allow her to "be herself" and be "important" without sneaking suspicions of inferiority. Helga assumes that the smiles and attention she receives hold no malevolence. Eventually, even this wears thin and reaches the breaking point with artist Axel Olsen's marriage proposal. His remarks, which serve to exoticize and objectify Helga, spark an awareness of her complexity—"a sensual being with something of the primitve hidden beneath her controlled exterior"—and her need for a cultural identification with African-Americans.[45] Helga returns to New York.

Underlying much of this movement (Naxos, Chicago, New York, Copenhagen, New York) is a struggle for identity and empowerment in terms of the racial/cultural and sexual self. Symbolized by Helga's broken engagement to Naxos teacher James Vayle (done before leaving Naxos), unremitted attraction to Dr. Anderson (former head of Naxos, now New York resident), and her rejection of Axel Olsen's advances, the book is marked by repressed sexual desire. However, with the recognition, while in Copenhagen, of her need to culturally identity with Black Americans, Helga turns her attention to the fulfilment of her sexual self (through Dr. Anderson). These plans are frustrated (he is married to Anne Grey and unwilling to follow through on an advance he himself has made). After leaving her encounter with Anderson, Helga stumbles into a storefront church and is mesmerized by the sensual dance of the women possessed by the Holy Spirit. This encounter results in Helga's joining the church and marrying the minister, Reverend Pleasant Green. Within the context of the Black Christian church, Helga is freed from her inhibitions regarding self-expression.[46]

Moving south with Reverend Green, Helga attempts, in spite of the resistance of the church women, to fulfill the role of minister's wife. Helga was at peace with herself, community, and God. Although fear would surface at times:

> In the morning she was serene again. Peace had returned. And she could go happily, inexpertly, about the humble tasks of her household, cooking, dish-washing, sweeping, dusting, mending, and darning. And there was the garden. When she worked there, she felt that life was utterly filled with the glory and the marvel of God.[47]

This contentment does not last, and as before, she becomes restless. The flaws in Reverend Green's demeanor and appearance she easily overlooked before now become unbearable, and the intellectual and material poverty of her surroundings becomes sickening. In addition (and of tremendous importance), the expression of her sexuality held painful ramifications. The birth of her children ties her to the surroundings she despises and exposes her to a physical pain she had never before known. With the birth of her fourth child, Helga becomes very ill. Initially, Helga attempts to live by placing full responsibility for her well-being upon God; this was pyschologically comforting in the manner Major Jones affirms, yet it ultimately collapsed in the face of her unrelenting suffering.

Helga cannot graciously accept and delight in her suffering as the church women and Reverend Green would have her do. The prayers she prays to God and her continued suffering present a contradiction she cannot ignore and that is unresolvable through redemptive suffering arguments. Her suffering is undeniablely real and God's lack of attention to such suffering can only mean there is no God:

> The cruel, unrelieved suffering had beaten down her protective wall of artificial faith in the infinite wisdom, in the mercy, of God. For had she not called in her agony on Him? And He had not heard. Why? Because, she knew now, He wasn't there. Didn't exist.[48]

For Helga, humanism means asserting one's value as a human being and working to act upon this value. Rough times are dealt with through human strength, but without guarantee of success. History does not support the espousing of guarantees:

Life wasn't a miracle, a wonder. It was, for Negroes at least, only a great disappointment. Something to be got through with as best one could.[49]

Within *Black Boy*, Richard Wright outlines the sense of racism-based alienation and hunger (physical, mental, and emotional) experienced by himself and other African-Americans. The existing social order and its champions foster, in African Americans, an ontological and epistomological estrangement which recreates the world as an absurd place, lacking unity and meaning. In reality, the humanity of both the victims and the victimizers is damaged.

With a rather naturalistic tone, one that is lost in later works, Wright understands that humanity is "pushed" by environmental factors and therefore must seek redress through knowledge (in his case, self-education). The Black American's quest is to end meaninglessness and develop self and self-determination (freedom), in part through an epistomologically based rejection of subservience and subjection to assertions of false white superiority. In this way, one becomes a subject rather than an object. The opposite of this is humiliation, indicated by the surrender of will exemplified by Southern Blacks who grin and humbly accept the abuse of whites, manifesting a dangerous passivity.

According to Wright, some Blacks attempt to use religion as a means by which to address this meaninglessness and societal negation. He knows the failure of this approach first hand. Bigger Thomas, the protagonist in *Native Son*, expresses Wright's rejection of Christian solace. Bigger, after his arrest for the murder of his employer's daughter and his own girlfriend Bessie, rejects the comforting words of Reverend Hammond and his mother. These Christians offer solutions to life's complexity and absurdity that his experiences suggest are oversimplified and representative of a dangerous naiveté. Religious answers to life's meaninglessness promote an embracing of suffering which reinforces life's meaninglessness rather than ending it. A humble embrace, of God and God's ridiculous pedagogical use of Black suffering, mirrors for Wright and Bigger, deference to whites.[50] Christian principles are unfounded, and talk of God is trivial at best. For Bigger and Wright, the quest for self-identity and meaning must involve a total commitment to defiance and freedom, even if this defiance and exercise of freedom result in destruction.

This is certainly a tragic sense of life, yet it is, for Wright, a real-istic depiction that fully appreciates the inescapability of subjectivity and the value of self-knowledge. This deterministic appeal to nihilistic rebellion is problematic. However, this does not mean that the overall religious system of humanism is likewise flawed. An underlying message, represented by Bigger's demise within *Native Son*, speaks of the need to restrain human activity, since unchecked assertion damages the unity all humans seek. This message of restraint out of respect for communal bonds is further developed in Wright's subsequent work.

Wright grew up under the heavy influence of his grandmother's fundamentalist religion. He came to regard this strict religious piety as antithetical to growth in that it is narrow-minded and numbs believers to the disjointedness of existence; it encourages blind acceptance of existential dilemmas that are best dealt with through educated protest. Even the educational experience offered to Wright through the Seventh-Day Adventist religious school (taught by his aunt Addie) was merely a lesson in conformity. In a way, Wright felt it gave divine endorsement to the diabolical distinction between white and Black.

Wright rejects Black religion (symbolically presented by his grandmother's faith) because it does not result in an attitude of defi-ance toward oppressive structures. He does not experience God because God does not exist. Despite the efforts of his family to change his mind, Wright is not concerned with the existence of God. In keep-ing with Sartre's depiction of existentialism, Wright does not tire himself out trying to disprove God's existence. Rather, "[he] declares that even if God did exist, that would change nothing."[51] In the world of human affairs and struggles (symbolized by life in racist Southern society), God is irrelevant. In response to a friend who approaches him regarding salvation, Wright says:

> It would have been impossible for me to have told him how I felt about religion. I had not settled in my mind whether I believed in God or not; His existence or nonexistence never worried me. I reasoned that if there did exist an all-wise, all-powerful God who knew the beginning and the end . . . this God would surely know that I doubted His existence. . . . And if there was no God at all, then why all the commotion?[52]

Wright's viewpoint led him to believe that the creation of identity (with all its ramifications) would come about only through human effort.

Within the walls of the church, it is easy to be convinced of God's presence; however, the sounds, sights, and sorrows of the world outside the church's walls raise questions that only those blind to suffering can ignore. Concerning this, Wright says:

> Perhaps if I had caught my first sense of life from the church I would have been moved to complete acceptance, but the hymns and sermons of God came into my heart only long after my personality had been shaped and formed by uncharted conditions of life. I felt that I had in me a sense of living as deep as that which the church was trying to give me, and in the end I remained basically unaffected.[53]

Moral obligation and proper ethical conduct are not dictated by God but by a genuine concern with unified existence—ontological wholeness on the individual level and communal relations. Achievement of this goal is not certain, however; humanity must work toward it nonetheless. There is intrinsic value in the effort itself.

Within *American Hunger*, the other component of his autobiography, Wright is outside of the racist South. Still having the hunger for unity and knowledge, Wright connects with the Communist Party and within this context, attempts to further develop self. There is no real talk of God; even the mentioning of God would give God an importance that this mythical figure did not merit. Only what can be known and experienced are real. That is, "[he] believed that man should live by hard facts alone, and [he] had so long ago put God out of [his mind] that [he] did not even discuss Him."[54]

While Wright maintains his atheism, he becomes disillusioned with the Communist Party because of its racism and infighting. Ultimately, Communism did not resolve the African-American community's problem of alienation. His communist acquaintances, and the party by extension, did not appreciate his individualism, yet they offered no sustainable alternative. Communism did not, according to Wright, provide for the "human unity" that destroys life's pain and absurdity. Wright, alone in the world, committed himself to obtaining meaning, and thereby, human life, through words which express and give shape to the hunger for "the inexpressibly human."[55]

The nascent existentialism Wright expresses in *Native Son* and *Black Boy* comes to fruition in *The Outsider*. Within this novel Wright continues to face the absurdity of human oppression and the meaninglessness of life. Using the character Cross Damon, Wright responds to this dilemma through self-assertion and the radical exercise of human freedom. Once again, Wright does not spend a great deal of time denying the existence of God; existentialists do not engage in this activity. Rather, through Cross Damon, Wright suggests that if God exists, God is incompetent and of no use in securing liberation. And if God does not exist, theistic appeals to suffering-centered moral and ethical codes are invalid. As Cross Damon remarks:

> . . . Now what does this mean—that I don't believe in God? It means that I, and you too, can do what we damn well please on this earth. Many men have been doing just that, of course, for a long time, but they didn't have the courage to admit it.[56]

Either way, humans must struggle alone to forge their identity and thereby invest the world with meaning and find redemption. Nonetheless, the end Cross Damon meets suggests that self-assertion must be tempered with an interest in community (unity). That is, the humanist quest for liberation must engage values based upon an awareness that human activity carries enormous weight because of its consequences. Conscious of this, humanism as Wright presents it ultimately proposes an ethic of unifying action.

Although the nihilistic tone of Wright's novels is troubling, it is not, I would argue, a general characteristic of strong humanism. Humanism is by nature optimistic; as Sartre says of existentialism, it places human destiny in the hands of humans. That is:

> [Existentialism] can not be taken for a philosophy of quietism, since it defines [humanity] in terms of action; nor for a pessimistic description of [humanity]—there is no doctrine more optimistic, since [humanity's] destiny is within [itself]; nor for an attempt to discourage [humanity] from acting, since it tells [humanity] that the only hope is in . . . acting and that action is the only thing that enables [humanity] to live. . . .[57]

We nonetheless gain insight from Wright into the diabolical nature of oppression that might cause nihilism, and into the need for human activity in the movement away from human oppression and meaninglessness. Finally, Wright teaches that the meaning of life is found in the human struggle for meaning. Hence, meaning is not housed in the spiritual platitudes of churches; nor is it given by God (whose existence is doubtful and unproven).[58] Humans are constantly in the process of becoming. This is the essential nature of his humanism.

Life for African-Americans has been historically defined by oppression and suffering. Reflecting upon this reality, Black folklore and modern Black literature often bring into question the theistic beliefs held dear by Black Christian religion. A system of religious thought truly committed to dealing with oppression must hold in tension the existence of God and operate according to a new hermeneutic—nitty-gritty hermeneutics—in order to avoid the theodical dilemma through which suffering is inevitably, and dangerously, labeled redemptive. Only such a system is of value in the struggle for liberation.

Strong humanism as presented here is such a system. By denying the existence of God, it is free from the dangerous doctrinal and theological obligations inherent in theistic responses to suffering. Strong humanism values experience above any allegiance to theological categories and platitudes.

This form of humanism understands suffering as wrong and sees it as being solely a result of human misconduct. Suffering is evil and it must end; contact with it and endurance of it do not promote anything benefical. To think otherwise is to deny the value of human life by embracing a demonic force that effectively mutates and destroys the quality of life. *Suffering Has No Redemptive Qualities*.

In removing even the most covert possibility of divine approval for suffering, strong humanism frees the oppressed to fight for social transformation. The importance of human struggle for change is highlighted and amplified by strong humanism because there are no external sources of assistance. Humanity has complete control over its destiny and therefore, one cannot hide behind God and plead that nonaction is a divine command.

Strong humanism need not be nihilistic or defeatist, if it sees potential for goodness within humanity. This system requires that humanity aggressively act to bring about meaning in a world defined by the absurdity of oppression. And this action is guided by a concern for the sanctity of life. That is not to say African-Americans can end their oppression if only they stop seeing suffering as redemptive. Furthermore, I am not arguing that genuine human effort will ultimately destroy oppression. To the contrary, I am asserting that redemptive suffering arguments set up false expectations and thereby eclipse sustainable liberation activity. Nonetheless, even sustained efforts provide only the possibility of total social transformation.

Sharon Welch asks a pertinent question: "What does it mean to work for social transformation in the face of seemingly insurmountable suffering and evil? How can we sustain energy, hope, and commitment in the face of an unrelenting succession of social and political crises?" In keeping with the ethical notions outlined in the blues, Welch argues that proper action does not arise out of notions of guaranteed success. It requires a sense of daring.[59] That is to say, strong humanism does not guarantee an end to oppression. Human effort without superhuman assistance does not allow for such claims. However, sustained struggle takes place and is shaped by the possibility of change. And victories are not won because of or through suffering, but in spite of suffering. Possibility is enough. For what are the true possibilities for transformation when God's intervention is not apparent, but is desperately appealed to? How strongly does one fight for change while seeking signs of God's presence? Humanity is far better off fighting with the tools it has—a desire for transformation, human creativity, physical strength, and untapped collective potential.

NOTES

INTRODUCTION

1. John H. Hick, "The Problem of Evil," in *Philosophy of Religion*, 4th ed. (Englewood Cliffs, N.J.: Prentice Hall, 1990), 39–40.

2. Ibid.

3. For a more detailed discussion of this position see *Philosophy of Religion*, 39–55; see also John H. Hick, *Evil and the God of Love*, 2d ed. (New York: Harper & Row, 1976; reissued, Macmillan, 1987).

4. Hick, *Philosophy of Religion*, 42.

5. Ibid., 44–48; Gen. 1:26. For a detailed account of this theodicy see Hick, *Evil and the God of Love.*

6. *Philosophy of Religion.*, 47.

7. Ibid., chaps. 2–4.

8. Ibid., 49.

9. Ibid., 48–55.

10. Ibid., 51.

11. Hick, "Arguments against the Existence of God," in *Philosophy of Religion*, 30.

12. I am not suggesting that all African-Americans have understood suffering within the rubric of redemptiveness. Rather, the understanding of suffering as fruitful is one of several perspectives evident in Black religious discourse. However, it is a strong and consistent line of reasoning which has not been sufficiently isolated and examined.

13. Clifford Geertz, "Religion as a Cultural System," 79–80, in *Reader in Comparative Religion: An Anthropological Approach*, ed. William A. Lessa and Evon Z. Vogt, 4th ed. (New York: Harper & Row, 1979).

CHAPTER 1: SPIRITUALS AS AN EARLY REFLECTION ON SUFFERING

1. For information regarding early religious activity in the South, see, for example, Albert Raboteau, *Slave Religion: The Invisible Institution in*

the Antebellum South (New York: Oxford University Press, 1978), chaps. 3–5.

2. Clarence Walker, *A Rock in a Weary Land: The African Methodist Episcopal Church During the Civil War and Reconstruction* (Baton Rouge: Louisiana State University Press, 1982), 277.

3. Gayraud Wilmore, *Black Religion and Black Radicalism: An Interpretation of the Religious History of Afro-American People*, 2d ed. (Garden City, N.Y.: Doubleday, 1972; Maryknoll, N.Y.: Orbis Books, 1983), 1–28. Also of interest, Gary Nash's *Race and Revolution* (Madison: Madison House, 1990).

4. John Lovell, Jr., *Black Song: The Forge and the Flame; The Story of How the Afro-American Spiritual Was Hammered Out* (New York: Macmillan, 1972), 9.

5. C. Eric Lincoln and Lawrence H. Mamiya, *The Black Church in the African American Experience* (Durham, N.C.: Duke University Press, 1990), 349.

6. Ibid.

7. See Benjamin Mays, *The Negro's God as Reflected in His Literature*, 3d ed. (Boston: Chapman and Grimes, 1938; New York: Atheneum, 1973), 19–30.

8. Lovell, 9.

9. It must be noted that an exact time frame for the appearance of the spirituals in the United States cannot be provided. During my research, I was unable to locate any resources that provided positive dates for the completion of the canon of spirituals. Often, it is indicated that the spirituals were created as early as the seventeenth century through the mid-nineteenth century. Others place the beginning of their formation in the eighteenth century. Some would suggest that the creation of the spirituals ceased with the emancipation proclamation and that those songs proposed by R. Nathaniel Dett, John Wesley Work, and others are not true spirituals because of the individual nature of the singing. This point is debatable. See Zora Neale Hurston, *The Sanctified Church* (Berkeley, Calif.: Turtle Island, 1981), 79–84.

10. Edward Henry Krehbiel, *Afro-American Folk Songs: A Study in Racial and National Music*, 4th ed. (New York: G. Schirmer, 1914; Portland, Me.: Longwood Press, 1976), 24.

11. Harold Courlander, *Negro Folk Music, U. S. A.* (New York: Columbia University Press, 1969), 38.

12. Christopher Small, *Music of the Common Tongue* (New York: Riverrun Press, 1987), 259.

13. See George Pullen Jackson, ed., *Down-East Spirituals, and Others* (New York: J. J. Augustin, 1939).

14. Raboteau, 251.

15. R. Nathaniel Dett, ed., *Religious Folk-Songs of the Negro* (Hampton, Va.: Hampton Institute Press, 1927; New York: AMS Press, 1972), xiii.

16. Lovell's text *Black Song* provides one of the best accounts concerning the formation and development of the spirituals in relation to other forms of musical expression. Also see: Dena J. Epstein's *Sinful Tunes and Spirituals: Black Folk Music to the Civil War*, (Urbana: University of Illinois Press, 1977); Portia K. Maultsby's "Afro-American Religious Music: 1619–1861" (Ph.D. diss., University of Wisconsin (Madison), 1974).

17. Hildred Roach, *Black American Music; Past and Present* (Boston: Crescendo Publishing Co., 1976), 21.

18. Paulo Freire, foreword to *A Black Theology of Liberation*, by James Cone (Philadelphia: Lippincott, 1970; 2d ed., Maryknoll, N.Y.: Orbis Books, 1986), 1.

19. Early opposition to this statement is found in Joseph Washington's *Black Religion: The Negro and Christianity in the United States*, (Boston: Beacon Press, 1964), 206–7. He writes:

    It has been argued that, given the independent movement of the Negro in religion, there is no reason why he could not have developed an independent theology, the most likely source being the spirituals. But while, in a deep sense, spirituals were songs of great belief, perhaps of hope, they were neither songs of faith, nor songs of a growing body of critical theology.

20. Mays, 19.

21. James Weldon Johnson and J. Rosamond Johnson, eds., *The Books of American Negro Spirituals*, Volumes 1 and 2 (Viking Press, 1969; New York: Da Capo Press, 1977), 1:145–47.

22. Ralph Ellison, *Shadow and Act* (New York: Vintage Books, 1969), 198.

23. Johnson and Johnson, 2:30–33.

24. Ibid., 2:34–36.

25. Howard Thurman, *Deep River* (Port Washington, N.Y.: Kennikat Press, 1969; Richmond: Friends United Press, 1975), 45.

26. Johnson and Johnson, 1:51–53.

27. Lovell, 387.

28. William Francis Allen, Charles P. Ware, and Lucy M. Garrison, eds., *Slave Songs of the United States* (New York: A. Simpson and Co., 1867), 104.

29. James Cone, *The Spirituals and the Blues: An Interpretation*, 2d ed., (New York: Seabury Press, 1972; Maryknoll, N.Y.: Orbis Books, 1991), 35.

30. Ibid., 189.

31. Raboteau, 260.

32. Johnson and Johnson, 2:136–37.

33. Allen et al., 59.

34. Johnson and Johnson, 1:184–87.

35. Ibid., 1:71–73.

36. Ibid., 2:110–13.

37. Cone, *The Spirituals and the Blues,* 91.

38. James Cone, *God of the Oppressed* (San Francisco: Harper & Row, 1975), 2.

39. Raboteau, 261.

40. Ibid., 1:114–17.

41. Johnson and Johnson, 1:134–35.

42. Ibid., 1:80–81

43. Lovell, 294.

44. Cone, *The Spirituals and the Blues,* 32–33.

45. Ibid., 103.

46. Ibid., 16–19.

47. Ibid., 58–59.

48. Ibid., 113.

49. Ibid.

50. Johnson and Johnson, 1:148–51.

51. Ibid., 2:140–41.

52. Cone, *The Spirituals and the Blues* , 52.

53. Ibid., 96.

54. Johnson and Johnson, 2:74–77.

55. Ibid., 2:160–61.

56. Cited in Stephen Angell, *Bishop Henry McNeal Turner and African-American Religion in the South* (Knoxville: University of Tennessee Press, 1992), 23.

57. Eileen Southern, *The Music of Black Americans: A History,* 2d ed. (New York: W. W. Norton & Co., 1971, 1983), 82.

CHAPTER 2: NINETEENTH-CENTURY BLACK THOUGHT ON BLACK SUFFERING

1. For an early example of statements to this end see: W. P. Harrison, *The Gospel among the Slaves* (Nashville: Publishing House of the M.E. Church, South, 1893), 93.

2. Carol V. R. George, *Segregated Sabbaths: Richard Allen and the Rise of Independent Black Churches, 1760–1840* (New York: Oxford University Press, 1973), 127.

3. Ibid., 126; citing Richard Allen, *Address to the Public and People of Colour* (Philadelphia: n.p., 1808).

4. This discussion focuses on the activities of the African Methodist Episcopal Church because it was the most active of the Black denominations working in the South. The Baptist churches had internal dilemmas that prevented aggressive missionary work (see James Washington's *Frustrated Fellowship: The Black Baptist Quest for Social Power* [Macon, Ga: Mercer University Press, 1986]). Clarence Walker's *A Rock in a Weary Land* (Baton Rouge: Louisiana State University Press, 1982), provides a good discussion of the rivalry between AME missionaries and African Methodist Episcopal Zion (AME Zion) missionaries.

5. See Harry Richardson's *Dark Salvation; The Story of Methodism as It Developed among Blacks in America* (Garden City, N.Y.: Anchor Press/ Doubleday, 1976), Part III.

6. See Clarence Walker, *A Rock in a Weary Land.*

7. David Walker, *David Walker's Appeal, in Four Articles: Together with a Preamble, to the Coloured Citizens of the World, But in Particular, and Very Expressly to Those of the United States of America*, edited with an introduction by Charles M. Wiltse (New York: Hill and Wang, 1965; original ed., Boston, 1829).

8. Ibid., 5.

9. Ibid., 12.

10. Ibid., 25.

11. Ibid., 26.

12. Ibid., 22.

13. Ibid., 28.

14. Ibid., 43.

15. See Jacqueline Jones, *Labor of Love, Labor of Sorrow; Black Women, Work, and the Family from Slavery to the Present* (New York: Vintage Books, 1985); Paula Giddings, *When and Where I Enter: The Impact of Black Women on Race and Sex in America* (New York: Bantam Books, 1984); Angela Davis, *Women, Race, and Class* (New York: Random House, 1981).

16. Bert J. Loewenberg and Ruth Bogin, eds., *Black Women in Nineteenth Century American Life: Their Words, Their Thoughts, Their Feelings* (University Park: Pennsylvania State University Press, 1976), 235; citing Sojourner Truth, "Ain't I a Woman?" from Elizabeth Cady Staton, et al., *History of Woman Suffrage* (Rochester, N.Y., 1881), I, 116. Also see Giddings, pt. I.

17. For more information on the Exodus in Black theological thought, see Albert Raboteau "African-Americans, Exodus, and the American Israel," in *African-American Christianity: Essays in History*, ed. Paul E. Johnson (Berkeley: University of California Press, 1994), 1–17.

18. Clarice Martin, "Biblical Theodicy and Black Women's Spiritual Autobiography: 'The Miry Bog, the Desolate Pit, a New Song in My

Mouth,'" in *A Troubling in My Soul: Womanist Perspectives on Evil and Suffering,* ed. Emilie M. Townes (Maryknoll, N.Y.: Orbis Books, 1993), 18–21.

19. Ibid., 23.

20. Maria Stewart, "Religion and the Pure Principles of Morality, The Sure Foundation On Which We Must Build," from the *Productions from the Pen of Mrs. Maria W. Stewart* (Boston: Friends of Freedom and Virtue, 1835), in Maria Stewart, *Maria Stewart; America's First Black Woman Political Writer,* ed. Marilyn Richardson (Bloomington: Indiana University Press, 1987), 35.

21. Ibid., 38.

22. Ibid., 69.

23. Maria Stewart, "Farewell Address to Her Friends in the City Of Boston," September 21, 1833, in ibid., 72.

24. Bert Loewenberg and Ruth Bogin, eds., *Black Women in Nineteenth Century American Life* (Philadelphia: Penn. State University, 1987), 264; citing Fannie Barrier Williams, address, "The Intellectual Progress of the Colored Women of the United States Since the Emancipation Proclamation," *World's Congress of Representative Women,* ed., May Wright Sewall (Chicago, 1893).

25. Loewenberg and Bogin, 246; citing Frances Harper, address, "Woman's Political Future," *World's Congress of Representative Women,* ed. May Wright Sewall (Chicago, 1893).

26. Frances E. W. Harper, "The Two Offerings," in *A Brighter Coming Day: A Frances Ellen Watkins Harper Reader,* ed. Frances Smith Foster (New York: Feminist Press at City University of New York, 1990), 107–8.

27. Ibid., 108.

28. Anna J. Cooper, *A Voice from the South* (Xenia, Ohio, 1892; New York: Oxford University Press, 1988).

29. If men show similar sympathies and talents, it is because they have been trained by women. Ibid., 60.

30. Ibid., iii. Of interest is Karen Baker-Fletcher's "Soprano Obligato: The Voices of Black Women and American Conflict in the Thought of Anna Julia Cooper," 172–89, in *A Troubling in My Soul,* ed. Emilie Townes.

31. Cooper, 144–45.

32. Ibid.

33. Wilson Moses, *Black Messiahs and Uncle Toms; Social and Literary Manipulations of a Religious Myth* (University Park: Pennsylvania State University Press, 1982), 10.

34. George, 165; citing Miller, "Sermon on the Abolition of the Slave Trade: Delivered in the African Church, New York, on the First of January, 1810" (New York: John C. Totten, 1810), 10.

35. Absalom Jones, "A Thanksgiving Day Sermon, Preached on January 1, 1808, in St. Thomas's, or the African Episcopal Church, Philadelphia: On Account of the Abolition of the Slave Trade." Cited in George, 165.

36. Additional information on Black nationalist thought during the nineteenth century can be secured from John Bracey's *Black Nationalism in America* (Indianapolis: Bobbs-Merrill, 1970); Lawrence Levine, *Black Culture and Black Consciousness: Afro-American Folk Thought from Slavery to Freedom* (New York: Oxford University Press, 1977); Edwin Redkey, *Black Exodus; Black Nationalist and Back to Africa Movements, 1890–1910* (New Haven: Yale University Press, 1969); Sterling Stucky, *Slave Culture: Nationalist Theory and the Foundation of Black America* (New York: Oxford University Press, 1987).

37. Some did not agree with this. For example, Rev. F. Grimke thought it was nonsense to attribute the dehumanization of Africans to Providence.

38. Wilson Moses, *The Wings of Ethiopia: Studies in African-American Life and Letters* (Ames: Iowa University Press, 1990), 168–69; citing Alexander Crummell, "The Destined Superiority of the Negro," in *The Greatness of Christ and Other Sermons* (New York: Whittaker, 1882), 351.

39. Moses, *Wings of Ethiopia*, 168.

40. Alexander Crummell, "The Regeneration of Africa," in *Afro-American Religious History: A Documentary Witness*, ed. Milton Sernett (Durham, N.C.: Duke University Press, 1985), 255.

41. Ibid.

42. Turner first met Crummell during Crummell's visit to Washington, D.C. on May 6, 1862.

43. He was elected bishop in 1880.

44. See Stephen Angell's *Bishop Henry McNeal Turner and African-American Religion in the South* (Knoxville: University of Tennessee Press, 1992), epilogue; Henry McNeal Turner's *Catechism: Being a Series of Questions and Answers upon some of the Cardinal Topics of Christianity*, ed. B. T. Tanner (Philadelphia: AME Book Concern, 1917). For information on Turner's ideas regarding Church structure see Turner's *The Genius and Theory of Methodist Polity, or the Machinery of Methodism. Practically Illustrated Through A Series Of Questions and Answers* (Philadelphia: Publications Department, AME Church, 1885; reprinted by AMEC Sunday School Union, 1978), chap. 35.

45. Turner's diary covering Jan. 22, 1859 to Dec. 13, 1862. This diary is available through the Turner Collection of the Moorland-Springarn Research Center, Howard University, Washington, D.C., Manuscript Department. I thank Dr. Stephen Angell for access to his transcribed notes from this diary.

46. Angell, 45.

47. Henry McNeal Turner, "A Speech on the Benefits Accruing from the Ratification of the Fifteenth Amendment, and Its Incorporation into the United States Constitution" (Macon Ga., April 19, 1870).

48. Turner had been elected a member of the Georgia Senate. However, like the other Black men elected to this position, he was denied an opportunity to exercise his duties. See Angell, 82–99.

49. In Henry McNeal Turner, *Respect Black: The Writings and Speeches of Henry McNeal Turner*, ed. Edwin Redkey (New York: Arno Press and New York Times, 1971), 42. Originally printed in *African Repository*, 51/2 (April 1875): 39.

50. Henry McNeal Turner, "On the Anniversary of Emancipation," Augusta, Georgia (January 1, 1866); cited in Turner,*Respect Black*, 7.

51. Edwin Redkey, "Bishop Turner's African Dream," in *Black Apostles: Afro-American Clergy Confront the Twentieth Century*, ed. Randall Burkett and Richard Newman (Boston: G. K. Hall & Co., 1978), 233.

52. Angell, 263; citing Henry Turner, *The Negro in All Ages* (Savannah, 1873); *Christain Recorder*, September 21, 1876.

53. Much of Turner's rhetoric concerning the beauty and wealth of Africa was based upon second-hand information. However, with the end of the nineteenth century approaching, Turner added to his glowing recommendation of Africa, first-hand exposure to the continent through four AME Church-sponsored trips to Africa (1891, 1893, 1895, and 1898). He sent back reports of glorious possibilities for those eager for progress. One letter suggested that he could not understand any hesitance to emigrate "unless it be for the reason that they do not find scullion employment or some white man to curse and kick them around. . . .This is no place for the mere kitchen pimp nor for the Cargo Negro" (Turner, *Respect Black*, 118; Letter from Africa, November 29, 1891).

54. Redkey, *Black Exodus*, 91.

Chapter 3: Black Suffering in the Twentieth Century

1. John Hope Franklin, *From Slavery to Freedom: A History of Negro Americans*, 5th ed. (New York: Alfred A. Knopf, 1980), 310.

2. C. Vann Woodward, *The Strange Career of Jim Crow* (New York: Oxford University Press, 1957), 64.

3. Franklin, 310.

4. Thomas Dixon, *The Clansman: An Historical Romance of the Ku Klux Klan* (1905; reprinted, Lexington: University Press of Kentucky, 1970). Cited in Gossett 1968, 272.

5. Examples of the pseudosciences include phrenology (the reading of skulls) and physiognomy (the reading of faces). See Cornel West, *Prophesy Deliverance! An Afro-American Revolutionary Christianity* (Philadelphia: Westminster Press, 1982), 57–65.

6. Ibid., 333.

7. Ibid., 345.

8. For a tongue-in-cheek depiction of the layout and arrangement of Jim Crow segregation, see Stetson Kennedy, *Jim Crow Guide to the U.S.A.: The Laws, Customs and Etiquette Governing the Conduct of Nonwhites and Other Minorities as Second-Class Citizens* (London: Lawrence and Wishart, Ltd., 1959), esp. 228–300.

9. David Gord Nielson, *Black Ethos: Northern Negro Life and Thought, 1890–1930* (Westport, Conn.: Greenwood Press, 1977), 49.

10. Gayraud Wilmore, *Black Religion and Black Radicalism: An Interpretation of the Religious History of African-American People*, 2d ed. (Anchor Press/Doubleday, 1972; Maryknoll, N.Y.: Orbis Books, 1983), 135.

11. For more information on his life and ministry see: Reverdy C. Ransom, *The Pilgrimage of Harriet Ransom's Son* (Nashville: Sunday School Union, 1949); Calvin Morris, *Reverdy Ransom: Black Advocate of the Social Gospel* (New York: University Press of America, 1990); David Wills, "The Making of an AME Bishop," In *Black Apostles: Afro-American Clergy Confront the Twentieth Century*, ed. Randall Burkett and Richard Newman (Boston: G. K. Hall & Co., 1978).

12. Ransom, 49.

13. Ibid., 82.

14. S. P. Fullinwider suggests that a more liberal theological stance during the late nineteenth and twentieh century resulted in clergy such as Reverdy Ransom replacing an all-powerful God with a "weak" deity who needed human assistance. This is an overstatement based on a lack of awareness of God conceptions in Black religion. It is true that some Black clergy persons suggested a coworker relationship with God; yet, they would not have considered their God weak. They still considered God in control of history, and working out a plan. Human participation arose as a result of human freedom and consequential responsibility, not God's weakness. Nonetheless, even this freedom must fall in line with God's immanence. Fullinwider suggests that this coworker status is a type of break with Black tradition, a tradition stemming back to the spirituals. My reading of this tradition suggests a counterconclusion. From the spirituals on, there have been Black theological opinions suggesting a copartnership with God. See: S. P. Fullinwider, *The Mind and Mood of Black America: 20th Century Thought* (Homewood, Ill: Dorsey Press, 1969), 34–46.

15. Ransom met Josiah Strong and Washington Gladden during the World Parliament of Religions and had also listened to Strong during the 1900 AME general conference. See Morris, "Reverdy Ransom, the Social Gospel and Race," *The AME Church Review*, 102/329 (January–March, 1988): 27. This is reprinted from *The Journal of Religious Thought* 4/1 (Spring–Summer, 1984).

16. Glenn Bucher, "Social Gospel Christianity and Racism," *Union Seminary Quarterly Review*, 28/1 (Fall, 1972): 146–57. In opposition to the opinion that social gospelers were not interested in race problems, Ralph E. Luker *The Social Gospel in Black and White; American Racial Reform, 1885–1912* (Chapel Hill, N.C.: University of North Carolina Press, 1982), 2, suggests a modified position. He argues that this perspective is valid only when: "the social gospel is looked at from one perspective—the Schlesinger framework. Yet, if it is seen as an extension of antebellum home missions and social reform movements, one notices that social gospel leaders were conservative but not unconcerned with race issues." Furthermore, he states that the Anglo-Saxon superiority rhetoric of Strong is not race-based but culture-based and this position was abandoned by Strong (*Our Country*, ed. Jurgen Herbst [1891; reprinted, Cambridge, Mass.: Belknap Press of Harvard University Press, 1963, 274). Nonetheless, racist remarks about Blacks remained fashionable. It appears to me that the recorded remarks, however labelled, suggest a position justifying the poor treatment of Blacks and a maintenance of the status quo.

17. Jacob Henry Dorn, *Washington Gladden: Prophet of the Social Gospel* (Columbus: Ohio State University Press, 1966), 302; in Bucher, 150,

18. Josiah Strong, *Our Country*, ed. Jurgen Herbst (1891; reprinted, Cambridge, Mass.: Belknap Press of Harvard University Press, 1963), xxiv.

19. Ibid., 215.

20. Ibid.

21. Ibid.

22. Morris, *Reverdy Ransom: Black Advocate*, 33.

23. Reverdy C. Ransom, "The Institutional Church," *The Christian Recorder*, March 7, 1901.

24. Reverdy C. Ransom, "The Negro and Socialism," in *The African Methodist Church Review* XIII, 1896–97. Reprinted in *Black Socialist Preacher*, ed. Philip S. Foner (San Francisco: Synthesis Publications, 1983), 282–89.

25. Ibid., 284.

26. Ibid., 289.

27. Quoted in Morris, *Reverdy Ransom: Black Advocate*, 50.

28. Reverdy Ransom, *The Negro: The Hope or the Despair of Christianity* (Boston: Ruth Hill Publisher, 1935), 22–25.

29. Ransom agreed with popular thought that African-Americans experienced some difficulty in finding their place in North American society. Yet, he attributed this to a racist environment rather than Social Darwinian inherent inferiority. Ransom continuously encouraged Black Christians to make this critique (see Ransom, *The Pilgrimage of Harriet Ransom's Son*, 299).

30. Ransom, *The Negro*, 91.

31. Ibid., 91; 95.

32. Ibid., 97. Also see: "The Spirit of John Brown," Second Annual Meeting of the Niagara Movment, Harper's Ferry, W. Virginia, August 17, 1906, 24-25; John GreenLeaf Whittier, "Plea for Political Equality." Centennial Oration, Fanueil Hall, Boston, Mass., December 17, 1907, 31–34. Both are located at the Schomberg Research Center, New York City.

33. Ransom, *The Negro*, 18.

34. For additional information on Wells life, see: Ida B. Wells, *Crusade for Justice; The Autobiography of Ida B. Wells*, ed. Alfreda M. Duster (Chicago: University of Chicago, 1970); Mildred Thompson, *Ida B. Wells-Barnett: An Exploratory Study of an American Black Woman, 1893–1930* (Brooklyn, N.Y.: Carlson Pub., 1990).

35. Quoted in Emilie Townes, "Because God Gave Her Vision: The Religious Impulse of Ida B. Wells-Barnett," in *Spirituality and Social Responsibility: Vocational Vision of Women in The United Methodist Tradition*, ed. Rosemary Skinner Keller (Nashville: Abingdon Press, 1994), 156.

36. Ida B. Wells, "The Negro's Case in Equity," *Independent*, April 26, 1900. Reprinted in Thompson, *Ida B. Wells-Barnett*.

37. From Ida B. Wells, "Crusade for Justice: The Arkansas Riot," quoted in Emilie Townes, "Because God Gave Her Vision," 163.

38. Ida B. Wells-Barnett, *Selected Works of Ida B. Wells-Barnett*, compiled with an introduction by Trudier Harris (New York: Oxford University Press, 1991), 37.

39. For information concerning the difficulties faced by Black women after slavery see: Jacqueline Jones, *Labor of Love, Labor of Sorrow; Black Women, Work and the Family from Slavery to the Present* (New York: Vintage Books, 1985); Paula Giddings, *When and Where I Enter: The Impact of Black Women on Race and Sex in America* (New York: W. Morrow, 1984); Angela Davis, *Women, Race, and Class* (New York: Random House, 1981).

40. Wells-Barnett, *Selected Works*, 40.

41. According to Townes: "Wells-Barnett joins those who reject suffering as God's will and believe that it is an outrage that suffering exists at all," (Emilie Townes, *Womanist Justice, Womanist Hope* [Atlanta: Scholars Press, 1993]), 171.

42. Ibid., 196.

43. Ibid., 195–96.

44. Ibid., 197.

45. Ibid., 194–96.

46. Ibid.

47. Ibid., 197.

48. Ransom, *The Negro*, 22.

49. Townes, *Womanist Justice, Womanist Hope*, 196.

50. For a concise biographical treatment of Martin King, Jr. and the King family, see Clayborne Carson, introduction to *The Papers of Martin Luther King, Jr.*, vol 1, by Martin Luther King, Jr. (Los Angeles: University of California Press, 1992).

51. "An Autobiography of Religious Development", Boston University, King Collection, Box 106, folder 22. Also in King, *Papers*, 363.

52. See King, "Autobiography of Religious Development".

53. John J. Ansbro, *Martin Luther King, Jr.: The Making of a Mind* (Maryknoll, N.Y.: Orbis Books, 1982), 1–2.

54. Ibid., 3.

55. King, *Papers*, 262.

56. Influences on King's theological development: Ansbro, *Martin Luther King, Jr.: The Making of a Mind*; Lewis Baldwin, *There is a Balm in Gilead: The Cultural Roots of Martin Luther King, Jr.* (Minneapolis: Fortress Press, 1991); John C. Harris. "The Theology of Martin Luther King, Jr." (Duke University, Ph.D. diss., 1974); Walter Muelder, "Philosophical and Theological Influences in the Thought and Action of Martin Luther King," in David Garrow, ed., *Martin Luther King, Jr.: Civil Rights Leader, Theologian, Orator*, vol. III (New York: Carlson Press, 1989); John Rathbun, "Martin Luther King: The Theology of Social Action," in Garrow, vol. III, 1989; James Cone, "The Theology of Martin Luther King, Jr." Garrow, vol. I, 1989. This article by Cone and the text by Baldwin, for example, balance the Eurocentric perspective of Ansbro by stating the Black religious roots of King's thought.

57. See Ansbro, 77–86;

58. King's strong opinion concerning the connection between religion and social action comes across, for example, in his response to a question by an *Ebony* reader he addressed. See "Ebony Questions and Answers," July 29, 1958, Boston University, King Collection, Box 80. X.43.

59. The Southern Christian Leadership Conference grew out of the Montgomery Improvement Association.

60. It must be noted that King's stance on nonviolence went through several stages of development. During the first stage in Montgomery, King had to wrestle with the issue of self-defense. He at one point possessed a gun for safety. However, with the encouragement of Bayard Rustin, King recognized the inappropriateness of the leader of a nonviolent movement possessing a firearm.

61. For examples of this cosmic companionship, see "Remaining Awake Through a Great Revolution," in *A Testament of Hope: The Essential Writings of Martin Luther King, Jr.*, ed. James Washington (San

Francisco: Harper & Row, 1986), 270; King, "Our God Is Able," in King, *Strength to Love* (New York: Harper & Row, 1963); "Statement to the Press" at beginning of the Youth Leadership Conference, April 15, 1960, Raleigh, North Carolina in Boston University, King Collection, Box 3.1–11 (folder 5 out of 7); The Final Examination for the Course "Christian Theology for Today" (Crozer Theological Seminary, Dr. Davis), essay number II, King, *Papers*, 290.

62. David Garrow (cited in Baldwin, 11–13 nn. 24, 27; and Cone, 123) argues that a proper understanding of King's thought cannot be obtained through his published works. He asserts that published materials were written with the maintenance of financial support from northern white liberals in mind and were also completed largely with the assistance of ghost writers such as Bayard Rustin. However, I tend to agree with Lewis Baldwin who argues that although the best approach is the use of unpublished materials and published materials, there are no contradictions or inconsistencies between the two sets of materials. For this project both materials published and materials contained in Boston University's collection of King papers have been used. However, even Cone acknowledges that King's thought on redemptive suffering remains consistent in published and unpublished documents. A more revealing example of the private v. public writings is Booker T. Washington, whose donations to various Black organizations and private comments reveal a rather modified version of his public conciliatory rhetoric.

63. King, *Papers*, 419.

64. Untitled Montgomery Improvement Association Address, 1959, Boston University, King Collection, Box 2, 1–11, Folder 2. This address mentions the type of abuse those fighting for liberation encounter. Along these lines, King often had his person and character attacked, being accused of communist leanings. See, for example, David Garrow, *The FBI and Martin Luther King, Jr.* (New York: W. W. Norton, 1981) for governmental resentment accounts; Billy James Hargis, "Unmasking the Deceiver," Boston University, King Collection, Box 80, X.43.

65. "Suffering and Faith," in *A Testament of Hope: The Essential Writings of Martin Luther King Jr.*, ed. James Washington (San Francisco: Harper & Row, 1986), 41.

66. Martin L. King, Jr., "Shattered Dreams," Boston University, King Collection, Box 119a. XVI. 16, 10.

67. Martin Luther King Jr., *Where Do We Go From Here: Chaos or Community?* (Boston: Beacon Press, 1967), 37.

68. "Love, Law, And Civil Disobedience," in Washington, 47.

69. "Eulogy for the Martyred Children," in ibid., 221–22.

70. Baldwin, 8, 237–39.

71. King, *Where Do We Go From Here?*, 134.

72. One who continued King's philosophy was Pauli Murray. Reverend Murray makes direct mention of King and his redemptive suffering

perspective without alteration. The distinction is that Pauli Murray includes in this analysis the issues raised by being a Black woman. However, this added dimension does not distinguish her thought from that of King or Ida Wells-Barnett. For additional information on Murray see: Pauli Murray, *Pauli Murray: The Autobiography of a Black Activist, Feminist, Lawyer, Priest, and Poet ([Song in a Weary Throat]* (New York: Harper & Row; Knoxville: University of Tennessee Press, 1987); Pauli Murray, *Proud Shoes: The Story of an American Family* (New York: Harper and Brothers, 1956); Pauli Murray Collection, Harvard University, Schlesinger Library; Pauli Murray, *Dark Testament and Other Poems* (Norwalk, Conn.: Silvermine, 1970); "An Alternative Weapon," *South Today* (Winter 1942): 53–57; "An American Credo," *Common Ground* 5/2 (Winter 1945): 22–24; Pauli Murray, "Black Theology and Feminist Theology: A Comparative View," *Anglican Theological Review* 60/1 (January 1978): 3–24. To my knowledge few pieces have been written on Murray's theological development. That project still awaits a writer.

73. Joseph Washington, *Black Religion: The Negro and Christianity in the United States* (Boston: Beacon Press, 1964).

74. It should be noted that Washington is not opposed to violence because God is able to use violence for God's divine plans. See Joseph Washington, *The Politics of God* (Boston: Beacon Press, 1967, 1969), 161–62.

75. Ibid., 26.

76. Ibid., 27.

77. Ibid., 29.

78. Ibid., 254–57.

79. Ibid., 158.

80. Ibid., 161.

81. Albert Cleage, *The Black Messiah* (New York: Sheed & Ward, 1968), 6–7.

82. Ibid., 95–96.

83. Ibid., 7.

84. King speaks of Black courage; however, he does not separate it from suffering. See King, *Why We Can't Wait* (New York: Harper & Row, 1964), 31.

85. Cleage, 208.

86. Ibid., 162.

87. James Cone, *My Soul Looks Back* (Nashville: Abingdon, 1982), 44.

88. This text caused a great deal of controversy. Many white scholars considered it racist and a manipulation of the gospel. The exposure Cone received as a result of this text resulted in his being offered a position at Union Theological Seminary (New York City). In moving to New York, Cone gained the opportunity to further explore Black culture. In addition, Union provided an opportunity to bring his thought into dialogue with some of America's most influential white theologians. See

James Cone, *Black Theology and Black Power*, 20th anniv. ed., with a foreword by Paulo Freire (New York: Seabury Press, 1969; San Francisco: Harper & Row, 1989), preface 1989 ed., ix.

89. Chapter one of the present work provides, in connection to the spirituals, an outline of Cone's major theological contensions; and so, they will not be repeated here.

90. Cone, *My Soul Looks Back*, 51–52.

91. Cone, *Black Theology and Black Power*, preface 1989 ed., ix.

92. Ibid., 37.

93. Ibid., 14–16.

94. The scene had been set for this by the National Conference of Black Churchmen's 1966 statement on Black power and the teachings of Albert Cleage. Although many ministers and academics felt an emotional connection to King, the end of his ministry and the powerful voice of Blackness called into question the SCLC's methodology. Some, as Gayraud Wilmore recounts, believed it to be imbalanced, weighed too heavily toward the welfare of white America, even to the detriment of Black people (see James Cone and Gayraud Wilmore, *Black Theology: A Documentary History, 1966–1979* [Maryknoll, N.Y.: Orbis, 1979], pts. one and two).

95. James H. Cone, *A Black Theology of Liberation*, 2d ed., (Philadelphia: Lippincott, 1970: Maryknoll, N.Y.: Orbis, 1986), 63–66.

96. Ibid., 14–16.

97. Ibid., 143.

98. Ibid., 40.

99. Ibid., 113.

100. Ibid., 123–24.

101. Ibid., 125.

102. Ibid.

103. Ibid., 16–17.

104. Ibid., 56–7.

105. Ibid., 81.

106. Ibid., 110.

107. It should be noted that Emilie Townes (*Womanist Justice, Womanist Hope*) apparently misunderstands Cone's notion of suffering if she believes that he seeks only to relieve pain. For Cone, suffering can be a liberating force that moves through existential conditions and transforms one's life options. Here we have positive suffering, as opposed to negative suffering–the substance of oppression. My reading of Townes suggests that her analysis, borrowed from Audre Lorde, is in keeping with Cone's hermeneutical dualism. Suffering as discussed by Townes seems to mirror Cone's first pole (negative suffering) and pain mirrors the positive suffering pole. The actual distinction seems to arise as a result of a failure to

acknowledge the complexity of Cone's definition of suffering. Cone would agree that negative suffering (understood by Townes as suffering in general) is nonliberative and reactive. And that pain (Cone would label this positive suffering) is active and transforming. If one substitutes the word pain in the second sentence and puts in positive suffering (struggle) this quotation from Townes could as easily be attributed to Cone:

> Suffering [negative suffering], and any discussion that accepts suffering as good is a tool of oppression. Pain [positive suffering] allows the victim to examine her or his situation and make a plan for a healthy future (Townes, *A Troubling in My Soul* [Maryknoll, N.Y.: Orbis Books, 1993], 197).

108.　James Cone, *The Spirituals and the Blues: Aan Interpretation* (New York: Seabury Press, 1972), 62.

109.　James Cone, *God of the Oppressed* (San Francisco: Harper & Row, 1975). It should be noted that Cone writes this text as well as *The Spiritual and the Blues* during a period in the writing of history in which the contribution of African-Americans to American society is highlighted. Accompanying this is a theory of the creation of Black culture which suggests that it arose out of the crucible of slavery. This thinking often resulted in an overly romanticized depiction of Black history (see Clarence Walker, *De-romantizing Black History: Critical Essays and Reappraisals* (Knoxville: University of Tennessee Press, 1991) and Wilson Moses, "Creating a Happier Past," in *The Wings of Ethiopia: Studies in African-American Life* (Ames: Iowa State University Press, 1990). Cone's work is better understood with this backdrop in place.

110.　Cone is criticized by Warren McWilliams for not addressing the origin of evil. See: "Theodicy According to James Cone," *Journal of Religious Thought* 36/2 (Fall–Winter 1979–80): 45–54.

111.　Cone, *God of the Oppressed*, 177.

112.　Ibid., 193.

113.　Ibid., 177.

CHAPTER 4: ALTERNATIVE THEOLOGICAL VIEWS ON SUFFERING

1.　See William R. Jones, *Is God a White Racist?: A Preamble to Black Theology* (Garden City, N.Y.: Anchor Press, 1973), xiii; 169–72. It should be noted that Black Process thought has addressed this issue. However, Black Process thinkers such as Henry Young and Theodore Walker find the Process God anemic and weak on racism and classism. Their alternative approach involves a partnership with God to combat such evils. I find this very similar to the partnership proposed by James Cone. See *Process Thought*, 18/4 (Winter, 1989); Henry Young, "Black Theology: Providence and Evil," *Duke Divinity School Review* 40 (Spring 1975): 87–96; Henry Young, *Hope in Process: A Theology of Scoial Pluralism* (Minneapolis: Fortress Press, 1990). The earliest example of Black

Process theology is Eulalio R. Baltazar, *The Dark Center: A Process Theology of Blackness* (New York: Paulist Press, 1973).

2. Ibid., 66.

3. For an earlier analysis of this issue in which Jones establishes the natural centrality of the problem of evil for Black theology of liberation see: William Jones, "Theodicy and Methodology in Black Theology: A Critique of Washington, Cone, and Cleage," *Harvard Theological Review* 64 (October 1971): 541–57; "Theodicy: The Controlling Category for Black Theology," *Journal of Religious Thought* 30/1 (Summer 1973): 28–38.

4. Regarding this Jones says: "The general issue of theodicy and the particular issue of divine racism are central because of the status black theologians assign to black suffering. Theodicy and divine racism are controlling issues because black oppression and suffering are made the starting point for theological analysis" (Jones, *Is God a White Racist?*, 73).

5. Ibid., 61. For material on theology's "threshold question" see 62-64. Also in the same volume, see "Divine Racism: Explicit and Implicit," 72–78.

6. Ibid., 65.

7. Ibid.

8. Ibid., 75. Jones argues that Black theologians must involve themselves in a "reconstruction" effort which seeks to obliterate harmful concepts and beliefs, and provides more useful paradigms. He labels this process "Gnosiological conversion":

    Gnosiological here means the shift is primarily one of concepts and beliefs it relates to one's "knowledge." Thus the object of the theologian's analysis should be what his black sisters and brothers believe to be true about themselves and the universe of nature and society, for it is this knowledge that regulates their actions (67).

9. Ibid., 9.

10. Ibid., 16–17.

11. See ibid., 20–22.

12. Cone, *God of the Oppressed* (New York: Harper & Row, 1975), n. 23, 267–68.

13. Ibid., 191–92.

14. Ibid., n.23, 268. For evidence of what Jones means by internal criticism, see *Is God a White Racist?*, chap. 4; "Purpose and Method in Liberation Theology: Implications for an Interim Assessment," in *Liberation Theology: North American Style*, ed. Deane William Ferm (New York: International Religious Foundation, 1987), 137–64; "The Religious Legitimation of Countervillance; Insights from Latin American Liberation Theology," in *The Terrible Meek: Religion and Revolution in Cross Cultural Perspective*, ed. Lonnie D. Kliever (New York: Paragon

House, 1987), 189–215. Also of interest: "Toward an Interim Assessment of Black Theology," *The Christian Century*, May 3, 1972, 513–17.

15. Cone, *God of the Oppressed* , 191–92. For additional responses to Jones which suggest this same rationale see for example: Major Jones, *The Color of G.O.D.: The Concept of God in African-American Thought* (Macon, Ga.: Mercer University Press, 1987), chap. 6; Roberts, "Liberation Theism," in *Black Theology II: Essays on the Formulation and Outreach of Contemporary Black Theology*, ed. Calvin Bruce and William Jones (Lewisburg, Pa.: Bucknell University Press, 1978), chap. 9; James Evans, *We Have Been Believers: An African-American Systematic Theology* (Minneapolis: Fortress Press, 1992), 58–78. For a process perspective see Henry Young's "Black Theology and the Work of William R. Jones," *Religion in Life*, 44 (Spring 1975):14–28.

16. Jones, *Is God a White Racist?*, 119.

17. Ibid., 92.

18. Ibid., 118.

19. For the nature of the Prolegomenon, see ibid., 169–72.

20. William Jones, "The Case for Black Humanism," in *Black Theology II: Essays on the Formation and Outreach of Contemporary Black Theology*, ed. Calvin Bruce and William Jones (Lewisburg, Pa.: Bucknell University Press, 1978).

21. Jones, *Is God a White Racist?*, 172.

22. Ibid., 173.

23. However Jones does admit that humanocentric theism does not fulfill all demands (ibid., 185–86). It is not a flawless system, yet is "more trustworthy than the theological models that inform the extant black theologies" (186).

24. Ibid., 187.

25. Ibid., 186–94. Howard Burkle, *The Non-Existence of God* (New York: Herder and Herder, 1969); Harvey Cox, *The Secular City* (New York: Macmillan Co., 1968).

26. Jones, *Is God a White Racist?*, 192; citing Burkle 1969, 207.

27. Ibid., 195.

28. William Jones, "Is Faith in God Necessary for a Just Society? Insights from Liberation Theology," in *The Search for Faith and Justice in the Twentieth Century*, ed. Gene G. James (N.Y.: Paragon House, 1987), 82–96.

29. Jones, *Is God a White Racist?*, 195.

30. Ibid., 196.

31. Ibid., 200.

32. Cited in ibid., 193; Burkle, 214–16.

33. See Jones, *Is God a White Racist?*, 15–20.

34. Ibid., 64–67.

35. Cited in ibid., 7–8; Albert Camus, *The Rebel*, trans. by Anthony Bower (New York: Alfred A. Knopf, 1956), 32–34.

36. Jones, *Is God a White Racist?*, 196–97; 201.

37. Terrence Tilley's *The Evils of Theodicy* (Washington, D.C.: Georgetown University Press, 1991) argues against viewing the Book of Job as a theodicy. Tilley asserts that the Book of Job argues against the feasibility of theodicy. Nonetheless, in addition to the Book of Job, I would suggest that the story of Abraham and the potential sacrifice of his son also support my contention (Gen. 22:1–19).

38. Job 1:12, RSV.

39. Ibid., 2:6.

40. Ibid., 42:10, RSV.

41. Jones, *Is God a White Racist?*, 196.

42. Ibid., 201.

43. Jacquelyn Grant, "Black Theology and the Black Woman," in *Black Theology: A Documentary History, 1966–1979* (Maryknoll, N.Y.: Orbis Books, 1979), 420–21.

44. See Delores Williams "Womanist Theology: Black Women's Voices," 267–70, in *Black Theology: A Documentary History, 1980–1993*, vol. II, ed. James Cone and Gayraud Wilmore (Maryknoll, N.Y.: Orbis Books, 1993).

45. Jacquelyn Grant, "Black Theology and the Black Woman," 1979, 430–31.

46. A notable exception to the overwhelming support of this term comes from Cheryl Sanders, who questions the feasibility of this "secular" term for Black church related efforts. This term she argues may have damaging consequences if Black theology is to foster a relationship with Black church morality and ethics. See her article in Jones and Wilmore, *Black Theology* vol. II, first published as "Christian Ethics and Theology in Womanist Perspective," *Journal of Feminist Studies in Religion* 5/2 (Fall 1989): 83–91. The same volume of this journal contains responses to Dr. Sanders from Emilie Townes, Katie Cannon, Cheryl Gilkes, M. Shawn Copeland, and bell hooks.

47. Alice Walker, *In Search of our Mother's Gardens: Womanist Prose* (New York: Harcourt Brace Jovanovich, 1982), xi.

48. Delores Williams, *Sisters in the Wilderness* (Maryknoll, N.Y.: Orbis Books, 1993).

49. Because of its commitment to the maintenance of Black life, this tradition can also be called the "survival/quality-of-life tradition of African-American biblical appropriation" (Williams, *Sisters*, 6).

50. In her biography of Richard Wright (for example, see chap. 25), Margaret Walker states that Richard Wright held a very low opinion of Black women in general and that this attitude is prevalent in his writings:

There is not one whole black woman in Wright's fiction whom he feels deserves respect. . . . One feels he hates black women; one senses early in his writing an unconscious hatred of black women (Margaret Walker, *Richard Wright, Daemonic Genius: A Portrait of the Man, a Critical Look at His Work* (New York: Warner Books, 1988), 179.

With this in mind and combined with his harsh feelings towards religion, one begins to understand the background for his statements concerning the effect of religion on Black women.

51. Richard Wright, *Native Son* (New York: Harper & Row, 1940). For this dissertation, I have made use of the Perennial Library (1987) ed..

52. Williams, *Sisters*, 48; citing Wright, *Native Son*, 246.

53. Alice Walker, *The Color Purple: A Novel* (New York: Harcourt Brace Jovanovich, 1982).

54. Williams, *Sisters*, 53.

55. Ibid., 54; citing Alice Walker *The Color Purple*, 170.

56. Gen. 16:5–6, RSV.

57. Gen. 16:9–10, RSV.

58. Delores Williams, "Black Women's Surrogacy Experience and the Christian Notion of Redemption," 1–14, in *After Patriarchy: Feminists Transformation of the World Religions*, ed. Cooey et al., (Maryknoll, N.Y.: Orbis Books, 1991).

59. Ibid., 5.

60. Williams, *Sisters*, 73.

61. Ibid., 78.

62. Ibid., 79.

63. Ibid., 80.

64. Of interest: Michele Wallace's *Black Macho and the Myth of the Superwoman* (New York: Dial; London: John Calder, 1979).

65. Williams, "Black Women's Surrogacy," 1, 8.

66. Gen. 16:7–9, RSV.

67. Williams, *Sisters*, 165, 166.

68. Ibid., 164.

69. Ibid., 167.

70. Ibid., 162.

71. Ibid., 169.

72. Ibid., 146.

73. Ibid., 148.

74. Ibid., 144–53.

75. Ibid., 161.

76. Ibid., 196–99.

77. Ibid., 197.

78. Ibid., 198.

79. Ibid., 145.

80. Ibid., 113.

81. Ibid., 200; Joanee Carlson Brown and Rebecca Parker, "For God So Loved the World?" 1–30, in *Christianity, Patriarchy, and Abuse*, ed. Joanne Carlson Brown and Carole R. Bolin (New York: The Pilgrim Press, 1989).

82. Williams, *Sisters*, 200.

83. Ibid., 198.

CHAPTER 5: BLUES, RAP, AND NITTY-GRITTY NERMENEUTICS

1. Terrence Tilley, "The Uses and Abuses of Theodicy," *Horizons* 11 (Fall 1984): 304–19; *The Evils of Theodicy* (Washington, D.C.: Georgetown University Press, 1991). For reviews of Tilley's *The Evils of Theodicy*, see: "Review Symposium," *Horizons*, 18 (Fall 1994):.290–312 .

2. Tilley, "The Uses and Abuses of Theodicy," 318. Tilley argues that theists must content themselves with defending religious belief as opposed to offering theodicies (304).

3. Tilley, *The Evils of Theodicy*, 249.

4. Ibid., 219; 3. Several Black theologians have already objected to "theodicy" as a theological tool. See for example James Cone's *The Spirituals and the Blues* and Cone's *God of the Oppressed*. However, these objections revolve around the sufficiency of the Christ event as proof of God's praxis and a lack of concern for the "origin" of evil. This is certainly the case for James Cone and many of his students. Others argue that "theodicy" is moot because of the way Blacks understand their suffering and struggles. In short, it is a White contextual tool. However, these complaints miss the crux of the inadequacies. "Theodicy" is inappropriate precisely because it confirms warped understandings of suffering, not because Blacks do not use it. "Theodicy's" short-comings do not revolve around its failure to be a "Black thang"; rather, because it is a masochistic "thang".

5. Ibid., 251.

6. Peter Hodgson, *God in History: Shapes of Freedom* (Nashville: Abingdon Press, 1989), 229.

7. Lerone Bennett, Jr., *Confrontation: Black and White* (Baltimore: Penguin, 1965), 198.

8. Although my use of nitty-gritty as a hermeneutical device was developed independently, it bears some resemblance to Henry Mitchell's use of

nitty-gritty as descriptive of the Black preacher's exposition of the gospel
("'hermeneutic' is a code word for putting the gospel on a tell-it-like-it-is,
nitty-gritty basis"). In both cases, it is understood that nitty-gritty
denotes the rawest layer of truth. However, my use of the term is distinctive in that it does not necessarily indicate a support for/reading of the
gospel message; rather, nitty-gritty hermeneutics often brings into question the theological and religious assumptions of Christian doctrinal
structures and the Scriptures. Furthermore, my term arises from the
undercurrents of Black religion usually labelled secular and serves as a
methodology for the exploration of the full scope of Black religion—
including the aforementioned undercurrents. In a word, nitty-gritty
hermeneutics, as I understand it, is not inherently Christian (nor theistic) in nature and scope. Furthermore, as Gayraud Wilmore indicates,
Mitchell saw the need for this new hermeneutic, but he did not construct
it. What is required is the exploration/excavation of Black cultural production that Mitchell acknowledged as necessary but does not complete.
My hermeneutic seeks to take Mitchell's suggestion to its full conclusion—theistic and nontheistic. See Gayraud Wilmore, *Black Religion and
Black Radicalism* (Maryknoll, N.Y.: Orbis Books, 1983), 235–37; Henry
H. Mitchell, *Black Preaching* (New York: Harper & Row, 1979), 23–31.

9. Kurt Mueller-Vollmer, ed., *The Hermeneutics Reader: Texts of the
German Tradition from the Enlightenment to the Present* (New York:
Continuum, 1985), 1–3.

10. James Cone, *A Black Theology of Liberation*, twentieth Anniversary ed.
(Maryknoll, N.Y.: Orbis Books, 1993; J. B. Lippincott Co., 1970), 38.

11. I thank one of my students, Abraham Wheeler, for valuable information
on certain blues figures.

12. Paul Oliver, *The Meaning of the Blues* (New York: Collier Books, 1960,
1963), 26.

13. LeRoi Jones, *Blues People: The Negro Experience in White America and
the Music that Developed from It* (New York: Morrow Quill Paperbacks,
1963), 63–68.

14. Charles Keil, *Urban Blues* (Chicago: University of Chicago Press, 1966), 57.

15. James Cone, *The Spirituals and the Blues: An Interpretation* (New
York: Seabury Press, 1972), 78.

16. Oliver, 118. Although I agree with Oliver in part, I disagree with his
contention that the blues lack spiritual values. As this chapter demonstrates, Oliver's remark betrays a limited understanding of Black religion. I argue that the blues form of musical expression is not areligious.

17. Part of this critique involves the sarcastic lampooning of repressive
Christian sex codes. The blues responds to this aspect of Black religion
by openly celebrating expressed sexuality as a vital component of freedom. Using easily deciphered metaphors such as "jelly rolling," blues
artists promoted sexuality as a vital and invaluable aspect of humanity.
In this way, blues figures such as Ma Rainey, Robert Johnson, Muddy

Waters, Koko Taylor, and others moved away from provincial (church-inspired) ethical codes and restraining sensibilities and embraced the full depiction of their being in the world. This implies a norm of interpretation or hermeneutic that examines tradition and rejects religion's allegiance to nineteenth century codes of conduct that problematized Black sexuality. Such codes deny African-Americans a full range of human expression. Nitty-gritty hermeneutics, as expressed in the blues, interprets the meaning of proper religious conduct codes as encouraging the full expression of one's humanity as a symbol of freedom. Religious systems and practices that hamper full human expression are inherently hypocritical.

18. Cited in James Cone, "The Blues: A Secular Spiritual," in *Sacred Music of the Secular City: From Blues to Rap*, a special issue (edited by Jon Michael Spencer) of *Black Sacred Music: A Journal of Theomusicology* 6/1 (Spring, 1992): 93.

19. Cited in Oliver, 118.

20. Ibid., 128.

21. Cited in Jerry G. Watts, *Heroism and the Black Intellectual: Ralph Ellison, Politics, and Afro-American Intellectual Life* (Chapel Hill: University of North Carolina Press, 1994), 54–55.

22. This blues-rap continuum extends the spiritual-blues impulse discussed by Cornel West in the article "On Afro-American Popular Music: From Bebop to Rap," 177–88, in *Prophetic Fragments* (Grand Rapids: William B. Eerdmans Co., 1988).

23. Tricia Rose, *Black Noise: Rap Music and Black Culture in Contemporary America* (Hanover: Wesleyan University Press/University Press of New England, 1994), 21–25.

24. Break dancing and graffiti art did not remain exclusively within the Black community. Movies such as *Breakdance* and *Wild Style* commercialized these art forms and brought them to a larger audience. As Rose points out (46), Fab 5 Freddy's graffiti art, for example, was eventually displayed in New York city galleries.

25. Rose, 73.

26. See for example: Gil Scott-Heron, "The Revolution Will Not Be Televised," *The Best of Gil Scott-Heron* (New York: Arista Records, 1984) and The Last Poets, "Before The White Man Came," *Chastisement* (New York: Celluloid, 1992). The Henderson quotation is cited in Ronald Jemal Stephens, "The Three Waves of Contemporary Rap Music," in *The Emergency of Black and the Emergence of Rap*, a special issue (edited by Jon Michael Spencer) of *Black Sacred Music: A Journal of Theomusicology* 5/1 (Spring 1991): 27.

27. It should be noted that other rap songs recorded during this early period include "King Tim III" by Fatback. However, this and others like it were small releases that did not make the same impact as "Rapper's Delight."

28. Rose, 51–57.

29. Brian Cross, *It's Not about a Salary . . . Rap, Race and Resistance in Los Angeles* (New York: Verso, 1993), 19; 20–21.

30. Ibid., 108.

31. Ibid., 24. Houston's Geto Boys also present a strong example of "gangsta" rap. ScarFace, formerly of the Geto Boys, continues this image as a solo artist (e.g., "The Return of Mr. ScarFace" and "The Diary").

32. The distinction between the two schools of rap must not be too strongly stated. In fact, it should be noted that the line between East and West is blurred as a result of rapid growth and blending of styles.

33. This is a commonly used term not originating with me.

34. Cited in B. Adler and Janette Beckman, eds., *Rap: Portraits and Lyrics of a Generation of Black Rockers* (New York: St. Martin's Press, 1991), 41.

35. Ibid., 59.

36. Cheryl James—Salt; Sandy Denton—Pepa; and, Dee Dee Roper—Spinderella (the DJ).

37. Cited in Adler and Beckman, 55.

38. Michael Eric Dyson, "Rap Culture, the Church, and American Society," in *Sacred Music of the Secular City: From Blues to Rap*, a special issue of *Black Sacred Music* 6/1 (Spring 1992): 270.

39. Ibid., 93.

40. See for example, Eldridge Cleaver's "Domestic Law and International Order," 128–37 in Cleaver, *Soul on Ice* (New York: Delta Book, 1968).

41. Ibid., 75. "Ice-T" (from Los Angeles), "Freedom of Speech" (1990).

42. Jonathan Gold, "Dr. Dre and Snoop Doggy Dogg: One Nation Under a G Thang," *Rolling Stone*, no. 666 (September 30, 1993): 124.

43. bell hooks, "Gangsta Culture-Sexism and Misogyny: Who Will Take the Rap," 117, in *Outlaw Culture* (New York: Routledge, 1994).

44. Rose, 101.

45. Gangsta rap is not devoid of this explicit critique. Pieces such as Ice Cube's "When I Get to Heaven" and ScarFace's "Mind Playin' Tricks on Me, 1994" provide this type of critique.

46. Adler and Beckman, 19.

47. William Eric Perkins, "Nation of Islam Ideology in the Rap of Public Enemy," in *The Emergency of Black and the Emergence of Rap,*. a special issue of *Black Sacred Music* 5/1 (Spring 1991): 41-42 Other rap groups such as Poor Righteous Teachers embrace the philosophy of the 5% Nation, a Nation of Islam splinter group formed by Clarence 13X. This group argues that 85% of the people are ignorant; 10% are capable of initiating liberation but fail to do so; and, 5% have the truth and are poor righteous teachers.

48. Arrested Development, "Fishin' 4 Religion," *3 Years, 5 Months and 2 Days in the Life of*... (New York: Chrysalis Records., 1992).

49. Ibid.

50. Ibid.

51. Ibid.

52. The African basis of their religiosity is hinted at in the group's makeup which includes the Baba (Ojay) figures. This name—Baba—is given to African spiritual advisors.

53. Arrested Development, "Washed Away," *3 Years*.

54. "Dropping the Science" entails presenting the hard truth as a source of liberative knowledge.

55. Charles Long, *Significations: Signs, Symbols, and Images in the Interpretation of Religion* (Philadelphia: Fortress Press, 1986).

56. Ibid., 7.

57. George Cummings, "Slave Narratives, Black Theology of Liberation (USA), and the Future," in *Cut Loose Your Stammering Tongue: Black Theology in the Slave Narratives*, Dwight Hopkins and George Cummings, eds. (Maryknoll, N.Y.: Orbis Books, 1991), 147.

58. Dwight Hopkins, *Shoes that Fit Our Feet: Sources for a Constructive Black Theology* (Maryknoll, N.Y.: Orbis Books, 1993), 89–90.

59. Long, 7.

CHAPTER 6: BLACK HUMANISM AND BLACK RELIGION

1. Patricia Hill Collins, *Black Feminist Thought: Knowledge, Consciousness, and the Politics of Empowerment* (Unwin Hyman, 1990; London: Harper Collins Academic, 1991), 37. Taken from Filomina Steady "The Black Woman Cross-Culturally: An Overview," in *The Black Woman Cross-Culturally*, ed. Filomina Chioma Steady (Cambridge, Mass.: Schenkman Pub. Co., 1981), 7–42; Filomina Steady, "African Feminism: A Worldwide Perspective," in *Women in Africa and the African Diaspora*, ed. Rosalyn Terbory-Penn, et al. (Washington, D.C.: Howard University Press, 1987) 3–24.

2. Collins, 39. Henry Louis Gates, Jr., provides a similar vision of humanism, in "A Liberalism of Heart and Spine," *New York Times*, Op-Ed, March 27, 1994, sec. 4, p.17.

3. Charles Rowell, "An Interview with Margaret Walker," *Black World* 25/2 (1975): 12.

4. Cornel West, "Philosophy and the Afro-American Experience," *Philosophical Forum* 9 (Winter–Spring 1977–78): 117–48; Cornel West, *Prophesy Deliverance: A Prophetic Black Christianity* (Philadelphia: Westminster Press, 1982), chap. 3.

5. West, "Philosophy and the Afro-American Experience," 139.

6. West, *Prophesy Deliverance!*, 146.

7. Trudier Harris, "Three Black Writers and Humanism: A Folk Perspective," 50–74, in *African-American Literature and Humanism*, ed. R. Baxter Miller (Lexington, Ky.: University Press of Kentucky, 1981), 52.

8. Sharon D. Welch, *A Feminist Ethic of Risk* (Minneapolis: Fortress Press, 1990).

9 Riggins R. Earl, *Dark Symbols, Obscure Signs: God, Self, and Community in the Slave Mind* (Maryknoll, N.Y.: Orbis Books, 1993), 153; citing Abraham D. Rogers, *African Folktales: Selected and Retold by Abraham Rogers* (New York: Pantheon Books, 1983), 55.

10. Earl, 153–54.

11. Ibid, 154.

12. Ibid. This seems reminiscent of Delores Williams theory of survival as God's objective.

13. Ibid.

14. In addition to stories dealing solely with the concept of God, there are also numerous stories lampooning church structure and leadership. See, for example Daryl Cumber Dance, *Shukin' and Jivin': Folklore from Contemporary Black Americans* (Bloomington: Indiana University Press, 1978), chap. 5.

15. Zora Neale Hurston, *Mules and Men* (Philadelphia: J. B. Lippincott, Co., 1935; New York: Perennial Library, 1990), 70.

16. Ibid.

17. Ibid., 72.

18. Hurston, "Ole Massa and John Who Wanted to Go to Heaven," 72.

19. See Dance, 41–42.

20. Mel Watkins, *On the Realside: Laughing, Lying, and Signifying: The Undergound Tradition of African-American Humor that Transformed American Culture, from Slavery to Richard Pryor* (Simon and Schuster/A Touchstone Book, 1994), 27; 33; 40; 444.

21. Ibid., 475.

22. Major J. Jones, *The Color of G.O.D.: The Concept of God in Afro-American Thought* (Macon, Ga.: Mercer University Press, 1987), 51–73.

23. A prime example of this exclusion—I do not think his isolation is self-imposed—is the "position" (or lack thereof) held by William R. Jones within Black theological circles. His attempt to break with traditional claims and opinions through an, albeit aborted, questioning of God's goodness ("Is God a white racist?") resulted in his "banishment" from formative Black theological discussions. Many have asserted and defended the Christian nature of Black theology and therefore William Jones' alternative perspective is a theological virus swiftly disposed of.

Although mentioned in several current books (written over the past ten years) on Black theology, he is, to the detriment of Black religious thought, far from recognized as an important player in Black theology's constructive project.

24. Ibid., 51.

25. Ibid., 48.

26. Ibid., 36.

27. One of the difficulties with this text is the manner in which Jones fluctuates between acceptance of a limited God and his demand for an all-powerful God. See for example pages 73 and 66.

28. Ibid., 66.

29. Ibid. 73.

30. Watkins, 450.

31. J. Mason Brewer, ed., *American Negro Folklore* (Chicago: Quadrangle Books, 1968), 114–16.

32. George P. Rawick, "Interview with Jeff Davis," *American Slave: A Composite Autobiography*, vol. 6, pt. 1, (Westport, Conn.: Greenwood Pub., Co., [1973–1976]), 418.

33. For a discussion of this term see: Nicholas Cooper-Lewter and Henry Mitchell, *Soul Theology: The Heart of American Black Culture* (San Francisco: Harper & Row, 1986).

34. Brewer, 115.

35. Ibid.

36. Ibid., 116.

37. Ibid.

38. Ibid., 266.

39. Ibid., 268.

40. Dwight Hopkins, *Shoes That Fit Our Feet: Sources for a Constructive Black Theology* (Maryknoll, N.Y.: Orbis Books, 1993), 121.

41. See, for example, Richard Wright, *Native Son* (New York: Harper and Brothers, 1940); *Black Boy: A Record of Childhood and Youth* (1937; reprinted, New York: Harper & Row, 1945); *The Outsider* (New York: Harper & Row, 1953); and, Nella Larsen, *Quicksand and Passing*, ed. Deborah E. McDowell (New Brunswick, N.J.: Rutgers Unversity Press, 1994). (*Quicksand* is Larsen's novel outlining humanism and is therefore the one of interest here.) As Thadious M. Davis acknowledges in his biography, Nella Larsen "maintained that she did not 'believe in religion, churches, and the like'." See Davis, *Nella Larsen, Novelist of the Harlem Renaissance: A Woman's Life Unveiled* (Baton Rouge: Louisiana State University Press, 1994), 59.

42. Larsen, 3.

43. Helga's only "accepting" (in a paternalistic manner) relative, Uncle Peter, lives in Chicago. She believes, although she is proven wrong, that Uncle Peter will help her to financially begin a new life. His new wife, however, forces a separation between the two that is only bridged by an inheritence check he sends her at a later point.

44. Larsen, 47.

45. Davis, 265–67.

46. Ibid., 267–68.

47. Larsen, 120–21.

48. Ibid., 130. Larsen, through Helga, identifies God as white. However, there is no evidence in the text that she wants to replace a white God with a Black God. This does not appear to be a distinction between "true religion" and "false religion."

49. Ibid.

50. Robert L. Douglas, "Religious Orthodoxy and Skepticism in Richard Wright's *Uncle Tom's Children* and *Native Son*," in C. James Trotman, ed., *Richard Wright: Myths and Realities* (New York: Garland Publishing., 1988), 80.

51. Jean-Paul Sartre, *Existentialism and Human Emotions* (New York: Carol Publishing Group/Philosophical Library Inc., 1990), 51.

52. Richard Wright, *Black Boy (American Hunger)* (New York: Harper Collins Publishers/The Library of America, 1991), 134.

53. Ibid., 131.

54. Ibid., 335.

55. Ibid., 453.

56. Cited in Nick Aaron Ford, "The Ordeal of Richard Wright," in *Five Black Writers: Essays on Wright, Ellison, Baldwin, Hughes, and LeRoi Jones*, ed. Donald B. Gibson (New York: New York University Press, 1970), 32.

57. Sartre, 35–36.

58. Michel Fabre, "Beyond Naturalism," in *Richard Wright,* ed. Harold Bloom (New York: Chelsea House Publishers, 1987), 42.

59. Welch, *A Feminist Ethic ,* 1, 68.

SELECT BIBLIOGRAPHY

Adams, Marilyn McLord. "Redemptive Suffering: A Christian Approach to the Problem of Evil." In *Rationality, Religious Belief, and Moral Commitment*, ed. Robert Audi and William J. Wainwright. 248–67. Ithaca: Cornell University Press, 1986.

African Methodist Episcopal Church. *African Methodist Episcopal Church Hymnal*. Nashville: African Methodist Episcopal Church, 1984.

Adler, B. and Janette Beckman, eds. *Rap: Portraits and Lyrics of a Generation of Black Rockers*. New York: St. Martin's Press, 1991.

Allen, Norm R. Jr., ed. *African-American Humanism: An Anthology*. Buffalo, N.Y.: Prometheus Books, 1991.

Allen, William F., Charles P. Ware and Lucy M. Garrison, eds. *Slave Songs of the United States*. New York: A Simpson and Co., 1867.

Andrews, William L., ed. *Sisters of the Spirit: Three Black Women's Autobiographies of the Nineteenth Century*. Bloomington: Indiana University Press, 1986.

Angell, Stephen. *Bishop Henry McNeal Turner and African-American Religion in the South*. Knoxville: University of Tennessee Press, 1992.

Ansbro, John J. *Martin Luther King, Jr.: The Making of a Mind*. Maryknoll, N.Y.: Orbis Books, 1982.

Baer, Hans A. *The Black Spiritual Movement: A Religious Response to Racism*. Knoxville: University of Tennessee Press, 1984.

Baker, Houston A., Jr. *Black Studies, Rap, and the Academy*. Chicago: University of Chicago Press, 1993.

Baldwin, Lewis. *There is a Balm in Gilead: The Cultural Roots of Martin Luther King, Jr.* Minneapolis: Fortress Press, 1991.

Barlow, William. *"Looking Up at Down": The Emergence of Blues Culture*. Philadelphia: Temple University Press, 1989.

Barton, William E., ed. *Old Plantation Hymns*. New York: Lamson, Wolffe and Co., 1899.

Battle, Michael A. "The Kerygmatic Ministry of Black Song and Sermon." *The Journal of Black Sacred Music*. 1/2 (Fall 1987):17–20.

Baxter, Miller R. *Black American Literature and Humanism*. Knoxville: University of Tennessee Press, 1981.

Bennett, Lerone, Jr. *Confrontation: Black and White*. Baltimore: Penguin, 1965.

Berlin, Ira. *Slaves Without Masters: The Free Negro in the Antebellum South*. New York: Oxford University Press, 1981.

Bleicher, Josef. *Contemporary Hermeneutics: Hermeneutics as Method, Philosophy and Critique*. Boston: Routledge and Kegan Paul, 1980.

Bloom, Harold, ed. *Richard Wright*. New York: Chelsea House, 1987.

Boles, John B. *Masters and Slaves, in the House of the Lord*. Louisville: University Press of Kentucky, 1988.

Bouleware, Marcus. *The Oratory of Negro Leaders: 1900–1968*. Westport, Conn: Negro Universities Press, 1969.

Branch, Taylor. *Parting the Waters: America in the King Years, 1954–63*. New York: Simon and Schuster, 1988.

Brewer, J. Mason, ed. *American Negro Folklore*. Chicago: Quadrangle Books, 1968.

Brooks, Tilford. *America's Black Musical Heritage*. Englewood Cliffs, N.J.: Prentice-Hall, 1984.

Brown, Joanee Carlson and Rebecca Parker. "For God So Loved the World?" In *Christianity, Patriarchy, and Abuse*, ed. Joanne Carlson Brown and Carole R. Bolin, 1–30. New York: Pilgrim, 1989.

Bucher, Glenn R. "Social Gospel Christianity and Racism." *Union Seminary Quarterly Review*. 28/1 (Fall 1972):146–57.

Burkett, Randall and Richard Newman, eds. *Black Apostles: Afro-American Clergy Confront the Twentieth Century*. Boston: G. K. Hall & Co., 1978.

Campbell, Jane. *Mythic Black Fiction: The Transformation of History*. Knoxville: University of Tennessee Press, 1986.

Cannon, Katie. *Black Womanist Ethics*. Atlanta, Ga.: Scholars Press, 1988.

Carby, Hazel. "On the Threshold of Woman's Era: Lynching, Empire, and Sexuality in Black Feminist Theory." *Critical Inquiry* 12 (Autumn 1985): 262–77.

Carmichael, Stokley and Charles V. Hamilton. *Black Power: The Politics of Liberation in America*. New York: Vintage Books, 1967.

Carver, Ronald P. "How Humanistic Are Humanists?" *Religious Humanism*. 18/1 (Winter 1984):41–45.

Cashman, Sean Dennis. *African-Americans and the Quest for Civil Rights, 1900–1990*. New York: New York University Press, 1991.

Clarke, Erskine. *Wrestlin' Jacob: A Portrait of Religion in the Old South*. Atlanta, Ga.: John Knox Press, 1979.

Cleage, Albert. *The Black Messiah*. New York: Sheed & Ward, 1968.

Collins, Patricia Hill. *Black Feminist Thought: Knowledge, Consciousness, and the Politics of Empowerment*. Unwim Hyman., 1990; second impression, London: Harper Collins Academic, 1991.

Cone, James H. *Black Theology and Black Power.* New York: Seabury Press, 1969; 20th anniv. ed., San Francisco: Harper & Row, 1989.

————. *A Black Theology of Liberation.* With a foreword by Paulo Freire. Philadelphia: Lippincott, 1970; 2d ed., Maryknoll, N.Y.: Orbis, 1986.

————. *The Spirituals and the Blues; An Interpretation.* New York: The Seabury Press, 1972; reprinted Maryknoll, N.Y.: Orbis Books, 1991.

————. *God of the Oppressed.* New York: Seabury Press, 1975.

————. *My Soul Looks Back.* Nashville: Abingdon, 1982.

————. *For My People: Black Theology and the Black Church.* Maryknoll, N.Y.: Orbis Books, 1984.

————. *Speaking the Truth: Ecumenism, Liberation, and Black Theology.* Grand Rapids, Michigan: William B. Eerdmans Publishing, 1986.

————. *Martin & Malcolm & America: A Dream or a Nightmare.* Maryknoll, N.Y.: Orbis Books, 1991.

————. *Black Theology: A Documentary History, 1980–1992*, Vol. 2. Maryknoll, N.Y.: Orbis Books, 1993.

Cooey, Paula M. et al., eds. *After Patriarchy: Feminist Transformations of the World Religions.* Maryknoll, N.Y.: Orbis Books, 1991.

Cooper, Anna J. *A Voice from the South.* Xenia, Ohio, 1892; New York: Oxford University Press, 1988.

Coulter, E. Merton. "Henry M. Turner: Georgia Negro Preacher-Politician during the Reconstruction Era." *The Georgia Historical Quarterly.* 48/4 (December 1964).

Courlander, Harold. *Negro Folk Music, U.S.A.* New York: Columbia University Press, 1969.

Crawford, Vicki et al., eds. *Women in the Civil Rights Movement: Trailblazers and Torchbearers, 1941–1965.* Brooklyn: Carlson Publishing Co., 1990.

Cross, Brian. *It's Not About A Salary . . . Rap, Race and Resistance in Los Angeles.* New York: Verso, 1993.

Crummell, Alexander. "The Regeneration of Africa." In *Afro-American Religious History: A Documentary Witness*, ed. Milton Sernett. 253–59. Durham, N.C.: Duke University Press, 1985.

Cummings, Melbourne S. "The Rhetoric of Bishop Henry McNeal Turner." *Journal of Black Studies.* 12/4 (June 1982).

Curtis-Burlin, Natalie, recorder. *Negro Folk-Songs, Books I and II.* New York: G. Schirmer., 1918.

Dance, Daryl Cumber. *Shuckin' and Jivin': Folklore from Contemporary Black Americans.* Bloomington: Indiana University Press, 1978.

Davis, Angela. *Women, Race, and Class.* New York: Random House, 1981.

Davis, Thadious M. *Nella Larsen, Novelist of the Harlem Renaissance: A Woman's Life Unveiled.* Baton Rouge: Louisiana State University Press, 1994.

de Lerma, Dominique Rene. *Reflections on Afro-American Music*. Kent, Ohio: Kent State University Press, 1973.

Dett, R. Nathaniel. *Negro Spirituals*. New York: John Church Co., 1920.

———. *.Religious Folk-Songs of the Negro*. Hampton, Va.: Hampton Institute Press, 1927; reprinted New York: AMS Press, 1972.

Dixon, Christa K. *Negro Spirituals; From Bible to Folk Song*. Philadelphia: Fortress Press, 1976.

Dixon, Thomas, Jr. *The Clansman: A Historical Romance of the Ku Klux Klan*. 1905; reprinted, Lexington: University Press of Kentucky, 1970.

Dje Dje, Jacqueline Cogdell. *American Black Spiritual and Gospel Songs From Southeast Georgia: A Comparative Study*. Los Angeles: Center for Afro-American Studies UCLA, 1978.

Dorn, Jacob Henry. *Washington Gladden: Prophet of the Social Gospel*. Columbus: Ohio State University Press, 1966.

DuBois, W. E. B. *The Souls of Black Folk*. New York: New American Library, 1969.

Dundes, Alan, ed. *Mother Wit from the Laughing Barrel: Readings in the Interpretation of Afro-American Folklore*. Englewood Cliffs, N.J.: Prentice-Hall, 1973.

Earl, Riggins R. Jr. *Dark Symbols, Obscure Signs: God, Self, and Community in the Slave Mind*. Maryknoll, N.Y.: Orbis Books, 1993.

Ellison, Ralph. *Shadow and Act*. New York: Vintage Books, 1969.

Epstein, Dena J. *Sinful Tunes and Spirituals: Black Folk Music to the Civil War*. Urbana: University of Illinois Press, 1977.

Evans, James H. *Black Theology: A Critical Assessment And An Annotated Bibliography*. New York: Greenwood Press, 1987.

———. *We Have Been Believers: An African-American Systematic Theology*. Minneapolis: Fortress Press, 1992.

Fisher, Miles Mark. *Negro Slave Songs in the United States*. New York: Russell and Russell, 1968.

Floyd, Preston L. "The Negro Spiritual: Examination of Some Theological Concepts." *Duke Divinity Review* 43 (Spring 1978): 102–11.

Foner, Philip S., ed. *The Black Panthers Speak*. New York: J. B. Lippincott Co., 1970.

———. *American Socialism and Black Americans: From the Age of Jackson to World War II*. Westport, Conn.: Greenwood Press, 1977.

———. *Black Socialist Preacher*. San Francisco: Synthesis Publications, 1983.

Foster, Frances Smith, ed. *A Brighter Coming Day: A Frances Ellen Watkins Harper Reader*. New York: Feminist Press at City University of New York, 1990.

Franklin, John Hope. *From Slavery to Freedom: A History of Negro Americans*. 5th ed. New York: Alfred A. Knopf, 1947, 1980.

Franklin, V. P. *Black Self-Determination: A Cultural History of the Faith of the Fathers*. Westport, Conn.: Lawrence Hill and Co., 1984.

Frazier, E. Franklin. *The Negro Church in America* and C. Eric Lincoln. *The Black Church Since Frazier*. New York: Schocken Books, 1963.

Frederickson, George. *The Black Image in the White Mind: The Debate on Afro-American Character and Destiny, 1817–1914*. New York: Harper & Row, 1972.

Fullinwider, S. P. *The Mind and Mood of Black American; 20th Century Thought*. Homewood, Ill: Dorsey Press, 1969.

Fulop, Timothy E. "The Future Golden Day of the Race: Millennialism and Black Americans in the Nadir, 1877–1901." *Harvard Theological Review* 84:1.

Garon, Paul. *Blues and the Poetic Spirit*. New York: Da Capo Press, 1975.

Garrow, David. *Bearing the Cross: Martin Luther King, Jr., and the Southern Christian Leadership Conference*. New York: William Morrow, 1986.

———, ed. *Martin Luther King, Jr.: Civil Rights Leader, Theologian, Orator*. vols. I–III. New York: Carlson Press, 1989.

Gates, Henry Louis, Jr., and K. A. Appiah. *Richard Wright: Critical Perspectives Past and Present*. New York: Amistad Press., 1993.

Gayle, Addison, Jr. *Black Expression*. New York: Weybright and Talley, 1969.

Geertz, Clifford. "Religion as a Cultural System." In *Reader in Comparative Religion: An Anthropological Approach*, eds. William A. Lessa and Evon Z. Vogt, 78–89. New York: Harper & Row, Publishers, 1979.

Geneovese, Eugene. *Roll Jordan Roll*. New York: Vintage Books, 1976.

Gennep, Arnold van. *The Rites of Passage*. Trans. Monika B. Vizedom and Gabriello L. Caffle. Chicago: University of Chicago Press, 1961.

George, Carol V. R. *Segregated Sabbaths; Richard Allen and the Rise of Independent Black Churches, 1760–1840*. New York: Oxford University Press, 1973.

Gibson, Donald B. *Five Black Writers: Essays on Wright, Ellison, Baldwin, Hughes, and LeRoi Jones*. New York: New York University Press, 1970.

Giddings, Paula. *When and Where I Enter: The Impact of Black Women on Race and Sex in America*. New York: Bantam Books, 1984.

Gold, Jonathan. "Dr. Dre and Snoop Doggy Dogg: One Nation Under a G Thang." *Rolling Stone*, no. 666, September 30, 1993.

Gordon, Robert Winslow. "Folk-Songs of America: The Spirituals." In *Folk-Songs of America. New York Times Magazine*, February 20, 1927.

Gossett, Thomas F. *Race: The History of an Idea in America*. New York: Schocken Books, 1963.

Grant, Jacquelyn. "Black Theology and the Black Woman." In *Black Theology: A Documentary History, 1966–1979*, ed. James Cone and Gayraud Wilmore, 418–33. Maryknoll, N.Y.: Orbis Books, 1979.

———. *White Women's Christ and Black Women's Jesus: Feminist Christology and Womanist Response*. Atlanta, Ga.: Scholars Press, 1989.

Hamilton, Charles V. *The Black Experience in American Politics*. New York: Capricorn Books; New York: G. P. Putnam's Sons, 1973.

Handy, James A. *Scraps of African Methodist Episcopal History*. Philadelphia: A.M.E Church, 1901; Ann Arbor, Michigan: University Microfilm, 1974.

Haney, Elly. "Pauli Murray: Acting and Remembering." *Journal of Feminist Studies in Religion*. 4 (Fall 1988): 75–79.

Harding, Vincent. *Hope and History: Why We Must Share the Story of the Movement*. Maryknoll, N.Y.: Orbis Books, 1990.

Harris, John C. "The Theology of Martin Luther King, Jr." Ph.D. diss., Duke University, 1974.

Harris, Robert. "The Free Black Response to American Racism." Ph.D. diss., Northwestern University, 1974.

Harris, Sheldon. *Black America and the African Return*. New York: Simon and Schuster, 1972.

Harris Trudier. "Three Black Writers and Humanism: A Folk Perspective." In *African-American Literature and Humanism*, ed. R. Baxter Miller. 50–74. Lexington, Ky.: University Press of Kentucky, 1981.

Harrison, Berry. *Slavery and Abolitionism as Viewed by a Georgia Slave*, ed. Maxwell Whitman. Philadelphia: Historic Publications, 1969.

Harrison, W. P. *The Gospel Among the Slaves. A Short Account of Missionary Operations among the African Slaves of the Southern States*. Nashville: Publishing House of the Methodist Church, South, 1893.

Herndon, Jane. "Henry McNeal Turner's African Dream: A Re-Evaluation." *Mississippi Quarterly: The Journal of Southern Culture*. 22/4 (Fall 1969).

Herskovits, Melville J. *The Myth of the Negro Past*. Boston: Beacon Press, 1958.

Herzog, Frederick. "God: Black or White?" *Review and Exposition*. 67 (Summer 1970): 299–313.

Hick, John H. *Philosophy of Religion*. 4th ed. Englewood Cliffs, N.J.: Prentice Hall, 1963, 1990.

———. *Evil and the God of Love*. 2d ed. New York: Harper & Row, 1976; reissued, Macmillan, 1987.

Higginson, Thomas Wentworth. *Army Life in a Black Regiment*. East Lansing: Michigan State University Press, 1960.

Hitchcock, H. Wiley and Stanley Sadie, ed. *The Grove Dictionary of American Music*. New York: Grove's Dictionaries of Music, 1986.

Hodgson, Peter C. *God in History: Shapes of Freedom*. Nashville: Abingdon Press, 1989.

Hofstader, Richard. *Social Darwinism in American Thought*. Boston: Beacon Press, 1992.

Hogue, W. Lawrence. *Discourse and the Other: the Production of the African-American Text*. Durham, N.C.: Duke University Press, 1986.

Holloway, Karla F. C. *Moorings and Metaphors: Figures of Culture and Gender in Black Women's Literature*. New Brunswick, N.J.: Rutgers University Press, 1992.

hooks, bell. *Outlaw Culture: Resisting Representations*. New York: Routledge, 1994.

Hopkins, Dwight N. *Black Theology USA and South Africa: Politics, Culture, and Liberation*. Maryknoll, N.Y.: Orbis Books, 1987.

———. *Shoes That Fit Our Feet: Sources for a Constructive Black Theology*. Maryknoll, N.Y.: Orbis Books, 1993.

——— and George C. L. Cummings, ed. *Cut Loose Your Stammering Tongue: Black Theology in the Slave Narratives*. Maryknoll, N.Y.: Orbis Books, 1991.

Hughes, Langston. *Selected Poems*. New York: Vintage Books, 1974.

——— and Arna Bontemps, eds. *The Book of Negro Folklore*. New York: Dodd, Mead & Co., 1958.

Hurston, Zora Neale. *Mules and Men*. Philadelphia: J.B. Lippincott, Co., 1935; reprinted New York: Perennial Liberary, 1990.

———. *The Sanctified Church*. Berkeley: Turtle Island, 1981.

Jackson, George Pullen, ed. *Down-East Spirituals and Others*. New York: J. J. Augustin, 1943.

Jackson-Brown, Irene V. "Afro-American Sacred Song in the 19th Century." In *The Black Perspective in Music*. New York: Foundation For Research in the Afro-American Creative Arts. Vol 4, Num. 1, Spring 1976.

Jacobs, Donald M. *Index to the American Slave*. Westport, Conn.: Greenwood Press, 1981.

James, William. *Pragmatism and The Meaning of Truth*. With an introduction by A. J. Ayer. Cambridge, Mass.: Harvard University Press, 1975.

Janheinz, John. *Neo-African Literature: A History of Black Writing*. New York: Grove Press., 1968.

Johnson, James Weldon and J. Rosamond Johnson, eds. *The Books of American Negro Spirituals*. Vol. 1 and 2., Viking Press, 1969; reprinted New York: Da Capo Press., 1977.

Johnson, Paul E. *African-American Christianity: Essays in History*. Los Angeles: University of California Press, 1994.

Johnston, Ruby F. *The Development of Negro Religion*. New York: Philosophical Library, 1954.

Jones, Absalom. "A Thanksgiving Sermon In St. Thomas's, or The African Episcopal Church, Philadelphia: An Account of the Abolition of the African Slave Trade, on that Day By The Congress of the United States." In *Afro-American History Series*, ed. Maxwell Whitman. Philadelphia: Rhistoric Publications, 1969.

Jones, Jacqueline. *Labor of Love, Labor of Sorrow; Black Women, Work and the Family from Slavery to the Present.* New York: Vintage Books, 1985.

Jones, LeRoi. *Blues People: The Negro Experience in White American and the Music that Developed from It.* New York: Morrow Quill Paperbacks, 1963.

——. *Black Music.* Westport, Conn.: Greenwood Press, 1980.

Jones, Major J. *The Color of G.O.D.: The Concept of God in Afro-American Thought.* Macon, Ga.: Mercer University Press, 1987.

Jones, William R. "Theodicy and Methodology in Black Theology: A Critique of Washington, Cone and Cleage." *Harvard Theological Review.* 64 (October 1971): 541–57.

——. "Reconciliation and Liberation in Black Theology: Some Implications for Religious Education." *Religious Education.* (September–October 1972): 382–89.

——. "Toward An Interim Assessment of Black Theology." *Christian Century.* 89 (May 3, 1972): 513–17.

——. *Is God a White Racist?: A Preamble to Black Theology.* Garden City, N.Y.: Anchor Press, 1973.

——. "Theodicy: The Controlling Category for Black Theology." *Journal of Religious Thought.* 30/1: (Summer 1973): 28–38.

——. "Theism and Religious Humanism: The Chasm Narrows." *The Christian Century.* 92 (May 21, 1975): 520–25.

—— and Calvin E. Bruce, eds. *Black Theology II: Essays on the Formation and Outreach of Contemporary Black Theology*, Lewisburg, PA: Bucknell University Press, 1978.

Jordan, Winthrop D. *White over Black.* New York: Norton, 1977.

Katz, Bernard. *The Social Implications of Early Negro Music in the United States; with over 150 of the Songs Many of Them with Their Music.* New York: Arno Press, 1969.

Keil, Charles. *Urban Blues.* Chicago: University of Chicago Press, 1966; 2d ed., 1969.

Kennedy, Stetson. *Jim Grow Guide to the U.S.A.: The Laws, Customs and Etiquette Governing the Conduct of Nonwhites and Other Minorities as Second-Class Citizens.* London: Lawrence and Wishart, 1959.

King, Martin Luther, Jr. *The Measure of a Man.* Boston: Pilgrim Press, 1959.

——. *Strength to Love.* New York: Harper & Row, 1963.

——. *Why We Can't Wait.* New York: Harper & Row, 1964.

——. *The Trumpet of Conscience.* New York: Harper & Row, 1967.

——. *Where Do We Go From Here: Chaos Or Community.* Boston: Beacon Press, 1967.

——. *The Papers of Martin Luther King*, Jr. Vol. 1, ed. Clayborne Carson. Los Angeles: University of California Press, 1992.

Krehbiel, Henry Edward. *Afro-American Folk Songs: A Study in Racial and National Music*. New York: G. Schirmer, 1914; reprinted Portland, Me.: Longwood Press, 1976.

Larsen, Nella. *Quicksand and Passing*, ed. Deborah E. McDowell. New Brunswick, N.J.: Rutgers University Press, 1994.

Larson, Charles R. *Invisible Darkness: Jean Toomer and Nella Larsen*. Iowa City: University of Iowa Press, 1993.

Levine, Lawrence W. *Black Culture and Black Consciousness: Afro-American Folk Thought From Slavery To Freedom*. New York: Oxford University Press, 1977.

Lincoln, C. Eric and Lawrence H. Mamiya. *The Black Church in the African American Experience*. Durham, N.C.: Duke University Press, 1990.

Locke, Alain. *The Negro and His Music*. Washington, DC: Associates in Negro Folk Education, 1936.

Loewenberg, Bert J. and Ruth Bogin, eds. *Black Women in Nineteenth Century American Life: Their Words, Their Thoughts, Their Feelings*. University Park: Pennsylvania State University Press, 1976.

Lomax, Alan. *Folk Song: U.S.A.* New York: Duell, Sloan and Pearce, 1947.

Long, Charles. *Significations: Signs, Symbols, and Images in the Interpretation of Religion*. Philadelphia: Fortress Press, 1986.

Lovell, John Jr. *Black Song: The Forge and the Flame; The Story of How the Afro-American Spiritual Was Hammered Out*. New York: Macmillan Co., 1972.

Luker, Ralph. *The Social Gospel in Black and White; American Racial Reform, 1885–1912*. Chapel Hill: University of North Carolina Press, 1982.

Lynch, Michael F. *Creative Revolt: A Study of Wright, Ellison, and Dostoevsky*. New York: Peter Lang,1990.

Marks, Morton. "Uncovering Ritual Structures in Afro-American Music". In *Religious Movements in Contemporary America*, ed. Zaretsky and Leon. 60–134. Princeton: Princeton University Press, 1974.

Marriott, Michel. "Hard-Core Rap Lyrics Stir Black Backlash." *The New York Times* Metro. Sunday, August 15, 1993, 1, 42.

Martin, Sandy. "Black Baptists, Foreign Missions, and African Colonization, 1814–1882". In *Black Americans and the Missionary Movement In Africa*, ed. Sylvia Jacobs. Westport, Conn.: Greenwood Press, 1982, 63–76.

Maultsby, Portia K. "Afro-American Religious Music; 1619–1861," University of Wisconsin (Madison), Ph.D. diss., 1974.

———. "Black Spirituals." In *The Black Perspective In Music*. New York: Foundation for Research in the Afro-American Creative Arts. 4/1 (Spring 1976).

Mays, Benjamin E. *The Negro's God: As Reflected in His Literature*. With a preface by Vincent Harding. New York: Atheneum, 1938; 3d ed., 1973.

McFague, Sallie. *Models of God: Theology for an Ecological, Nuclear Age.* Philadelphia: Fortress Press, 1987.

McLaughlin, Andr'ee Nicola and Joanne M. Braxton. *Wild Women in the Whirlwind: Afra-American Culture and the Contemporary Literary Renaissance.* New Brunswick: Rutgers University Press, 1990.

McWilliams, Warren. "Theodicy According to James Cone." *Journal of Religious Thought.* 36/2 (Fall–Winter 1979–1980): 45–54.

Meier, August and Elliott Rudwick, eds. *The Making of Black America: Essays in Negro Life and History.* New York: Atheneum, 1969.

Metzger, Bruce and Herbert May, eds. *The New Oxford Annotated Bible.* New York: Oxford University, 1973.

Mitchell, Henry H. Black Preaching. New York: Harper & Row, 1979.

——— and Nicholas C. Cooper-Lewter. *Soul Theology: The Heart of American Black Culture.* New York: Harper & Row, 1986.

Mitchell, Mozella G. "Howard Thurman: Literary/Humanist Theologian." *The Journal of the Interdenominational Theological Center.* 9/2 (Spring 1984): 31–56.

Morris, Calvin. "Reverdy Ransom, the Social Gospel and Race." *The A.M.E. Church Review.* 102/329 (January-March 1988): 27; reprint from *The Journal of Religious Thought.* 4/1 (Spring-Summer, 1984).

———. *Reverdy Ransom: Black Advocate of the Social Gospel.* New York: University Press of America, 1990.

Morrison, Roy D. "The Emergence of Black Theology in America." *The A.M.E. Zion Quarterly Review.* 94/3 (October 1982): 2–18.

Moses, Oval L. "The Nineteenth-Century Spiritual Text: A Source for Modern Gospel." In *Feel the Spirit*, ed. Keck and Martin. New York: Greenwood Press, 1988.

Moses, Wilson Jeremiah. *Black Messiahs and Uncle Toms; Social and Literary Manipulations of a Religious Myth.* University Park: Pennsylvania State University Press, 1982.

———. *Alexander Crummell; A Study of Civilization and Discontent.* New York: Oxford University Press, 1989.

———. *The Wings of Ethiopia: Studies in African-American Life and Letters.* Ames: Iowa State University Press, 1990.

Mueller-Vollmer, Kurt. *The Hermeneutics Reader: Texts of the German Tradition from the Enlightenment to the Present.* New York: Continuum, 1985.

Murray, Albert. *The Omni-Americans.* New York: Outerbridge and Dienstfrey Press, 1970.

Murray, Pauli. *Dark Testament and Other Poems.* Norwalk, Conn.: Silvermine, 1970.

———. "Minority Women and Feminist Spirituality." *Witness.* 67 (February 1984): 5–9.

Nash, Gary B. and Richard Weiss, eds. *The Great Fear: Race in the Mind of America*. New York: Holt, Rinhehart & Winston, 1970.

National Baptist Convention. *National Baptist Hymnal*. Nashville: National Baptist Publishing Board, 1977.

Nelson, Havelock and Michael A. Gonzales. *Bring the Noise: A Guide to Rap Music and Hip Hop Culture*. New York: Harmony Books, 1991.

Nelson, H. and R. Yokley, eds. *The Black Church in America* New York: Basic Books, 1971.

Nielson, David Gord. *Black Ethos: Northern Negro Life and Thought, 1890–1930*. Westport, Conn.: Greenwood Press, 1977.

Odun, Howard W. and Guy B. Johnson. *Negro Workaday Songs*. Chapel Hill, N.C.: University of North Carolina Press, 1926.

Oliver, Paul. *Blues Fell This Morning: The Meaning of the Blues*. With a foreword by Richard Wright. New York: Cambridge University Press, 1979; 2d rev. ed., 1990.

Onunwa, Udobata R. "Humanism: The Bedrock of African Traditional Religion and Culture." *Religious Humanism*. 25/2 (Spring 1991): 66–72.

Ownes, J. Garfield. *All God's Children: Meditations on Negro Spirituals*. New York: Abingdon Press, 1971.

Palmer, Robert. *Deep Blues*. New York: Viking Press, 1981.

Payne, Daniel Alexander. "Daniel Payne's Protestation of Slavery." *Lutheran Herald*. 1/15 (August 1, 1839): 113–15.

———. *History of the AME Church*. New York: Arno Press, 1969.

———. *Sermons and addresses, 1853–1891*, ed. Charles Killian. New York: Arno Press, 1972.

———. *Recollections of Seventy Years*, Salem, N.H.: Ayer Co., 1991. Originally published by Arno Press, 1968.

Parrish, Lydia. *Slave Songs of the Georgia Sea Islands*. Athens: University of Georgia Press, 1992.

Paul, Nathaniel. "African Baptist Celebrate Emancipation in New York State." In *Afro-American Religious History, A Documentary Witness*, ed. Milton Sernett. 180–87. Durham, N.C.: Duke University Press, 1985.

Pinn, Anthony B. "Cross and Crown: An Analysis of Black Theological understandings of and Responses to Suffering." Master's thesis, Harvard Divinity School, 1989.

Pitts, Walter. "Keep the Fire Burnin': Language and Ritual in the Afro-Baptist Church." *Journal of the American Academy of Religion*. 56 (Spring 1988): 77–97.

Ponton, M. M. *Life and Times of Henry M. Turner*. New York: Negro Universities Press, 1917.

Potter, Ronald C. "A Comparison of the Conceptions of God in Process and Black Theologies." *Journal of the Interdenominational Theological Center*. 7 (Fall 1984/Spring 1985): 50–61.

Raboteau, Albert J. *Slave Religion: The Invisible Institution in the Antebellum South.* New York: Oxford University Press, 1978.

——. "Black Christianity in North America." In *Encyclopedia of the American Religious Experience: Studies of Traditions and Movements,* eds. Charles Lippey and Peter Williams. New York: Charles Scribner's Sons, 1988.

Ramirez, Anne. "To Her that Overcame: A Tribute to Pauli Murray." *Daughters of Sarah.* 17 (October 1991): 24–27.

Ransom, Reverdy C. *The Disadvantages and Opportunities of the Colored Youth.* Cleveland: Thomas and Mattill Printers, 1894.

——. "Bishop Henry McNeal Turner." *A.M.E. Review.* 32 (July 1915): 45–47.

——. *The Spirit of Freedom and Justice: Orations and Speeches.* Nashville: AME Sunday School Union, 1926.

——. *The Negro: The Hope or the Despair of Christianity.* Boston: Ruth Hill, 1935.

——. *The Pilgrimage of Harriet Ransom's Son.* Nashville: Sunday School Union, 1949.

——. "The Industrial and Social Condition of the Negro." *The A.M.E. Church Review.* Vol. CII, No. 329, (January-March 1988): 9–18.

——. *Duty and Destiny.* L. I. Jenkins, Printer, n.d.

Rauschenbusch, Walter. *A Theology for the Social Gospel.* Macmillan Co., 1917; Nashville: Abingdon Press, 1978.

Rawick, George R., ed. *The American Slave: A Composite Autobiography.* Vols. 1–19. Westport, Conn.: Greenwood Publishing Co., 1973–76.

Redkey, Edwin. *Black Exodus: Black Nationalist and Back-to-Africa Movements, 1890–1910.* New Haven: Yale University Press, 1969.

——. "Bishop Turner's African Dream." In *Black Apostles: Afro-American Clergy Confront the Twentieth Century,* ed. Randal Burkett. Boston: G. K. Hall & Co., 1978.

Reeves, Gene, ed. *Process Theology and the Black Experience,* a special issue of *Process Thought,* 18/4 (Winter 1989).

Richardson, Harry V. *Dark Salvation; The Story of Methodism as It Developed among Blacks in America.* Garden City, N.Y.: Anchor Press/Doubleday, 1976.

Ricks, George Robinson. *Some Aspects of the Religious Music of the United States Negro: An Ethnomusicological Study with Special Emphasis on the Gospel Tradition.* New York: Arno Press, 1977.

Roach, Hildred. *Black American Music: Past and Present.* Boston: Crescendo Publishing Co., 1976.

Roberts, J. Deotis. *Liberation and Reconciliation.* Philadelphia: Westminster Press, 1971.

——. *A Black Political Theology.* Philadelphia: Westminster Press, 1974.

——. *Black Theology in Dialogue.* Philadelphia: Westminster Press, 1987.

Roberts, John W. *From Trickster to Badman: The Black Folk Hero in Slavery and Freedom*. Philadelphia: University of Pennsylvania Press, 1989.

Rose, Tricia. *Black Noise: Rap Music and Black Culture in Contemporary America*. Hanover, N.H.: Wesleyan University Press/University Press of New England, 1994.

Rose, Willie Lee. *A Documentary History of Slavery in North America*. New York: Oxford University Press, 1976.

Rowell, Charles H. "An Interview with Margaret Walker." *Black World*. 25/2 (December 1975): 4–20.

Ruether, Rosemary Radford and Rosemary Skinner Keller, eds. *Women and Religion in America, Vol. Two: The Colonial and Revolutionary Periods; A Documentary History*. San Francisco: Harper & Row, 1983.

Sander, Cheryl J., ed. *Living the Intersection: Womanism and Afrocentrism in Theology*. Minneapolis: Fortress Press, 1995.

Sartre, Jean-Paul. *Existentialism and Human Emotions*. New York: Carol Publishing Group/A Philosophical Library Book, 1990.

Seward, Theodore and George L. White. *Jubilee Songs: As Sung by the Jubilee Singers*. New York: Biglow and Main, 1884.

Silber, Irwin, ed. *Songs of the Civil War*. New York: Columbia University Press, 1960.

Small, Christopher. *Music of the Common Tongue: Survival and Celebration in Afro-American Music*. New York: Riverrun Press, 1987.

Smith, Archie. "A Black Response to Sontag's 'Coconut Theology'." *The Journal of Religious Thought* 36/2 (Fall–Winter, 1979–1980): 13–25.

Smith, Timothy L. "Slavery and Theology: The Emergence of Black Christian Consciousness in Nineteenth-Century America." *Church History*. 41, (1972):497–512.

Sontag, Frederick. "Coconut Theology: Is James Cone the 'Uncle Tom' of Black Theology?" *Journal of Religious Thought*. 36/2 (Fall–Winter, 1979–1980): 5–12.

Southern, Eileen. *Readings in Black American Music; Black Sacred Music and Social Change*. Valley Forge, Pa.: Judson Press, 1979.

———. *The Music of Black Americans: A History*. New York: W. W. Norton, 1971; 2d ed., 1983.

Spencer, Jon Michael. *Protest and Praise; Sacred Music of Black Religion*. Minneapolis: Fortress Press, 1990.

———. *Theological Music: Introduction to Theomusicology*. New York: Greenwood Press, 1991.

———. *Blues in Evil*. Knoxville: University of Tennessee Press, 1993.

———, ed. *The Theology of American Popular Music*. A special issue of *Black Sacred Music: A Journal of Theomusicology* 3/2 (Fall 1989).

————, ed. *The Emergency of Black and the Emergence of Rap*. A special issue of *Black Sacred Music: A Journal of Theomusicology* 5/1 (Spring 1991).

————, ed. *The R. Nathaniel Dett Reader*. A special issue of *Black Sacred Music: A Journal of Theomusicology* 5/2 (Fall 1991).

————, ed. *Sacred Music of the Secular City: From Blues to Rap*. A special issue of *Black Sacred Music: A Journal of Theomusicology* 6/1 (Spring 1992).

Sterling, Dorothy. *We Are Your Sisters: Black Women in the Nineteenth Century*, New York: W. W. Norton, 1984.

Stewart, Maria. *Maria W. Stewart, America's First Black Woman Political Writer*. Ed. Marilyn Richardson. Bloomington: Indiana University Press, 1987.

Still, William Grant. *Twelve Negro Spirituals*. New York: Handy Brothers Music Co., 1937.

Strong, Josiah. *Our Country*. Ed. Jurgen Herbst. Cambridge, Mass.: Belknap Press of Harvard University Press, 1963.

Stuckey, Sterling. *Slave Culture: Nationalist Theory and the Foundations of Black America*. New York: Oxford University Press, 1987.

Surin, Kenneth. *Theology and the Problem of Evil*. New York: Blackwell, 1986.

Taylor, John E. "So Let Us Watch: An Interpretation of Antebellum Spiritual Texts." *Hymn* 38 (April 1987): 7–13.

Thurman, Howard. *The Negro Spirituals Speak of Life and Death*. Richmond: Friends United Press, 1975.

Tilley, Terrence W. "The Use and Abuse of Theodicy." *Horizons*. 11/2 (Fall 1984): 304–19.

————. *The Evils of Theodicy*. Washington, D.C.: Georgetown University Press, 1991.

Tinney, James S. "Singing from the Soul: Our Afro-American Heritage." *Christianity Today*. 23 (May 1979): 16–19.

Townes, Emilie. *Womanist Justice, Womanist Hope*. Atlanta: Scholars Press, 1993.

————, ed. *A Troubling in My Soul: Womanist Perspectives on Evil and Suffering*. Maryknoll, N.Y.: Orbis Books, 1993.

Trotman, C. James. *Richard Wright: Myths and Realities*. New York: Garland Publishing., 1988.

Trulear, Harold Dean. "The Lord Will Make a Way Somehow: Black Worship and the Afro-American Story." *Journal of the Interdenominational Theological Center* 13 (Fall 1985): 87–102.

Turner, Henry M. "The Civil and Political Status of the State of Georgia, and Her Relations to the General Government, Reviewed and Discussed in a Speech Delivered in the House of Representatives of the Georgia Legislature." Atlanta: New Era Printing Establishment, 1870.

————. "A Speech on the Benefits Accruing from the Ratification of the Fifteenth Amendment, and Its Incorporation into the United States Constitution." Macon: April 19, 1870.

————. "A Speech On the Present Duties and Future Destiny of the Negro Race," Atlanta: Lyceum, 1872.

————. *Respect Black: The Writings and Speeches of Henry McNeal Turner*, ed. Edwin Redkey. N.Y.: Arno Press and the New York Times, 1971.

Turner, Victor. *The Ritual Process: Structure and Antistructure*. New York: Aldine, 1969.

Vora, Erika. "Revolution of Race: A Synthesis of Social and Biological Concepts," *Journal of Black Studies* 12/2 (December 1981).

Walker, Alice. *The Color Purple: A Novel*. New York: Harcourt Brace Jovanovich, 1982.

————. *In Search of our Mothers' Gardens*. San Diego: Harcourt Brace Jovanovich, 1983.

Walker, Clarence. *A Rock in a Weary Land: The African Methodist Episcopal Church during the Civil War and Reconstruction*. Baton Rouge: Louisiana State University Press, 1982.

————. *Deromanticizing Black History: Critical Essays and Reappraisals*. Knoxville: University of Tennessee Press, 1991.

Walker, David. *David Walker's Appeal to the Coloured Citizens of the World, but in Particular, and Very Expressly, to Those of the United States of America*. Edited with an introduction by Charles M. Wiltse. New York: Hill & Wang, 1965. (Original publication: Boston, 1829.)

Walker, Margaret. *Richard Wright, Daemonic Genuis: A Portrait of the Man, a Critical Look at His Work*. New York: Warner Books, 1988.

Walker, Wyatt Tee. *Somebody's Calling My Names: Black Sacred Music and Social Change*. Valley Forge, Pa.: Judson Press, 1979.

Washington, Joseph R. *Black Religion: The Negro and Christianity in the United States*. Boston: Beacon Press, 1964.

————. *The Politics of God*. Boston: Beacon Press, 1967.

Washington, James, ed. *A Testament of Hope: The Essential Writings of Martin Luther King., Jr*. San Francisco: Harper & Row, 1986.

Watkins, Mel. *On The Real Side: Laughing, Lying, and Signifying; The Underground Tradition of African-American Humor That Transformed American Culture, from Slavery to Richard Pryor*. New York: Simon and Schuster/A Touchstone Book, 1994.

Watts, Jerry Gafio. *Heroism and the Black Intellectual: Ralph Ellison, Politics, and Afro-American Intellectual Life*. Chapel Hill: University of North Carolina Press, 1994.

Welch, Sharon D. *A Feminist Ethic of Risk*. Minneapolis: Augsburg Fortress Press, 1990.

Wells-Barnett, Ida. *Selected Works of Ida B. Wells-Barnett.* Compiled with an introduction by Trudier Harris. New York: Oxford University Press, 1991.

West, Cornel. "Philosophy and the Afro-American Experience." *Philosophical Forum.* 9/2–3 (1977–1978): 117–48.

———. *Prophesy Deliverance!: An Afro-American Revolutionary Christianity.* Philadelphia: Westminster Press, 1982.

———. "On Afro-American Popular Music: From Bebop to Rap." In *Prophetic Fragments.* 177–88. Trenton, N.J.: Eerdmans Pub. Co/Africa World Press, 1988.

———. *Keeping Faith: Philosophy and Race in America.* New York: Routledge, 1993.

Williams, Delores S. "Black Women's Surrogacy Experience and the Christian Notion of Redemption." In *After Patriarchy: Feminists' Transformation of the World Religions,* ed. Cooey et al., 1–14. Maryknoll, N.Y.: Orbis Books, 1991.

———. *Sisters in the Wilderness: The Challenge of Womanist God-Talk,* Maryknoll, N.Y.: Orbis Books, 1993.

Williams, George W. *History of the Negro Race in America, 1619–1880.* New York: Arno Press, 1968.

Williams, Preston N. "James Cone and the Problem of a Black Ethic." *Harvard Theological Review.* 65 (October 1972): 483–94.

Williams, Walter L. *Black Americans and the Evangelization of Africa, 1877–1900.* Madison: University of Wisconsin Press, 1981.

William-Jones, Pearl. "Afro-American Gospel Music: A Crystallization of the Black Aesthetic." *Ethnomusicology.* 19 (September 1975): 373–85.

Wills, David. "The Making of an AME Bishop." In *Black Apostles: Afro-American Clergy Confront the Twentieth Century.* ed. Randall Burkett and Richard Newman. Boston: G. K. Hall & Co., 1978.

———. *Black Apostles at Home and Abroad: Afro-Americans and the Christian Mission from the Revolution to Reconstruction.* Boston: G .K. Hall & Co., 1982.

Wilmore, Gayraud. *Black Religion and Black Radicalism: An Interpretation of the Religious History of Afro-American People.* Garden City, N.Y.: Doubleday, 1972; 2d ed., Maryknoll, N.Y.: Orbis Books, 1983.

Woodson, Carter. *The History of Christian Church.* Washington, D.C.: Washington D.C.'s Associated Publishers, 1972.

Woodward, C. Vann. *The Strange Career of Jim Crow.* New York: Oxford University Press, 1957.

———. *Origins of the New South, 1877–1914.* Baton Rouge: Louisiana State University Press, 1971.

Work, John Wesley. *American Negro Songs and Spirituals.* New York: Bonanza Books, 1940.

———. *Folk Songs of the American Negro.* New York: Negro Universities Press, 1969.

Wright, Richard. *Native Son*. New York: Harper & Row, 1940; Perennial Library, 1966; reissued 1987.

———. *Black Boy (American Hunger)*. New York: HarperPerennial/Library of America, 1993. (Original date of publication, 1944.)

———. *The Outsider*. New York: HarperPerennial/Library of American, 1993. (Original date of publication, 1953.)

Yee, Shirley. *Black Women Abolitionists; A Study in Activism*, 1828–1860. Knoxville: University of Tennessee Press, 1992.

Young, Henry J. "Black Theology and the Work of William R. Jones." *Religion in Life*. 44 (Spring 1975): 14–28.

———. "Black Theology: Providence and Evil." *Duke Divinity School Review*. 40 (Spring 1978): 87–96.

NEWSPAPERS AND JOURNALS

Liberator, 1831–1833

Christian Recorder, 1862–1915

A.M.E. Church Review, 1850–1930

MANUSCRIPT COLLECTIONS

Martin Luther King, Jr. Collection, Boston University, Murgar Library, Boston, Massachusetts.

Pauli Murray Papers, Radcliffe College, Harvard University, Schlesinger Library, Cambridge, Massachusetts.

Maria Stewart. *Productions from the Pen of Mrs. Maria W. Stewart*. Rare Books and Manuscripts Division, Boston Public Library, Copley Square Branch, Boston, Massachusetts.

PARTIAL DISCOGRAPHY

Arrested Development. *Three Years, 5 Months, and 2 Days in the Life of. . .* New York: Chyrsalis Records, 1992.

———. *Zingalamaduni*. New York: Chyrsalis Records, 1994.

Boogie Down Productions. *Ghetto Music: The Blueprint of Hip Hop*. New York: BMG Music, 1989.

Ellis, Shirley. "The Nitty Gritty." *A Collection of Sixties Soul Classics: Soul Shots*. Vol. 4. Santa Monica: Rhino Records., 1987; by permission of MCA Records., 1954.

Ice Cube. *Bootlegs and B Sides*. Los Angeles: Priority Records, 1994.

Pittman, Sampson. *The Devil Is Busy*. Norwood, N.J.: Continental Communications Corp., 1992.

Public Enemy. *It Takes a Nation of Millions to Hold Us Back*. New York: Columbia Records., 1988.

———. *Apocalypse 91 . . . The Enemy Strikes Black*. New York: Sony Music Entertainment, 1991.

———. *Muse Sick-N-Hour Mess Age*. New York: Def Jam Records, 1994.

Taylor, KoKo. "Nitty Gritty." *KoKo Taylor*. University City, Calif.: MCA Records., 1969, 1987.

Muddy Waters. "I'm Your Hoochie Coochie Man," *I'm Ready*. Blue Sky Stereo Cassette. New York: CBS., 1978.

COPYRIGHT ACKNOWLEDGMENTS

INDEX